THE BIG 50

PHILADELPHIA PHILLIES

THE BIG 50
PHILADELPHIA PHILLIES

The Men and Moments That Made
the Philadelphia Phillies

Scott Lauber

TRIUMPH
BOOKS

Library of Congress Cataloging-in-Publication Data available upon request

This book is available in quantity at special discounts for your group or organization. For further information, contact:

Triumph Books LLC
814 North Franklin Street
Chicago, Illinois 60610
(312) 337-0747
www.triumphbooks.com

Printed in U.S.A.
ISBN: 978-1-62937-753-7

Design by Andy Hansen
All photos courtesy of AP Images unless otherwise indicated.

To Becca & Jake, the loves of my life

[Contents]

Foreword

"You're only young once, but you can be immature forever."

That was one of the many "shallow thoughts" that I shared with late, great Hall of Famer Harry Kalas, my first broadcast partner. It's also basically how I choose to live my life. But living a life of immaturity doesn't mean I'm not cognizant of the things going on around me, such as *The Big 50: Philadelphia Phillies*, a fabulous book by Scott Lauber.

You may remember the old commercial for the financial investment company E.F. Hutton. The gist of the ad was this: "When E.F. Hutton talks, people listen." People generally don't listen when Scott talks. But when Scott Lauber writes, people read.

Scott has covered baseball since 2006, including two stints in Philadelphia that featured three Phillies playoff appearances and two World Series. In between, he was in New England covering Red Sox Nation. Because of that, and the fact that I believe Boston and Philly are two of the country's greatest sports towns, it gives credence to what he writes about in *The Big 50*.

This book looks at 50 people and moments that have defined the Phillies over their first 136 seasons. Now, there isn't any shortage of Phillies books out there. Even Scott admits, "With so many of these topics, so much has been written that I knew there wasn't much new ground to cover." So what did he do? Whenever possible, he found different points of view, perspectives that others haven't considered. And that is what sets this book apart.

Could you imagine going to work and being told you're taking the place of a legend, the best employee in the history of the company—even though that employee still works there? That's precisely the predicament Rick Schu was in, trying to replace Michael Jack Schmidt.

Scott talked at length with Rick about what it was like to follow a future Hall of Famer while also being his teammate.

Or how about getting to know more about another Hall of Famer, Chuck Klein, who, believe it or not, was before my time? Just hearing the name, I know I'm going to learn about some astronomical number put up by the legendary slugger. But Scott reached out to Chuck's nephew for the ultimate insider's perspective on all things Chuck Klein.

In the chapter about Steve Carlton, Scott talked to Lefty's batterymates Tim McCarver and Bob Boone. Both caught more than just a few of Carlton's starts, but surprisingly, they had vastly different experiences working with the Hall of Famer.

I feel like I have a pretty good grasp on Phillies baseball, at least for the last 40–50 years. Yet in reading *The Big 50*, I'm learning more about things I thought I already knew.

When you read about John Vukovich and Larry Bowa, you'll learn about some of what made them tick. Losing was not part of the equation and the mere mention of it brought boiling blood to the veins in their neck. Not working hard was not an option. You had to work for it, just like they did their whole lives. Well, that's not completely true, at least not for Vuke, always worried that he wasn't getting his due. He often told me about his business philosophy: "Get something for nothing and make 'em feel like they didn't do enough for ya." That didn't exactly entail hard work!

Did I mention they also had a sense of humor? I remember my last big-league hit. I fouled off a couple of pitches against Dan Plesac, who would later become a Phillie. After the first foul ball sailed over the first-base dugout, I looked down to the third-base coach's box for any signs that Bowa might want to relay. Instead, I see him facing left-center field with his shoulders bouncing up and down as though he's laughing. Surely that wasn't the case, or at least I didn't think so. Then I fouled off a second ball. Again, I look down to my third-base coach. This time, Bowa was laughing hysterically with his hands on his knees and his entire back facing the batter's box where I was standing. Well, I showed him, and after I got my last big-league hit and was walking back to the dugout, Bowa walks by and says, "That was [blanking] embarrassing." You fill in the blank.

Growing up, I had dreams of what it would be like to play in the major leagues. At the ripe old age of 40, those very dreams finally came to fruition with the '93 Phils.

What made that team so special to me? It started with policing our own clubhouse, followed by playing a game the way it is supposed to be played and having fun doing it. Maybe more importantly, we talked. We talked before the game; we talked during the game. But we really talked after the game.

There were usually a minimum of 10 players congregating in the trainers' room after the game, win or lose. Lenny Dykstra on the floor, towel draped over his lap and legs to give him a safe landing spot for his tobacco juice; Krukky (John Kruk) in trainer Jeff Cooper's red vinyl chair, and nobody sat there but him; Dutch (Darren Daulton) on a trainer's table icing his carved-up knees; the rest of us on tables or the floor, most with an adult beverage in hand. The only exception: Terry "Mo" Mulholland, who usually just stood while drinking hot coffee. Go figure!

We talked and talked. We covered our game that night, other games that day, who's our next victim, and of course, down the stretch, we talked standings. And this is why my dreams came true. We sat around and talked ball. Isn't it amazing that something that simple, something I dreamed about when I was much younger, took 23 years of pro ball to actually be a part of?

Oh, how I yearn for those days, to just sit around and talk baseball. For this retired former big leaguer and countless other retired players, that is the part that is missed the most—the camaraderie, the bonding, the talking.

The bonding for that '93 team started early in spring training, and by mid-spring we knew we had something special. Dutch had just signed an $18 million contract a couple weeks earlier. We were on the east coast of Florida, headed back to Clearwater. In the rear of the bus sat "Macho Row" members, along with their iced-up cooler. In discussing that day's game, Krukky blurts out, "Hey Dutch, with all that money from your new contract, why don't you build a big mansion and we'll just have parties and play baseball all year long?"

No sooner did those words leave Krukky's lips than "Inky" (Pete Incaviglia) chimed in, "If you build it, we will come."

That '93 team took Philadelphia by storm, and the fans reciprocated with passion like we've never seen before. That brings me to what I believe is most important to a player, a team, an organization: the fans. You can't put a price on the importance of having passionate fans, and having played all over this country, I can attest to the fact that there are no fans more passionate than Phils fans. As players, it's important to play the game the right way, which means giving 100 percent.

The fans in the Delaware Valley deserve a winner, and that is precisely what you get with *The Big 50: Philadelphia Phillies*.

—Larry Andersen

THE BIG 50
PHILADELPHIA PHILLIES

1

1980

Pete Rose had been through this all before. Twice, in fact. From the pile of humanity on the field to the champagne shower in the clubhouse and the subsequent victory parade through downtown, Rose had been here. He had done this.

Surely, then, he knew what to expect on October 21, 1980, after Tug McGraw threw one last fastball by Willie Wilson and turned the Phillies into World Series champions.

"I thought I had some idea," said Rose, a two-time winner with Cincinnati's Big Red Machine in 1975 and '76, "but I never saw anything like that post–World Series parade in Philly. You had a million people in the streets, and when we got to JFK [Stadium], we had 150,000 people waiting for us. And they all had the same expression on their face, whether they were 90 or whether they were nine. They were all smiling. I'll never forget that."

That's what happens when a city waits 97 years for one crowning moment.

Ninety-seven years. Think about that. The Phillies were founded in 1883. By 1980, they were the oldest one-name, one-city franchise in baseball. But for three generations they were marked by abject failure. Compared to the Phillies, the hexed Chicago Cubs and the cursed Boston Red Sox were charmed. So what if those teams hadn't won the World Series since 1908 and 1918, respectively? At least they had won.

The Phillies? In 97 years, they had 31 seasons of at least 90 losses, including 14 with 100 or more. They captured two pennants (1915 and 1950) and won only one game in a World Series. Their first big star, pitcher Charlie Ferguson, died of typhoid at the age of 25. Their second, outfielder Ed Delahanty, was found dead beneath Niagara Falls at age 35. Their ballpark, Baker Bowl, burned down in 1894. One of their owners, Horace Fogel, was banned from baseball in 1912 for alleging that games were fixed. A subsequent owner, Gerry Nugent, had to sell the office furniture just to scrape together enough cash to pay for a

Tug McGraw leaps into the air after striking out Willie Wilson to win the 1980 World Series. (AP Photo / Staff)

trip to spring training. One of their managers, Ben Chapman, opposed integration and shouted racial slurs at Jackie Robinson from the dugout. They had 30 losing seasons in a 31-year span from 1918 to 1948. They blew a 6½-game lead with 12 games to play in 1964. When they finally built a contender, they lost in the National League Championship Series three years in a row from 1976 to '78.

As prolific author and devout Phillies fan James A. Michener wrote in the *New York Times* in 1978, "It is traditional to say, 'I supported them in good years and bad.' There were no good years. I cheered in bad and worse."

Nobody knew quite what to do, then, at 11:29 PM as Wilson flailed at strike three. Even McGraw appeared confounded. The closer windmilled his left arm, flung both arms in the air, faced the third-base visitors' dugout, and took five disbelieving hops before his teammates swarmed him in front of the mound.

"Tug used to say, 'I pounded my glove on my thigh because I was nervous and afraid to go out there,'" former Phillies left fielder Greg Luzinski recalled. "That does enter your mind a little bit. You think, *What could go wrong*? But obviously it was a great, great moment."

It didn't come easy, though. These were, after all, the Phillies.

Never mind that they won 101, 101, 90, and 84 games in the previous four seasons. Or that they were led by dominant ace Steve Carlton and a homegrown nucleus that consisted of Hall of Fame third baseman Mike Schmidt, feisty shortstop Larry Bowa, erudite catcher Bob Boone, and barrel-chested slugger Luzinski. Or that they signed Rose as a free agent two years earlier to help push them over the top.

There was a palpable feeling, at least in the clubhouse, that this golden age of Phillies baseball—the first in franchise history—had an expiration date. If they didn't win the World Series in 1980, ownership would demand changes, maybe even blow up the roster. Most players sensed it. Some knew it for sure.

"No 'maybe' about it. We were basically told," Bowa said. "Our owner, Ruly Carpenter—probably the best owner I ever played for—I had a lot of one-on-ones with him [and] he said, 'We've got to win this year or I've got to start breaking this thing up.' And I said, 'You're right.' We knew going in that this could be the last time we played together."

The threat of change created a complex clubhouse dynamic. The Phillies spent only 25 days in first place and never led the division by more than two games. They were six games off the pace on August 11, one day after hard-driving manager Dallas Green's obscenity-filled tirade that was so ear-splitting it penetrated the walls of the visitors' clubhouse between games of a doubleheader at Three Rivers Stadium in Pittsburgh. They endured the shroud of a potential players' strike in spring training and a drug scandal in July when investigators found that a physician in Reading, Pennsylvania, wrote 23 prescriptions for the amphetamine Desoxyn to several players and their wives, including Carlton, Rose, and Luzinski. The players denied relationships with the doctor and the story fizzled.

But the 1980 Phillies bonded over one thing: their abhorrence of Green.

At 6-foot-5 and 210 pounds, Green was a mountain of a man with a shock of silver hair and a booming voice. He oversaw the Phillies' minor-league system until the Friday of Labor Day weekend in 1979, when general manager Paul Owens tapped him to replace manager Danny Ozark.

Ozark was more mild-mannered than Philadelphians tend to like in their baseball managers. He was prone to malaprops—"Even Napoleon had his Watergate," he once said—but had a nurturing effect on a young team, steering the Phillies to back-to-back-to-back NL East titles from 1976 to '78. But when they fell below .500 in 1979, Owens made a change.

It didn't get more drastic than Green.

"You talk about two different personalities," Bowa said. "It was like chocolate ice cream and vanilla ice cream."

And Green wasn't the players' flavor of choice, even though many played for him in the minors.

In his first team meeting after taking the reins, Green said, "The Phillies didn't fire Danny Ozark. You guys fired Danny Ozark." He delegated strategy and even some lineup decisions to bench coach Bobby Wine, his old teammate with the ill-fated 1964 Phillies, and made clear that he was there to help Owens change the clubhouse culture by weeding out anyone who didn't fall in line.

"Well, he definitely changed the culture," former reliever Dickie Noles said. "There were players in there that definitely didn't buy into him."

Green came to spring training in 1980 with a mantra of *"We, Not I,"* but it was plain that he intended on ruling with an iron fist. He didn't care about making friends or bruising egos. He once benched Boone, Luzinski, and Gold Glove center fielder Garry Maddox—lineup staples on the winningest teams in franchise history—in favor of Keith Moreland, Del Unser, and Lonnie Smith, respectively.

Moreover, Green wasn't beneath ripping players in the press. Maddox and Luzinski, in particular, feuded with the manager and fired back publicly. By midsummer, Luzinski compared Green's tactics to the "f—ing Gestapo." Shortly thereafter, players nominated Luzinski to go into Green's office and tell him to stop airing dirty laundry in the media.

Guess how that went?

"Not real good," Luzinski said, chuckling. "I told him, 'You said it was an open-door policy. Why don't you come out the other way and, if you're mad, tell us before we've got to read about it?' There was a little rift there."

Bowa puts it another way. "I do think we said, 'Hey, f— you, Dallas.'"

It all added to the angst that was building in a pressure-cooker of a clubhouse.

"Dallas beat on us pretty good, but as a team, we knew we had to win no matter whether Dallas yelled at us or not," Boone said. "We felt like it was do-or-die. And that's how we played every game."

They played 60 one-run games, earning the nickname "Cardiac Kids," and won 32 of them. They had 13 extra-inning victories and outscored their opponents by a total of only 89 runs.

The Phillies won 19 of 27 games down the stretch, clinched the division title on the season's second-to-last day, then came from behind to beat Nolan Ryan in Game 5 of an epic best-of-five NLCS against the Houston Astros.

After all that, the World Series felt more like a coronation than a competition.

"I wasn't taking Kansas City light, but once we got through Houston it was like somebody lifted something off our shoulders, threw it off and said, 'Go have fun,'" Bowa said. "I just felt it was our time."

The Phillies won the first two games at Veterans Stadium, lost Game 3 in Kansas City, and were trailing 4–0 after the first inning of an eventual Game 4 loss. But Noles changed the tenor of the rest of the Series by knocking down Royals star George Brett with a heat-seeking fastball early in Game 4. The Phillies came back to win Game 5 with two runs in the ninth inning against dominant closer Dan Quisenberry and went home with two chances to clinch.

With the Phillies leading 4–1 in the ninth inning of Game 6, McGraw loaded the bases on a walk and two singles. A call went down to the bullpen, and amid 65,838 delirious fans—and a few dozen police dogs on the field to help subdue potential chaos—Noles began to loosen. Well, sort of. You try to warm up in the midst of total bedlam.

"I stopped throwing," Noles said. "I don't think anybody wasn't going to stop and take in that scene. You've got the dogs in the bullpen barking. You've got police all around the ballpark. I looked up and there's people everywhere. I can see it just as though I was there now. Everybody in those stands knew Tug had already gotten Willie Wilson before he struck him out. And that was unique for Philadelphia to feel that way. When he struck out Willie, it's one of the loudest roars I've ever heard. It was unbelievable."

But it was nothing compared to the next day.

"Winning it, I guess, is the highlight of my career, but the real highlight was the parade," Boone said. "That's something that I'll never forget, having my kids and my wife there on the trucks going to JFK, just people everywhere and everyone being so happy, it was just unbelievable."

Rose had a hunch it might be unforgettable. When the Phillies' celebration spilled from the field to the clubhouse, Rose grabbed Noles by the shirt.

"He goes, 'Pie'—he always called me 'Pie'—'don't go out and party too much tonight. This thing tomorrow, you're going to see something you've never seen before. It's going to be the parade of all parades,'" Noles said. "And he was right. I don't know if I'll ever see anything like that. This was bigger than the players on the field. This was a city that never won. Ever. What happened was bigger than us."

It was 97 years in the making.

And there's nothing the Phillies can ever do to top it.

2

2008

Like most kids from Souderton, Pennsylvania, Jamie Moyer grew up loving the Phillies. A few times each year, his dad would buy them tickets and make the 35-mile drive to Veterans Stadium. Moyer idolized Steve Carlton and had his heart broken by playoff losses in 1977 and '78. And when the Phillies finally won the World Series in 1980, he played hooky from high school, took the train into the city, and watched the parade pass by on Broad Street.

It only made sense, then, when Moyer pitched for his hometown team 28 years later, that he made sure his high school–aged sons had a backstage pass for all the biggest moments.

"Division Series, Championship Series, World Series, when we clinched, they would sneak down the concourse and come into the clubhouse," Moyer told the *Philadelphia Inquirer* in 2018. "I had uniforms in my locker. They would put them on, and we had a little deal going—'You guys come down in the eighth inning, put the stuff on, no scene, just kind of hang out, and Dad will come get you.'"

Dillon and Hutton Moyer had the routine down pat by the eighth inning on October 29, 2008. Game 5 of the World Series had begun two nights earlier but got suspended by rain with the score tied at 2–2. When play resumed in the bottom of the sixth inning, Geoff Jenkins doubled and scored the go-ahead run on Jayson Werth's single. After the Tampa Bay Rays tied it in the top of the seventh, the Phillies pulled ahead again on Pat Burrell's leadoff double and an RBI single by Pedro Feliz.

As Brad Lidge came to the mound in the ninth inning, Moyer snuck back to the video room, where his sons were waiting, and brought them as close to the dugout as possible without actually entering it. He didn't want them to miss this.

"Put your head down and don't let anybody stop you," Moyer told them. "If we win—and we're going to—have fun."

With two outs and the tying run on second base, Lidge got two strikes on pinch-hitter Eric Hinske. The Phillies' second World Series title was one pitch away, and the oldest player in baseball was losing his mind.

"I was never so nervous," said Moyer, 46 years old then and in his 22nd major-league season. "At strike two, I'm thinking it's going to happen. *What do I do? Do I hug my kids? Do I hug my teammates? Do I run on the field?*"

Or option D: All of the above.

When Hinske swung through a dirt-diving slider, Moyer wrapped his arms around his boys and dashed onto the field. After a few minutes, Dillon and Hutton were there, too, helping their father dig up the pitcher's rubber, the ultimate souvenir. This was, after all, a family affair.

When a franchise waits more than a quarter-century to win only its second World Series in 125 years, the masses share the joy. That's why, as Citizens Bank Park rocked that night, the celebration moved from the confines of a clubhouse soaked by Domaine Ste. Michelle outside to the field, where fans yelled and screamed, high-fived, embraced total strangers, and refused to go home until they got a glimpse of slugger Ryan Howard hoisting the World Series trophy over his head and catcher Carlos Ruiz waving a red "2008" flag and leading his teammates in a victory lap around the outfield.

"I tell all my buddies that are around me back in Phoenix, I'm like, if you could ever take your best friend and just spray champagne profusely at each other and then at the fans and whoever's out there, it was one of the coolest out-of-body experiences," Jenkins said. "You're trying to grasp the moment and just kind of be in it."

Two titles in 125 years also invite comparisons of the championship teams, and there were many similarities between 1980 and 2008. Start here: Both rosters were overwhelmingly homegrown. If the 1980 club was built around Mike Schmidt, Larry Bowa, Bob Boone, and Greg Luzinski, the core of the 2008 group was Jimmy Rollins, Chase Utley, Howard, and Cole Hamels, all of whom were drafted by the Phillies and developed through the farm system.

"That was probably the biggest satisfaction I got," former Phillies assistant general manager Mike Arbuckle said, "just knowing that these kids had grown up and figured out how to do things the right way."

Also like 1980, 2008 represented the culmination of an incremental build-up. The Phillies narrowly missed the playoffs in 2005 and '06. In 2007, they finally broke through with a furious late-season rally to overtake the swooning New York Mets and win the National League East, but got swept out of the Division Series in three games by the scorching-hot Colorado Rockies. It was every bit the motivation that the 1977 and '78 NL Championship Series disappointments were to the 1980 team.

General manager Pat Gillick inherited the homegrown nucleus from predecessor Ed Wade. But he added supporting pieces, notably signing Werth, a non-tendered outfielder, before the 2007 season; trading for Moyer in 2006; and trading for starter Joe Blanton; and pinch-hitting savant Matt Stairs in 2008. Gillick added relievers Chad Durbin and J.C. Romero, and made a splash by trading for Lidge from Houston before the 2008 season.

They all made contributions, too. Werth broke through with 24 home runs and an .861 on-base plus slugging percentage; Moyer led the team with 16 wins and posted a 3.71 earned-run average; Blanton delivered six strong innings—and a home run, too—in Game 4 of the World Series; Lidge went 48-for-48 in save opportunities, including 7-for-7 in the postseason; Stairs crushed a pinch-hit, two-run homer against closer Jonathan Broxton to slay the Dodgers in Game 4 of the NLCS in Los Angeles.

But the biggest hits came from Shane Victorino. Nicknamed the "Flyin' Hawaiian" because of his boundless energy and unrelenting hustle, the center fielder belted a second-inning grand slam off indomitable CC Sabathia in Game 2 of the best-of-five Division Series against the Milwaukee Brewers. Eleven days later, his solo homer in the eighth inning of Game 4 against the Dodgers preceded Stairs' shot.

"I think it was just not being afraid to fail," Victorino said. "If you go by the numbers, I'm set up to fail there. CC was immortal. You think about what he did after the trade deadline in '08 [11–2, 1.65 ERA in 17 starts]. Nobody was going to beat CC and the Brewers."

Instead it became the moment when Gillick believed nobody was going to beat the Phillies.

Lidge felt that way much sooner, even though the Phillies weren't even a lock to make the playoffs on Labor Day. Going into September, they were two games behind the Mets. But Lidge took note of *how* the Phillies were winning. They had eight walkoff victories and 27 wins in one-run games. They scored 799 runs, second-most in the NL, and had a league-leading 3.22 bullpen ERA.

"The big thing for me was watching our team respond in close games. That was how I knew it was a special group," Lidge said. "I remember one game where we came back and won, we were in the clubhouse and Jimmy was like, 'You guys just keep it there, and we'll come back and score the runs.' He was so confident about that, and then we just kept doing it. It was really cool to watch."

The Phillies went 17–8 in September, winning 13 of their last 16 games. They overtook the Mets on September 16 and clinched the division title 11 days later.

Powered by Victorino's grand slam, which followed pitcher Brett Myers' nine-pitch walk against Sabathia, they took care of the Brewers in four games. Playing with heavy hearts after the deaths of manager Charlie Manuel's mother and Victorino's grandmother, they dumped the Dodgers in five games.

After all that, was there any doubt the Phillies would beat the Rays in the World Series?

Actually, yes.

The Phillies went 1-for-28 with runners in scoring position but somehow split the first two games in Tampa Bay. They returned home and won Game 3 on Carlos Ruiz's 40-foot chopper down the third-base line in the 11th inning, then won a 10–2 rout in Game 4. It took three days to finish Game 5, but a 46-hour rain delay was well worth it to a city that had waited 28 years for another World Series crown.

But the 2008 Phillies delivered more than that. They turned Philadelphia back into a baseball town. In 2009, the Phillies began a 257-game sellout streak that lasted into 2012.

"Even when we were winning, we felt like this was an Eagles town first," Rollins said before his retirement ceremony in 2019. "We got to a point where [fans] believed in us putting out a good product every single day. They showed up. We established that we're right up there with the Birds."

And if there were players who didn't already realize how much winning a World Series championship with the Phillies would change their lives, it hit them as soon as they walked out into that chilly South Philly night after Game 5.

"We get up to the player parking lot, and there's got to be 15,000, 20,000 people waiting out there like zombies. It's mayhem," Jenkins recalled. "Everyone's going to Burrell's penthouse. How are we getting down there? I asked a cop, 'Hey, is there any way you can give us a ride downtown?' He's like, 'Yeah, get in.' He puts us in the back and puts the sirens on and literally just goes about a mile an hour. People are shaking us, and I'm high-fiving people outside his SUV. Finally we get downtown. He parks right in the middle of the street. He gets us into the elevator. We get up top and the cop comes with us, and there are like 30 cops there because everybody had a cop take them. It was a really neat journey."

It was meant to be shared, between fathers and sons and mothers and daughters, but mostly between a team and its fans.

"My big question when someone starts talking about it is, 'Where were you?' Everyone has a story," Moyer said. "That's the coolest thing about it. Whether you were at the game, whether you were watching it at home, whether you were stuck on the subway or away on vacation, everyone has a story that relates to that special time. I really do believe that people are still relishing it and cherishing it."

3

MICHAEL JACK SCHMIDT

In the weeks and days leading up to his major-league debut, Rick Schu got plenty of tips about how to succeed as the Phillies' new third baseman. He was schooled on defensive positioning and handling tricky bounces on the artificial turf at Veterans Stadium, and briefed on how he might get pitched in the big leagues after putting up big numbers at Triple-A. But there was one thing that nobody thought to tell him before he ran onto the field to face the San Francisco Giants on September 1, 1984.

Duck!

"The very first time I went out to play third base, I was taking ground balls before the first inning and my name got announced," Schu recalled. "A golf ball comes down from the upper deck and hits right by me—and this is at our home field. I go, 'Oh my god. Uh-oh. They're here to see Mike Schmidt. They don't want to see me.' It was basically saying, 'Now *not* playing third base....' I wasn't ready for that."

It comes with the territory, though, when you're tasked with replacing the greatest player in franchise history, especially while he's still on the team.

Welcome to Philly, kid. You're no Schmitty!

But here's the crazy part: As a player, Schmidt was never universally beloved by Phillies fans, many of whom perceived him to be aloof, even standoffish. Early in his career, in fact, he got booed for seeming too cool in the midst of batting slumps, or for leading the league in strikeouts, or for going a combined 4-for-31 with no home runs in back-to-back National League Championship Series losses to the Los Angeles Dodgers in 1977 and '78 when he was the highest-paid player in baseball. It got so bad in 1985—after Schmidt called Phillies fans a "mob scene" and said they were "uncontrollable" and "beyond help"—that he resorted to taking the field the following night in a shoulder-length crimson wig and sunglasses, a disguise meant to disarm an anticipatory onslaught of jeers.

Indeed, Schmidt's relationship with the fans could be, well, complicated.

Schmidt's greatness was undeniable, though. A rundown of his accomplishments during an 18-year career spent entirely with the Phillies:

- 12 All-Star Game Selections
- NL most valuable player in 1980, 1981, and 1986
- 10 Gold Glove Awards
- 548 career home runs, seventh-most all-time when he retired in 1989
- Eight-time NL home-run king
- 1980 NLCS and World Series MVP
- Hall of Fame inductee in 1995

"Mike Schmidt was the best player I ever played with," said Pete Rose—and lest anyone forget, he played with Joe Morgan, Johnny Bench, Tom Seaver, and Steve Carlton.

Schmidt was still going strong, too, three weeks shy of his 35th birthday when Schu arrived as a September call-up in 1984. Schmidt finished that season with 36 home runs, 106 runs batted in, and a .919 on-base plus slugging percentage, league-leading numbers in each category. He won his ninth consecutive Gold Glove. There were no signs that his skills might be diminishing.

But the Phillies wanted to give Schu a chance. Besides, they figured they could extend Schmidt's career by moving him to first base, a position that might take less of a toll on his body.

"He was my idol, too," said Schu, born in Philadelphia but raised in Fair Oaks, California, near Sacramento. "I grew up a Phillies fan. It was surreal being in the same clubhouse with him, let alone throwing across the field to him. I knew he wasn't happy playing first. It was hard. He was a nice guy. I mean, he was the superstar of the team. One day he would tell me what the starting pitcher was going to do, another day he wouldn't talk to anyone. He could be kind of moody, I guess. But a great player. He tried to help me out whenever he could."

What Schu discovered, more than anything, was what so many teammates had come to learn over the years and Schmidt has admitted since his playing days.

"I was a bit of an insecure guy, my personality was," he said during spring training in 2019. "I masked a lot of that with my style on the field."

Never mind that the Phillies drafted Schmidt out of Ohio University in the second round in 1971. Or that they brought him to Veterans Stadium to work out with the major-league club one week later. Or that they pushed him to the big leagues at age 22. Or that they stuck with him as their third baseman in 1973 even though he batted .196 and, in his words, "could hit a fastball but that was about it." Or even that he led the league with 36, 38, and 38 homers from 1974 to '76.

To Schmidt, baseball was a nonstop battle to prove that he was worth the hype, the money, the accolades.

"I stood in front of the mirror one day and asked myself what I had done to deserve all of this success and wealth and good fortune," Schmidt said in a 2010 biography. "It just dawned on me that someone upstairs was taking good care of me."

Schmidt began taking Bible study classes in 1976, which helped him find inner peace. But it wasn't until 1979, when Rose walked through the doors of the Phillies' spring-training clubhouse in Clearwater, Florida, that he really began to believe how good he was.

For years, Rose watched Schmidt from the opposite dugout and admired his talent, both at the plate and in the field. But he also recognized that there was potential for more.

"When I got there for the '79 season, I thought Mike Schmidt was the best player in the league three or four days a week. And after playing with me for a year, he became the best player in the league seven days a week," Rose recalled. "I think what I did for Mike Schmidt—and I didn't try to do it; it just happened—was I made Mike understand that he's not going to hit home runs every day. You've got to lead with your defense. You've got to lead with your baserunning. You've got to lead with just being Mike Schmidt. I think he saw that and he did it. I understood Mike's value to the Phillies, and if I'm willing to accept Mike Schmidt as the team leader of the Phillies, [Larry] Bowa

October 19, 1980: Mike Schmidt clobbers a two-run homer in the fourth inning of Game 5 of the World Series against the Royals. (AP Photo / Ray Stubblebine)

and [Greg] Luzinski and [Bob] Boone and [Garry] Maddox are damn well going to."

It's no wonder that Schmidt reached even another level of greatness. During a six-year stretch from 1979 to 1984, he averaged 39 homers and 105 runs batted in per season. He led the league in walks four times and on-base percentage three times and won the first two of his MVP Awards.

"[Rose] told me that he thought I was the best player he ever played with and against," Schmidt said. "That just made my chest come out. I was insecure enough where, when Pete said that to me, that really changed my feeling of myself."

Schmidt's longtime teammates noticed. Luzinski, the middle-of-the-order slugger who often batted behind Schmidt, believes Rose "got in Mike's head and made him believe that he's one of the greatest third basemen to play the game. I think he consistently pounded it in Mike."

Rose was right about something else. Schmidt, at his peak, made everybody around him better. Listen to outfielder Gary Matthews, who was already an All-Star when he got traded to the Phillies in spring training of 1981 and batted in front of Schmidt for most of the next three seasons.

"One thing I learned with Mike was the importance of on-base percentage," Matthews said. "As a hitter, the better you know the strike zone, the better hitter you're going to be able to become. Mike made himself not a better hitter; he made himself a great hitter."

Schmidt remained productive long after the Phillies began to think he might be declining. He played first base for most of the 1985 season and topped the 30-homer mark for the seventh consecutive year. By 1986, with Schu struggling and relegated to the bench before eventually getting traded to the Orioles, he returned to third base and won his third MVP Award. Schmidt hit 37 homers in '86 and 35 in '87, including the 500th of his career on a 3-0 pitch with two runners on base, two outs, and the Phillies trailing by one run in the top of the ninth inning on April 18 at Three Rivers Stadium in Pittsburgh.

Harry Kalas' call—*"Swing and a long drive. There it is! Number 500. The career 500th home run for Michael Jack Schmidt!"*—still resonates with Phillies fans, who momentarily forgot their love-hate relationship with the best player in franchise history. He pumped his arms and legs in child-like delight as he reached first base. It was an emotional release that folks had waited nearly two decades to see.

"Mike was a little different," Luzinski said. "But I'm finding out, I played with Steve Carlton, I played with Mike Schmidt, I played with Carlton Fisk, I played with Tom Seaver, they're all Hall of Famers and they're all a little bit different. They've got that little streak in them. That's probably what made them great."

And in the history of the Phillies, nobody was greater than Schmidt.

4

LEFTY

One signature moment didn't transform a young, impressionable left-hander into such a dominant pitcher that he became known simply as "Lefty." But in pondering the evolution of Steve Carlton, there is one game that stands out in Tim McCarver's mind.

It was September 15, 1969, a Monday night in St. Louis. The Cardinals hosted the New York Mets at Busch Stadium. Carlton, 24 years old and already an All-Star, struck out 19 batters, a nine-inning major-league record that wouldn't be topped for 17 years. Yet the Cardinals somehow lost, a testament to the miraculousness of the '69 Mets' season.

"He was saying how the ball was shooting out of his arm," recalled McCarver, who was behind the plate that night. "It was a double rain delay, and as he was going to the dugout, he was looking at his arm and saying, 'What in the world is that ball doing coming out that fast with a slider that sharp?' It was the beginning of a decade and a half of just sheer power."

Indeed, from 1969 through 1983, Carlton recorded a 3.01 earned-run average, 47 shutouts, and 227 complete games. He racked up 3,333 strikeouts, second only to Nolan Ryan (3,538). Nobody worked more innings (4,056⅔) or won more games (270) than Carlton, who also bagged four Cy Young Awards, six 20-win seasons, and victories over the Kansas City Royals in both Game 2 and Game 6 of the 1980 World Series.

So, what was it like to catch the preeminent National League pitcher of the time?

Well, it depends who you ask.

McCarver wouldn't call it easy. But something about it was just so natural, even zen-like. Rarely were McCarver and Carlton not in sync. Seldom did they quarrel about how to attack a hitter. It almost felt as though they shared a brain. Two minds working as one.

"You're thinking in concert, really, and you can feel it," McCarver said. "There's a rhythm, there's a pulse, a feeling. You didn't think your way through it. You willed your way through it."

Put more simply, McCarver said, "It was an elevated game of catch."

It took Bob Boone years to feel that way.

Boone made his big-league debut as a September call-up in 1972. Carlton had been dealt to the Phillies seven months earlier for fellow lefty Rick Wise in the best trade in franchise history and was in the midst of a remarkable season. The Phillies won 59 games in 1972; Carlton won 27 of them while posting a 1.97 ERA.

"One of the most unbelievable seasons ever," Boone said.

Carlton worked the first half of the '72 season with McCarver, his old batterymate in St. Louis, and the second half with John Bateman, for whom McCarver was traded that June. Not once did he pair up with Boone. But Boone took over as the Phillies' top catcher in 1973, and coincidentally or not, Carlton slipped to 13–20 with a 3.90 ERA.

"Guess whose fault that was," Boone said, chuckling. "I had to live with that every day."

Fans and media weren't laying the blame, either. It came straight from Carlton. Idiosyncratic as it gets, Carlton trained in martial arts and Eastern meditation, stretched his left arm in a container of rice, and could be stubborn when it came to interacting with his catcher.

"The fact is, he didn't throw it so well," Boone recalled. "He battled me for a couple years that it was my fault any time something happened. I'd call a curveball and he'd hang it, and I'd be like, 'That's not the curveball that I called.' I got battered that first year in '73 catching Steve."

Things didn't get much better in '74 and '75. Carlton had good seasons, at least by ordinary pitchers' standards, with a 3.22 and 3.56 ERA, respectively, and led the league with 240 strikeouts in 1974. But he also had a league-leading 136 walks that season and the Phillies went 58–58 in his starts from 1973 to '75.

It was around that time that Carlton stopped talking to the media. He grants interview requests only slightly more often in retirement, and in 2018 he told *Newsday* that he and Boone "weren't seeing eye to eye." Carlton explained he didn't like that Boone, among other things, positioned his glove in the middle of the plate rather than where the pitch was supposed to go.

"Booney's a Stanford graduate and I'm a junior college guy, so I think we were outsmarting one another," Carlton said. "Booney and I were having problems communicating. I like to pitch quick. I don't like to sit there and wait for a sign."

Carlton and Boone clearly weren't working out, so when the Phillies brought back slugger Dick Allen in a May 7, 1975, trade with the Atlanta Braves, they also acquired catcher Johnny Oates. Two months later, they made their ace even more comfortable by re-signing McCarver, who had been released by the Boston Red Sox.

"Tim McCarver had kind of raised Steve in St. Louis, and Lefty just, whatever Timmy put down, of course that's what he threw," Boone said. "It was a little bruising to my ego at first, but I realized I had more time off when Steve pitched, which actually was fine with me because I caught so many games every year. I was like, 'Well, I'll take this break and I'll watch.' But they were a great combination."

Like peanut butter and jelly. Or spaghetti and meatballs.

McCarver caught 128 of Carlton's 140 starts from 1976 to '79, during which Carlton went 77–41 with a 3.05 ERA. He won his second Cy Young in 1977, when McCarver caught all 36 of his starts.

"The thing about it was, it had to work immediately," McCarver said. "I had to hit, he had to pitch, we had to win. It's that simple. And it worked. Immediately. I hit, he pitched, and we won. Not necessarily in that order, but it worked and it worked for a rather long time."

What was it, then, about McCarver that brought out the best in Carlton?

It helped that they built a rapport in St. Louis, even though their relationship developed the hard way. As a rookie in 1965, Carlton approached McCarver after a spring-training game and directed him to call more breaking balls. McCarver, who had caught more than 100 games in each of the previous two seasons, took offense, telling him to never question his game-calling again.

Carlton always told McCarver that it was the catcher's skill at bridge that got his attention. In particular, Carlton was impressed with McCarver's ability to remember the sequences of the cards.

"He used to kibbitz card games and we'd play bridge in rain delays and stuff like that," McCarver said. "He said if I could remember the cards, I could remember pitches to different hitters. That was a bit simplistic from my standpoint, but if Steve believed that, that was better for me and better for him, really."

McCarver attributes his symbiosis with Carlton to understanding the impact of his slider. Whereas Boone tended to treat Carlton like any other pitcher in that he used the fastball to set up the slider and curveball, McCarver recognized that the slider was Carlton's best pitch.

"I don't want to say anything about Booney; we're close friends. But Steve had had three years where he couldn't get together with Booney," McCarver said. "Booney's admitted it. Steve's admitted it. Look, we're not talking about brain surgery here. For whatever reason, Booney tried to set him up like a normal pitcher. But he's certainly a better-than-.500 pitcher."

All good things must end, though, and after the 1979 season, McCarver traded his catcher's mitt for a broadcaster's microphone. Left to work with Boone, Carlton went 24–9 with a 2.34 ERA and won his third Cy Young Award.

"He threw half the year and didn't make a single mistake with a pitch," Boone said. "If I called it outside, it was either on the corner or missed away. He never threw a slider and left it in the middle where somebody could hit it. And he did that for half a year. That's one of the most amazing things ever. He was incredible."

But Boone was never under any illusions about who was in charge of the game plan.

"He was going to do what he was going to do. There's no question about that," said Boone, the Washington Nationals' vice president of player development. "When I talk to young catchers I say, 'You don't fight with a pitcher. You have to have a relationship so that he knows what you guys have success with and that you trust each other.' That's a big thing that we didn't have in my early years with Steve. We had that later. He finally accepted that I was pretty good and knew what I was doing."

The Phillies sold Boone to the California Angels after the 1981 season. He played another nine seasons after leaving the Phillies, catching 2,225 games, third-most all-time. He worked with hundreds of pitchers, but only one went on to win 300 games.

"Steve was the best I ever caught," Boone said. "He's one of the all-time greats."

5

THE WHIZ KIDS

When Robin Roberts went to the mound at Ebbets Field on October 1, 1950, he brought along the hopes and dreams of a generation of Phillies fans who had never cheered for a winning team, much less a championship club.

But something else was at stake on that Sunday afternoon in Brooklyn.

"My wife, Mary, and I had planned on taking a vacation in Florida after the season with some of my World Series [bonus] money," Roberts wrote in the 1996 book *The Whiz Kids and the 1950 Pennant*, co-authored with C. Paul Rogers III, "and I remember for a brief moment thinking, *If we don't win this ballgame, we're not going to get to Florida.*"

Now *that's* pressure.

Never mind that the game was tied 1–1 in the bottom of the ninth inning, or that the Phillies were in jeopardy of blowing what had been a nine-game lead over the Dodgers with 10 games left in the season, or that they hadn't won a pennant since 1915 and wouldn't win another until 1980. Nothing puts a knot in a young man's stomach quite like not being able to afford a getaway with his wife for their first anniversary.

What ended up happening in the ninth and 10th innings was nothing short of the two most memorable plays in franchise history. And if either had unfolded differently, the "Whiz Kids" would have been remembered as one of the all-time worst flops rather than as one of the most beloved Phillies teams of all-time.

Not much was expected of the 1950 Phillies. The club endured 16 consecutive losing seasons from 1933 to 1948 and one winning season out of 31 dating to 1918. It was a remarkably depressing run, and by 1945, attendance at Shibe Park had bottomed out at 285,057 fans for the entire season.

But things were looking up. Under the new ownership of the Carpenter family (Delaware blue bloods related by marriage to the ultra-wealthy duPont family), the Phillies strengthened their farm system. Roberts, an ace pitcher, and speedy center fielder Richie Ashburn made their big-league debuts in 1948, two years after outfielder Del Ennis, a native Philadelphian. Third baseman Willie "Puddin' Head" Jones, shortstop Granny Hamner, pitchers Curt Simmons and Bubba Church, and reserve infielder Putsy Caballero also came through the system, while outfielder Dick Sisler and reliever Jim Konstanty were brought in from the outside. The average age of the roster going into the 1950 season was 26.4, prompting sportswriter Harry Grayson to dub them the "Whiz Kids," a moniker that caught on quickly and stuck once they got out to a fast start.

"That spring we had impressed none other than Branch Rickey, president of the Dodgers," Roberts wrote. "Rickey had watched us clobber the Fort Worth Cats, a Dodger farm club, during our swing through Texas, and he picked us to finish second behind Brooklyn."

By September 1, though, the Phillies led the National League by seven games and were greeted by about 30,000 swooning fans at the airport when they returned home for a Labor Day doubleheader, according to Roberts' retelling. Even after losing five games in a row, including three to the mighty Dodgers, the lead was still 4½ games on September 7, and the Phillies stretched it back to 7½ games on September 20.

"It was the first time that most of us realized how big a part of the city we were and how important our success was to the people of Philadelphia," Roberts wrote.

But the Phillies lost eight of 10 games from September 23 to September 30, slashing their lead over the Dodgers to one game entering the season finale on the first day of October.

Gulp.

Roberts learned he would be pitching that morning when manager Eddie Sawyer found him at his locker and handed him the ball. He dueled with the Dodgers' Don Newcombe, both aces allowing a run in the sixth inning and nothing more.

But Roberts got into trouble in the bottom of the ninth. Cal Abrams drew a leadoff walk on a close full-count pitch before Pee Wee Reese lined a single to left field. Duke Snider came to the plate and ripped the first pitch on a low line into center field.

Game over, right?

If not for Ashburn, probably. Not known for a strong throwing arm, Ashburn came up with the ball on one hop and threw a dart to catcher Stan Lopata, cutting down Abrams by 15 feet.

"Here was a guy who should not have been sent, with nobody out in the bottom of the ninth," Ashburn told Roberts and Rogers. "The third-base coach, Milt Stock, got fired because of that play. Oddly enough, he went from the Dodgers to St. Louis with his son-in-law, Eddie Stanky, who was managing the Cardinals. In one game when Milt Stock was coaching third base for the Cardinals, if memory serves me right, I threw out three guys from center field. He never thought I could throw, I guess."

After intentionally walking Jackie Robinson, Roberts retired Carl Furillo and Gil Hodges to get out of the ninth inning, then kickstarted the Phillies' 10th-inning rally with a single against Newcombe. Eddie Waitkus followed with a single before Ashburn bunted the runners over to bring Sisler to the plate.

The middle son of Hall of Fame slugger George Sisler, Dick was the Phillies' resident prankster. He kept the clubhouse loose either with his sense of humor or by leading his teammates in song in the shower or on the bus, according to Roberts. And he had already gotten three hits in the game against Newcombe.

"I was kind of glad to see Sisler up there," Ashburn said.

Newcombe attacked Sisler with fastballs and got ahead two strikes. Sisler, whose father was a Dodgers scout and in attendance at the game, fouled off the next pitch before Newcombe left one a little too far over the plate. Sisler launched it the other way to left field, clearing the wall and giving the Phillies a 4–1 lead.

If there's a bigger home run in Phillies history, well, good luck finding it.

"I didn't know it was a home run at first," Sisler told Roberts and Rogers. "I knew I had hit the ball good and I was hopeful that it was out, but I was past first base when I saw that it was a home run. Boy, that was the greatest feeling in the world. That was the greatest thrill I ever had in baseball."

Roberts retired Roy Campanella, Jim Russell, and Tommy Brown in the 10th inning, and the "Whiz Kids" won the pennant. In the celebration, Sawyer kissed Roberts on the cheek. Robinson came into the clubhouse to offer his congratulations. The Phillies returned home by train to a mob at 30th Street Station, then partied at the Warwick Hotel in Center City.

Not even getting swept in the World Series by the dynastic New York Yankees seemed to sour the Phillies' mood. With Simmons getting drafted into the National Guard late in the season, Konstanty, the National League Most Valuable Player that year, started Game 1 despite not starting a game all season and lost 1–0. Roberts gave up a 10th-inning homer to Joe DiMaggio in Game 2. The Phillies lost by one run in each of the first three games before falling 5–2 in Game 4 at Yankee Stadium.

It scarcely mattered. The Whiz Kids had arrived. Surely there would be more opportunities to win a World Series.

"My wife thought we would do this every year," Roberts told the *Wilmington News Journal* in 2009. "She thought, *My goodness, we'll be in it all the time.*"

Except they weren't. The Phillies didn't finish better than third place until 1964 and didn't reach the postseason again until 1976. Ashburn once suggested that it was because the Phillies refused to sign a black player until 1957, 10 years after Robinson's debut.

Whatever the reason, the Whiz Kids were a one-year wonder, the Phillies' only pennant winner in a 65-year span from 1915 to 1980, and adored by a generation of fans who never knew anything so wonderful as that singular season.

"Without Richie's throw, Dick's home run, and my getting the Dodgers out in the ninth and 10th innings, we might well have been just another Cinderella team that fell short," wrote Roberts, who died in 2010. "If that had occurred, I am afraid no one would remember the 1950 Phillies.

"Winning the pennant that day in Brooklyn gave me a feeling that I never had experienced in sports and, although I would pitch in the big leagues for another 16 years, I never really got that same feeling again. It was complete exhilaration, elation, and great relief all rolled together."

6

MACHO ROW

Frank Coppenbarger just wanted to go home.

As the Phillies' head clubhouse manager, Coppenbarger usually arrived for work by 11:00 AM for night games. He stayed through the final out, tended to the players' needs, then helped get everything in order for the next day. Thirteen- or 14-hour shifts were the norm.

But Coppenbarger began to notice something early in the 1993 season. He wasn't walking through the door of his South Jersey house until two or three in the morning, his postgame duties taking longer than ever to complete because, well, the players didn't want to leave.

"They were not in a hurry to get out of the clubhouse," Coppenbarger recalled. "They loved to spend time with each other."

Indeed, before the 1993 Phillies became one of the most beloved teams in franchise history, they turned the training room at Veterans Stadium into their private speakeasy. They bonded over baseball, beer, and (cigarette) butts. They played hard, lived harder, and didn't let up until Joe Carter and the Toronto Blue Jays vanquished them in Game 6 of the World Series.

Everything revolved around Darren Daulton, the former 25th-round pick who rose to become an All-Star catcher and respected leader. He endured nine knee surgeries during his 14-year career, so he typically made a beeline from the field to the training room and packed himself in ice.

Pretty soon he would be joined by John Kruk, the unkempt first baseman who brought the beer, and center fielder Lenny Dykstra, the tobacco-chewing hustler with the Southern California vocabulary and East Coast grit. Mitch Williams usually wandered in, especially if he had just completed another hair-rising save. So did scarily intense third baseman Dave Hollins and stocky slugger Pete Incaviglia, scrappy second baseman Mickey Morandini and wise-cracking reliever Larry

Andersen, mild-mannered starter Tommy Greene and outspoken ace Curt Schilling. On occasion, manager Jim Fregosi even stopped by.

They were characters, misfits with mullets and beards and nicknames like Dutch and Dude, Krukker and Wild Thing, Mikey and Inky. Their section of lockers was dubbed by local sportswriters as "Macho Row," and they embraced that persona. They were loud, irreverent and profane. They didn't suffer fools or back down from anybody.

And they would hang out nightly in trainer Jeff Cooper's room and review the game they just played, discuss the upcoming game, and just talk as much baseball as humanly possible.

"I think the thing that probably would surprise most people about that '93 team is we sat around—and I'm telling you, it was an hour and a half minimum every night—and we talked baseball," Andersen said. "The perception for that club is that we were just having our beers and talking about going out and partying and chasing women. To say that that wasn't even a part of it, that it never even came up, I think people would probably call BS. But I'd take a lie detector test. It was talking baseball with baseball players."

Coppenbarger eventually realized that the only way he would make it home before 3:00 AM was if the players could let themselves out. He went to general manager Lee Thomas, explained the situation, and before long, a new exit door was constructed, keys were cut, and the Macho Row stragglers could turn out the lights and lock the place up.

Nobody thought the '93 Phillies would amount to much. Well, nobody except for the '93 Phillies. Never mind that Thomas traded for starter Danny Jackson and signed Incaviglia, Andersen, and outfielders Jim Eisenreich and Milt Thompson as free agents to improve on a 92-loss season in 1992. The national media wasn't moved. Nearly every publication pegged the Phillies to finish last, just as they did in three of the previous five seasons.

From the start, then, the chip on the shoulders of the occupants of Macho Row stood out as prominently as the red pinstripes on their uniforms. Daulton declared, "We don't need to believe this crap." From the start of spring training, it was the Phillies against the world.

First, though, they had to get their house in order. Hollins led the majors in hit by pitches in 1992 and resented his teammates for not retaliating. It gnawed at him all winter long, so he stood up in the clubhouse in spring training and challenged Schilling, Greene, Jackson, and fellow starters Terry Mulholland and Ben Rivera.

"I had a short, quick statement to our pitchers that I didn't appreciate the fact that they didn't ever respond to anything. You know, a tit for a tat?" Hollins said. "I said, 'If you're worrying about a guy charging the mound, he's not going to beat me from third base. But you better worry about me and you after the game. That'll be the choice. You want me fighting [alongside] you, or me and you alone after the game?'"

Greene, for one, took it to heart. After St. Louis Cardinals pitcher Donovan Osborne hit Hollins in a spring-training game on a lazy Sunday in St. Petersburg, Florida, Greene drilled Osborne. When Cardinals reliever Paul Kilgus hit Ricky Jordan a few innings later, a brawl erupted.

"We kind of bonded right after that," Morandini said. "The pitchers became close with the position players and vice versa. The chemistry was right there from the beginning."

The Phillies swept the season-opening series in Houston and won eight of their first nine games. They went 17–5 in April and were 57–32 at the All-Star break. They went nearly wire-to-wire, spending 181 days in first place.

But it was also the way that they won. Kruk homered in the 14th inning to walk off the Padres on April 20 at the Vet. Nine nights later, Thompson leaped at the left-field wall to rob a grand slam in the eighth inning of a 5–3 victory in San Diego. One night after that, Morandini bailed Williams out of a bases-loaded, no-out mess in the ninth inning at Dodger Stadium by making a diving stab of a line drive and turning an unassisted double play. Mariano Duncan hit a grand slam off Cardinals closer Lee Smith in the eighth inning of a 6–5 win on May 9. Williams, of all people, hit an RBI single to win the second game of a rain-interrupted July 2 doubleheader at the Vet against the Padres that ended at 4:41 AM. Dykstra capped a 20-inning marathon against the Dodgers on July 7 with a ground-rule double in a 7–6 win.

Teams learned not to mess with the Phillies. After Giants reliever Bryan Hickerson spiked the ball to celebrate spearing Wes Chamberlain's line drive to end the sixth inning on April 26, the Phillies responded by rallying from an eight-run deficit for a 9–8 win in 10 innings.

"Once it started getting out that we didn't take any crap from anybody and we'll brawl if we have to, I think a lot of teams were a little bit intimidated by us," Morandini said. "Just the way we played the game—we grinded out at-bats, we took extra bases, we made diving plays, we grinded out wins—I think that scared people."

Dykstra batted .305 with 19 home runs and 37 steals, reached base at a .420 clip, led the league in runs (143), hits (194), and walks (129), and was runner-up to Barry Bonds in the voting for NL MVP. Daulton hit 24 homers. So did Incaviglia, in only 368 at-bats as part of a left-field platoon with Thompson. Greene began the season 8–0. Williams racked up 43 saves.

Kruk batted .316 with 14 homers and a .430 on-base percentage. He made $2.45 million in 1993, but might have worked for free. Coppenbarger once found more than $20,000 in uncashed checks wadded up in Kruk's locker.

"They finally came down and said, 'You're screwing up the books. You've got to cash these checks,'" Hollins said. "He would just throw 'em right in his locker."

But the most amazing thing about that team was that so many strong-willed personalities formed such a close brotherhood. Fregosi employed platoons in left field, right field, and second base, but there was never any grousing from players who weren't in the lineup every day.

"That was all Darren," Morandini said. "Darren nipped everything in the bud as soon as he saw something that could be an issue."

Here's the thing, though, about Macho Row: it wasn't built to last. No team can play that hard and expend even more energy off the field and expect to survive for more than one season. Human beings, even ones as tough as these, aren't capable of that. Those late-night, beer-filled bonding sessions led to seven divorces and countless other problems.

So, the Phillies outlasted the Greg Maddux/Tom Glavine/John Smoltz–led Atlanta Braves in six games in the NL Championship Series—"America's Team vs. America's Most Wanted," Schilling cracked—then overcame a crushing 15–14 defeat in Game 4 of the World Series and a 5–1 deficit in the sixth inning of Game 6 to push the Blue Jays to the brink of Game 7.

But Carter's three-run homer off Williams in the ninth inning was the brick wall that stopped a Phillies car that had been traveling at 100 mph for seven months.

And although the majority of Macho Row returned in 1994, it was never the same. The Phillies were 54–61 when a players' strike wiped out the rest of the season, including the World Series. They wouldn't have another winning season until 2001.

The '93 Phillies can't even have a proper reunion. Daulton died of brain cancer in 2017 at age 55. Fregosi, bench coach John Vukovich, pitching coach Johnny Podres, and first-base coach Mel Roberts are gone, too. Dykstra admitted to using steroids with the Phillies and is persona non grata at Citizens Bank Park after doing prison time for bankruptcy fraud, grand theft auto, and money laundering. Williams has declined invitations to come back.

As one-year wonders go, the '93 Phillies are the poster children.

"I tell people it took me 24 years to achieve my dream. It wasn't going to the World Series. It was being on a team like that," Andersen said. "But that was a one-time shot. You can't play that way again. It was all-out for a whole year, as much love for the game that you could have in one year. That was it."

Nothing more, and certainly nothing less.

7

ROBIN ROBERTS

Chris Welsh couldn't understand why his father insisted on taking him to Crosley Field on July 27, 1966. It was a night game in the middle of the week against the worst team in the league, hardly the hottest ticket in Cincinnati. And he had no earthly idea why his dad urged him to go to the bullpen before the game and ask for the Chicago Cubs starting pitcher's autograph.

But Welsh was an abiding son, to say nothing of a baseball-loving 11-year-old, so he played along. He grabbed his game program, wound his way through the bleachers, and waited for Robin Roberts to finish his warmup tosses, an exercise that the right-hander didn't complete until the top of the first inning had begun.

"Hey, Mr. Roberts," Welsh said, extending his arm. "Will you sign this for me?"

Roberts looked up. "Kid," he said, "I'm not allowed to sign it during the game. But I'll sign for you."

It wasn't the last favor that Roberts did for Welsh. Not by a long shot.

As a pitcher, Roberts' greatness was indisputable. He made 609 starts, 20th on the all-time list, and won 286 games in a major-league career that spanned 19 seasons, 14 with the Phillies. He threw 305 complete games, including a stretch of 28 in a row from 1952 to '53, a major-league record that will never fall. He was as dominant as any pitcher in the 1950s, reaching 300 innings and 20 wins in six consecutive seasons. He led the Phillies to the pennant in 1950 and started for the National League in the All-Star Game in 1950, '51, '53, '54, and '55. He was inducted into the Hall of Fame in 1976.

But Roberts' legacy goes beyond all of that. It can be found in Jim Palmer and Fergie Jenkins, fellow Hall of Fame pitchers who trace their success to Roberts' mentorship. It's evident in Welsh, too, a self-described "puss-armed left-hander with a good curveball" who nevertheless carved out a five-year big-league career by applying the hard lessons that Roberts imparted while coaching at the University of South Florida.

"Robin had such a positive impact," Jenkins said. "He was a power pitcher, and he wasn't a guy that gave in. He wanted to be dominant out there. What he did was transfer that to me. We struck an idea that I was going to try to do what he did in the '50s and part of the '60s, and I tried to do it as well as I could."

Roberts was innately talented and tough, qualities that aren't easily taught. It was important to him to try, though, and his devotion to the next generation of pitchers ran deep. At age 38, in his second-to-last major-league season, he stayed up late on the road and talked pitching with Palmer, his roommate and a touted 19-year-old rookie with the Baltimore Orioles. Palmer peppered Roberts with questions, and Roberts told tales from his Phillies days.

To wit: Roberts got so amped for starts that he often walked several miles back to the team hotel on the road to unwind after games and replay each pitch in his head, occasionally wandering into a bad neighborhood in the middle of the night. There were games when he would sometimes throw nothing but fastballs for seven innings before finally breaking out his slider for the third or fourth time through the batting order.

"Robin's message was to the point: 'The fastball is the best pitch in baseball. You've got a great one. And I hope you're smart enough to use it,'" Palmer wrote in *Nine Innings to Success*, his 2016 memoir. "Robin told me that I needed to think less about the velocity of my pitches and more about their location. He assured me that the ability to throw a well-placed fastball would translate into a lot of major league wins."

In 1966, staring at retirement after getting released by the Houston Astros, Roberts signed with the Cubs. But as much as they wanted him to make a few starts, they were even more interested in having him fill in for ailing pitching coach Fred Fitzsimmons. Roberts worked closely with Jenkins, Ken Holtzman, and the other impressionable pitchers on a Cubs team that wound up losing 103 games.

Roberts connected with Jenkins, in particular. Signed by the Phillies in 1962 and traded away four years later, Jenkins was used

mostly out of the bullpen in 1966 until Cubs manager Leo Durocher finally put him in the rotation in late August.

"I guess it proved to be the right direction to go because of the fact that, with three or four days' rest in between assignments, I threw the ball extremely well," Jenkins said. "I had a rubber arm. Robin could see that."

It takes one to know one. But if Roberts saw in Jenkins the characteristics of a durable workhorse, he also stressed the importance of a between-starts routine to build the stamina required to avoid missing a start. Roberts also focused on the mental side of pitching. He wasn't a big strikeout pitcher, averaging only 4.5 per nine innings. But he succeeded in controlling a game by studying hitters and staying ahead in the count to prey on their weaknesses.

"Robin Roberts was a big key to my career," Jenkins said. "When Robin got a hold of me, he reinforced, 'You've got a good fastball, you've got a good sinker. Get ahead with that fastball, and then, if you need to get people out with the slider, hey, throw it.'"

The Cubs offered to keep Roberts on as the pitching coach in 1967. But if he wasn't going to pitch, he didn't want to spend so much time away from his family. Besides, his influence on the Cubs was already profound. Jenkins went 20–13 with a 2.80 ERA and a league-leading 20 complete games in 289⅓ innings in '67 and was runner-up to Mike McCormick in the NL Cy Young voting; Holtzman went 9–0 with a 2.53 ERA; Rich Nye finished 13–10 with a 3.20 ERA. And the Cubs won 87 games, a 28-game improvement from the previous year.

After getting elected to the Hall of Fame on the first ballot in 1976, Roberts got an offer to move to Tampa and coach at South Florida. Welsh, a senior captain, was a student representative on the search committee. His father, who grew up in Wilmington, Delaware, and was a diehard Phillies fan, could hardly contain his excitement when Roberts got the job.

"It was hard to believe that, here's this guy who's in the Hall of Fame who was going to be my college coach," Welsh said. "And he was so down to earth, he was so helpful, and really cared about the kids. He knew he couldn't help some of them. They all had aspirations of being big leaguers. He knew that they weren't going to be. But he was still out there trying to help them."

Welsh figured he was right on track. After all, he had a strong enough junior year to get drafted by the Yankees in the 24th round. In deciding to return to school for his senior season he figured he would complete his degree and improve his draft stock.

But his new coach offered a reality check.

"Robin came in and, I remember this like it was yesterday, he watched me pitch in the bullpen and then in an intrasquad type game and he said, 'Hey Lefty, I got to tell ya, none of that stuff you've got is gonna work in pro ball,'" said Welsh, changing his inflection to exaggerate Roberts' folksy, midwestern twang. "I'm like, 'You're kidding, right?' He said, 'No, I'm not kidding. The way you're pitching is not going to work in pro ball.' So we worked on it. He got me to make some changes, and without those changes I probably would not have gotten to where I did as a professional pitcher."

Specifically, Roberts noticed that all of Welsh's pitches cut in the same direction. He was able to record outs against college hitters because he had a wicked curveball. But Roberts doubted that professional hitters would be similarly fooled, so he got Welsh to change his delivery to achieve different types of movement.

Many of Roberts' lessons were more intuitive. Roberts once explained to Welsh that he could overcome falling behind in the count to a dangerous slugger by flipping his wrist as he released his sinker and aiming for the edge of the plate. The ball would move "almost like a dead fish," Roberts said, causing the hitter to either roll over a ground ball or hit a weak popup. "If you do that every time you get a 3–1 count," Roberts would say, "you'll be successful." Welsh recalls that it bailed him out of several jams during his years with the San Diego Padres, Montreal Expos, Texas Rangers, and hometown Reds. But there were other times when Roberts fell short in adequately teaching pitchers who lacked his exceeding talent.

"He'd say, 'You get a man on third base and all you do is add a foot to your fastball when you need a strikeout,'" Welsh recalled, laughing. "I'd say, 'Coach, this is all I've got. I don't have an extra five inches much less an extra foot.' He had a hard time relating. I don't mean this in a bad way. He would be so simple in saying, 'You need to just keep the ball in this spot every time against this guy.' Well, most of us turds couldn't put into play what he was trying to teach."

That would gnaw at Roberts, his competitiveness as a player spilling into his coaching career. But he kept at it, guiding South Florida to conference championships in 1981 and 1982, and its first NCAA tournament appearance in '82, before retiring in 1985.

"He was such a special guy," Welsh said. "He had a big smile, a big heart, and he wanted to help everybody."

Indeed, for Roberts' wondrous pitching prowess, his desire to pay it forward proved to be his real legacy.

8

WHITEY

As a player, Richie Ashburn was so competitive, so fiery, that he often hollered at the opposing pitcher after making an out. Didn't matter whether it was Sandy Koufax or Bob Gibson or some journeyman who was out of baseball a year later. They were all on the receiving end of an Ashburn rant—"You ain't got nothing!" he would yell, irrationally—on his way back to the Phillies' dugout.

Later, during his 34-year run as a broadcaster, Ashburn could talk his way out of an on-air gaffe or into getting a pepperoni pizza from Celebre's in South Philly delivered to the television booth. He told it like it was in his homespun way and contributed several aphorisms to the lexicon, including his description of a "runnerish" baserunner who danced out to a big lead and his "Hard to believe, Harry" expression of incredulity to play-by-play partner and dear friend Harry Kalas.

Seldom during his 70 years was Ashburn at a loss for words.

Sit back, then, and let one of his longtime broadcast mates recall two of those times.

"I was in his company, right standing with him, one night when Willie Mays said, 'Richie Ashburn, you're the best center fielder I've ever seen,'" Chris Wheeler said. "Whitey just goes, 'C'mon, Willie.' And Willie says, 'No, Richie, you're the best I've ever seen.' Well, nothing much made Whitey step back, but that one took him back. That's a true story, not one of those old wives' tales that you hear."

Wheeler figures he told it on the air a few dozen times, often with Ashburn—known to friends as "Whitey" for his light-blonde hair—seated beside him. Actually, to hear Wheeler tell it, he owes his 36-year broadcasting career to Ashburn, who didn't feel very chatty during the second game of a doubleheader in Montreal on September 26, 1976.

The Phillies won the first game, 4–1, behind a complete game from Jim Lonborg to clinch the National League East title and celebrated with a sudsy postgame party in the clubhouse. But there was another game to play and, for Ashburn, nine more innings to call.

"I think Whitey wanted to keep drinking," Wheeler recalled with a laugh, and sure enough, Ashburn saw his chance when Wheeler entered the booth.

Wheeler worked in the Phillies' public relations department, and although he usually sat with the writers in the press box, he often stopped by to pass a note to Kalas or Ashburn.

"Whitey would give me the old, 'Here comes the PR guy, Chris Wheeler. He's the guy we tell you about that messes everything up all the time,'" Wheeler said. "Well, this time Whitey says, 'Wheels has always really wanted to do this, so I'm going to let him on the air.' He took his headset off and gave it to me. A big-league broadcast, and I'm sitting down next to Harry. And I had a ball."

Never mind that Wheeler was actually good at it. Or that the Phillies had an opening for a color commentator to work with Andy Musser on the radio. Or that team president Bill Giles saw the sense in promoting someone who was already on the payroll rather than hiring a new broadcaster.

By shutting his mouth, Ashburn gave rise to Wheeler's career.

"I don't know that I ever get on the air if Whitey hadn't gotten up that day and walked out," Wheeler said.

And if Ashburn wasn't already Wheeler's baseball hero, he surely would've ascended to that status. But like so many kids who grew up in the Philadelphia area in the 1950s, Wheeler wanted to be Ashburn, the small, scrappy, oh-so-speedy center fielder and leadoff man who made everything happen for the Phillies.

Ashburn spent 15 seasons in the big leagues, batting .308 with a .396 on-base percentage, 234 stolen bases, 1,198 walks, and only 571 strikeouts. He was a six-time All-Star and a two-time batting champion. In 1958, he went 14-for-21 in his final five games to hike his average to .350 and edge Mays, who went 10-for-21 and finished at .347. He was inducted into the Hall of Fame in 1995 along with Mike Schmidt.

In his 1996 book, *The Whiz Kids and the 1950 Pennant*, Hall of Fame pitcher Robin Roberts called Ashburn "the quintessential leadoff man" and "one of the best contact hitters to ever play the game." Roberts referred to Ashburn's "great speed and slashing hitting style" as skills that enabled him to collect the most hits (1,875) and third-most runs (952) of any player in the majors in the '50s. Ted Williams gave Ashburn the nickname "Putt-Putt" because he "ran so fast you would think he had twin motors in his pants." It hardly mattered that Ashburn hit only 29 career home runs.

"He had a great line about one year when they brought him in to redo his contract and they said, 'All you do is hit singles.' Whitey said, 'If I hit my singles any further, they'd be outs,'" Wheeler said. "He would tell that story a lot, and I'd laugh every time. Because that's what he did. He hit singles. And as kids we could identify with that because we were little guys who thought we could run. He was our guy. I was crushed when they traded him to the Cubs. Absolutely crushed."

Ashburn was the 23-year-old catalyst of the pennant-winning 1950 "Whiz Kids." Nine years later, though, the Phillies not only hadn't made it back to the playoffs but sunk to a 90-loss low. Ashburn had the worst year of his career in 1959 and was peddled to Chicago for pitcher John Buzhardt, aging All-Star infielder Al Dark, and third baseman Jim Woods.

It would've been an unpopular trade even if Ashburn hadn't had a mini-revival with the Cubs in 1960 or been an All-Star on a historically awful New York Mets team in 1962. If he hung on another two or three years, he likely would've gotten the 426 hits that he needed to reach 3,000. Instead, Phillies fans rejoiced in 1963 when he returned as a broadcaster alongside By Saam and Bill Campbell.

Wheeler met his hero in the mid-'60s. Ashburn was taping a commercial at the WCAU–1210 AM studios, where Wheeler was working while taking classes at Penn State.

"I was introduced to him and I was speechless," Wheeler said. "Dwight Eisenhower may as well have walked in at the same time, and I'd have rather talked to [Ashburn]."

Over the years, Wheeler recognized the same swoon from folks who met Ashburn either at the ballpark or charity events throughout the city. If Ashburn was the favorite player of Phillies fans in their sixties and seventies, he and Kalas became the soundtrack of summer to fans in their forties and fifties who knew him exclusively as a broadcaster.

"I would see other people come in the booth and react to Whitey the way that I had at one time," Wheeler said. "It could come back to me that this guy is really special to a lot of people. And he was to me, too."

Giles calls Ashburn "arguably the most beloved person ever to live in the Delaware Valley, at least since Ben Franklin—and Franklin couldn't hit a slider. I do not believe that I was ever in his company when he did not make me laugh or at least bring a big smile to my face."

Ashburn died suddenly of a heart attack at the Grand Hyatt in New York on September 9, 1997. But his memory endures in the Whitey-isms that might as well have served as the Phillies' answer to Yogi Berra.

"Right down the middle for a ball," Ashburn would say when he disagreed with an umpire's strike zone. *"It's a lead-pipe cinch, Harry,"* he would declare, an actual pipe hanging from his mouth.

And then there was this gem: Ashburn once surprised everyone by wishing former Phillies owner Ruly Carpenter a speedy recovery from a car accident. Between innings, public relations honcho Larry Shenk dashed into the television booth and asked, "Who told you Ruly was in a car accident?"

"I had dinner with some guy in the press room tonight, and he told me," Ashburn said.

One problem: The dinner companion was Shenk, and the victim of the car accident was his wife, Julie. Wheeler shook his head, wondering how they would correct the mistake on-air.

"Just leave it to me, pal," said Ashburn, who set the record straight as only he could.

"Fans, I'd like to correct something that was said last inning by yours truly. I was given some misinformation by Phillies PR man Larry Shenk, and I've heard that it was his wife, Julie, who was involved in the car accident and not former Phillies president Ruly Carpenter."

After wishing Julie well, Ashburn added that Shenk "needs to work on his enunciation," according to Wheeler.

Classic Ashburn. Never at a loss for words.

Well, almost never.

9

HARRY THE K

Todd Kalas was a nervous wreck.

It was October 19, 2008, a few hours before the first pitch of Game 7 of the American League Championship Series. Three days earlier, with a chance to win the pennant, the Tampa Bay Rays blew a seven-run lead at Fenway Park in Boston. The Red Sox won the next game, too. But the Rays had one last chance on their home turf, underneath the dome at Tropicana Field. It represented a seminal moment for the fledgling franchise.

For Kalas, though, the stakes were higher and more personal. As host of the pre- and postgame show on local Rays telecasts, it was an opportunity to call a World Series opposite his father, Harry Kalas, the beloved play-by-play voice of the National League–champion Phillies.

"I was pretty much as stressed and as excited as I'd ever been for any sporting event," Todd Kalas recalled. "I was just nuts that entire day. I remember as the game progressed and after the Rays won just how many emotions I had. I went back home after celebrating with everybody and just cried and bawled happy tears. I couldn't believe this was happening."

Oh, but it was about to get even better.

"Harry the K," as the elder Kalas was known to his adoring public, wasn't from Philadelphia. He grew up in a western suburb of Chicago, graduated from the University of Iowa, served in the United States Army, began his broadcasting career calling minor-league games in Hawaii, and got his big break with the Houston Astros. He even called the first game at the Astrodome on April 12, 1965.

Six years later, with the Phillies set to move into Veterans Stadium, they hired Kalas to replace popular Bill Campbell in a three-man booth with longtime announcer By Saam and former center fielder Richie Ashburn. Then-team president Bill Giles tried to pry Al Michaels from a play-by-play gig with the Cincinnati Reds. But when Michaels opted to stay put, Giles tapped Kalas, his "very, very close personal friend" with whom he worked previously in Houston.

Philadelphia is a notoriously parochial place, and fans were skeptical of an outsider on the mic. But they quickly fell for Kalas' leathery voice and easy manner, and for 38 years, they let him into their homes through both radio and television.

"I didn't really anticipate him being as popular as he turned out," Giles said, noting that Kalas was equally adored by sponsors. "Harry was a lovable guy, but he wanted everybody to like him and he went out of his way to be liked. It was a two-way street. [Fans] liked him and he liked them, and it was good for the Phillies."

Kalas had other jobs in broadcasting, notably following John Facenda as the lead voice of NFL Films. But the ballpark was his sanctuary, the Phillies his passion. Todd Kalas remembers his father being genuinely excited to leave for work every day. He often professed his affection for Philadelphia, and his adopted city loved him right back. He signed so many autographs and shook so many hands that fans felt like they knew him. It wasn't long before he became more popular than many Phillies players.

Growing up, Todd Kalas got the usual questions from classmates and teachers about whether he knew Mike Schmidt or Larry Bowa (he did). But that was nothing compared to the swoons whenever his father picked him up from school.

"Philadelphia fans can tell a phony from the real deal, and one thing about Dad is he was as genuine as they come," said Todd, the oldest of Harry's three sons. "Who he was in person and who he was on the air, who he was as a Phillies fan and broadcaster was genuine. He was one of the people cheering along with everybody else. He just happened to have a microphone in front of him."

His greatest call? Take your pick.

Many people are partial to April 18, 1987, in Pittsburgh: *"Swing and a long drive, there it is, number 500! The career 500th home run for Michael Jack Schmidt!"* There was also Kalas' tearful call with Tim McCarver after the Phillies outlasted the Astros in Game 5 in Houston to win the 1980 pennant, or his *"Could it be? Could it be?"* urging of Jim

Thome's 400th career homer in 2003, or even his disappointment over Joe Carter's walkoff homer to beat the Phillies in the '93 World Series.

And then there was this one, after Chase Utley hustled home from second base on an infield chopper on August 9, 2006, in Atlanta: *"Chase Utley, you are The Man!"*

Kalas called the first and last games at the Vet, the first game at Citizens Bank Park in 2004, and six no-hitters. He received the Hall of Fame's prestigious Ford C. Frick Award in 2002, and was inducted into the Phillies' Wall of Fame in 2009.

"I got really lucky that he and Ashburn were just awesome," Giles said. "I don't believe there has ever been a tandem of television or radio that was any better than the tandem of Richie and Harry. I had nothing to do with it. It just developed and happened."

One call that Kalas never got to make: the clinching moment from the Phillies' first World Series championship in 1980. Major League Baseball regulations forced local stations to air the national broadcast on CBS Radio, thereby keeping him out of the booth.

The rule was changed the following year, enabling Kalas to work the 1983 and 1993 World Series. But the Phillies were defeated both times. He was 72 when they finally returned to the Fall Classic in 2008, and with the Rays as the opponent, he wouldn't miss an opportunity to share the moment with his son.

Kalas asked Phillies manager of broadcasting Rob Brooks if he and Todd could work an inning together. Brooks agreed, and they settled on Game 1 in the Phillies' radio booth.

Harry Kalas: *"And we are back at Tropicana Field, Harry Kalas joined by my son, Todd, who works for the Tampa Bay Rays. It is 2-0, Phils, here in the fourth inning, and Shane Victorino will lead it off. Todd, this is quite an exciting time for us, involved in a World Series on opposite sides."*

Todd Kalas: *"This is absolutely the best."*

"Doing that inning together in the booth was just the best thing ever," said Todd, now the lead play-by-play announcer on Astros telecasts. "Just to be there with him was cool enough, but then to get to call an inning, I don't think in my broadcasting career if I worked another 25 or 30 years I could quite top that."

Todd Kalas recalls feeling oddly relaxed during the inning. If anything, he could sense that his dad was the anxious one. Always the gracious host, Harry set up Todd to talk about the Rays' surprising rise from 96 losses in 2007 to the first World Series in franchise history.

"It was totally his gig. I was just kind of along for the ride," Todd said. "I think Dad might've been a little more nervous because he was introducing me into a broadcast booth that is pretty much sacred ground. You have your Phillies announcers all year, and here comes this guy from another team.

"I was pretty laid back, I think. I knew how Dad usually paced out a game, so I was kind of used to his cadence and his rhythm in a broadcast. I thought we flowed pretty well. I just had a blast with it. I knew that this was a moment that I had to remember and cherish every second of because it was probably a once in a lifetime, and it was."

The Phillies won the Series in the rain-interrupted fifth game, and this time, Harry Kalas got to deliver the clinching call. Seated in the home radio booth and wearing a red wool Phillies jacket with white sleeves, he leaned into the microphone and zeroed in on closer Brad Lidge's two-strike pitch to Eric Hinske. It was 9:58 PM on October 29, 2008, when Kalas spoke the 110 words that he had been waiting for his entire career:

"*One strike away. Nothing-and-two, the count to Hinske. Fans on their feet. Rally towels are being waved. Brad Lidge stretches. The 0-2 pitch—swing and a miss, struck him out! The Philadelphia Phillies are 2008 world champions of baseball!*

"*Brad Lidge does it again and stays perfect for the 2008 season. 48-for-48 in save opportunities, and let the city celebrate! Don't let the 48-hour wait diminish the euphoria of this moment and the celebration. It has been 28 years since the Phillies have enjoyed a world championship, 25 years in this city that a team has enjoyed a world championship, and the fans are ready to celebrate. What a night!*"

Six months later, Kalas passed away. He had a heart attack and collapsed in the broadcast booth in Washington a few hours before a game. Team president David Montgomery put it best when he solemnly said that the Phillies had "lost our voice."

Kalas' legacy, though, carries on. A restaurant in left field at Citizens Bank Park is named "Harry the K's," and a seven-foot bronze statue of Kalas stands not far away on the outfield concourse. After a Phillies player hits a home run at home, Kalas' signature "Outta Here!" call blares over the ballpark sound system. When the Phillies win, a video of Kalas serenading the crowd with a rendition of his favorite song—Frank Sinatra's "High Hopes"—is played on the left-field scoreboard.

Todd Kalas got to see it in person on July 26, 2017, when the Phillies defeated the Astros in an interleague game at Citizens Bank Park.

"I love the fact that they still keep his memory alive," he said. "Half of today's players probably don't even know what the significance of that song is. But I know the Phillies are a special organization. I've known it since I was five years old when Dad joined the team. For them to carry the legacy on and keep that tradition going is really amazing."

Almost as amazing as a young broadcaster getting to call an inning in the World Series with his father by his side.

10

DALLAS & CHARLIE

As the celebration raged in the streets of Philadelphia, in the stands at Citizens Bank Park, and especially within the Phillies' clubhouse on the night of October 29, 2008, Charlie Manuel sat quietly in his office, a bottle of whiskey on his desk, and absorbed his new reality of being the manager of a World Series champion.

"I wanted our players to celebrate," Manuel recalled. "Believe me, I was probably happier than they were. But at the same time, too, I looked at it as, 'Hey, they did all the playing. Let them have the fun. Let me step back and get out of the way.'"

So, Manuel sat there in his office, like Vito Corleone at his daughter's wedding, and received a steady stream of congratulations. Harry Kalas, the Phillies' Hall of Fame broadcaster, dropped by. So did general manager Pat Gillick. Coaches, front-office staff, trainers, and support personnel came and went.

Then, after a while, it was just Manuel, that bottle of VO, a few reporters, and Dallas Green, the only person on the planet who knew exactly what Manuel was feeling.

Green managed the Phillies to their only other World Series title in 1980. He did it his way, which was considerably different from Manuel's, and there were moments when he openly criticized good ol' Charlie. Their relationship could be downright frosty. There was even a tense exchange around the batting cage in 2006 when Manuel told Green to knock it off—in far less polite language—after a denunciation on 94-WIP, Philadelphia's sports-talk radio station.

But now here they were, sharing a few drinks and a special bond.

"This is better than I imagined," Manuel said at the time. "It's better when you see the people that are happy and the people that enjoy it. It's good for everybody. It's good for the city, our fans, the organization, all our players. It definitely wasn't easy. But it was worth it."

Green nodded affirmatively like a churchgoer at a sermon.

"People think this is a piece of cake," Green said. "And the thing is, Charlie had to go through an extra playoff. I only went through one playoff. He went through two playoffs to get to the World Series."

Manuel interjected, "It's hard to win, period. You've got to have the talent but some fight comes into play."

This could've gone on all night, and it probably did. In the midst of a champagne- and beer-drenched championship party, it didn't get much cooler. And it cemented what became a good friendship between two men who, in their own ways, were larger than life.

Green had a middling eight-year career as a big-league pitcher for the Phillies, Washington Senators, and New York Mets. But it was his post-playing exploits as a scout, manager, general manager, and special adviser that earned him a place among the most colorful characters in baseball for six decades until his death from kidney failure in 2017 at age 82.

Born in Newport, Delaware, Green played for Conrad High School and the University of Delaware and was a favorite of Phillies owner Bob Carpenter and his son, Ruly, who were practically royalty in that state. He was working as the scouting director in 1979 when the Phillies canned Danny Ozark, the affable manager who led the club to back-to-back-to-back division titles but also three consecutive NL Championship Series losses from 1976 to '78, and promoted Green, pretty much his polar opposite.

A 6-foot-5 bear with a booming voice and a pull-no-punches attitude, he sparred with several players, including shortstop Larry Bowa. He benched slugger Greg Luzinski. He instituted a dress code, imposed a curfew, and banned drinking on team flights, an attempt to change the perception that the Phillies were too laid back under Ozark.

"He came in saying that we were a country-club team and he would come in with his whip. Well, all of us felt like that was a bunch of bull," catcher Bob Boone said. "The players resented that. He did what he said he was going to do, but I don't think there was anything in particular that he did."

The Phillies finished 19–11 under Green in 1979, then came back in 1980 and went 91–71. But they had to come from behind to win the division, and their chances weren't looking very good on August 10 when they got outscored 11–2 in a doubleheader sweep in Pittsburgh. Green blasted the players in a between-games clubhouse tirade and he got into a dugout fight with reliever Ron Reed during the second game. But the Phillies went 23–11 down the stretch, including a run of 12 wins in 16 games, overtook the Montreal Expos, and clinched the division on the final weekend. They won an epic NLCS against the Houston Astros to capture their first pennant since 1950, then vanquished the Kansas City Royals in the World Series.

And looking back, they might have done it all to spite their manager.

"We didn't feel that it was anything Dallas brought," Boone said. "He gave us somebody to not like in the clubhouse. But that, in a way, inspired us. Dallas brought a whole different mode to managing. He was like, 'I'm not here to be your friend. I'm here for us to win.'"

Bowa puts it this way: "Dallas pushed us. He pushed buttons. He knew we had a lot of All-Stars, guys who had good reputations. The first thing he said was, 'You guys think you're good. You're not as good as you think you are. Because if you were, you'd have a ring on your finger by now. You have nothing on your hand.' He would constantly bring that up."

Manuel's players would do anything for him. It just took the media and fan base considerably longer to come around.

A .198 hitter over parts of six big-league seasons, but a cult hero with Ruthian power for a half-dozen years in Japan, Manuel is a hitting savant in any country. Want to get him started? Ask him about the time that he got into a heated debate with none other than Ted Williams—over a few VOs, of course—in a hotel restaurant in Washington, D.C., about whether the top hand or the bottom is more important to a hitter.

After managing in the minor leagues, Manuel took over as hitting coach of the Cleveland Indians in the mid-'90s as young Manny Ramirez and Jim Thome were joining Albert Belle, Kenny Lofton, Carlos Baerga, and Omar Vizquel in a juggernaut lineup. He managed the Indians for 2½ seasons, leading them to a division title in 2001.

But when the Phillies hired him to replace Bowa after the 2004 season, it was viewed largely as a favor to Thome, the team's new star slugger, who regards Manuel as his baseball father. Mocked by fans for his Virginia twang and branded a rube by some in the media because of his homespun style—one radiohead cruelly dubbed him "Elmer Befuddled"—there were calls for the Phillies to dump Manuel after back-to-back postseason misses in 2005 and 2006.

"Never crossed my mind," former Phillies general manager Pat Gillick said.

It didn't matter, Gillick insists, that he inherited Manuel from predecessor Ed Wade. Or that he added ex-big-league managers Jimy

Former manager Dallas Green (left) hugs current manager Charlie Manuel after Green threw out the first pitch before Game 5 of the 2009 NLCS.
(AP Photo / Matt Slocum)

Williams and Davey Lopes to the coaching staff in 2007—prompting speculation that Manuel's replacement was on hand. Gillick recognized that the Phillies' personnel fit Manuel's area of expertise.

"He likes offensive clubs and we had an offensive club," Gillick said. "[Jimmy] Rollins, [Chase] Utley, [Ryan] Howard, [Pat] Burrell, [Shane] Victorino, [Jayson] Werth, that's an offensive-type team. That's the type of team that he works well with. It never crossed my mind to ever think about doing something with Charlie."

It helped Manuel's case, too, that most players would run through a wall for him. Aaron Rowand almost did, in fact. The hard-nosed (literally) center fielder broke his jaw and several orbital bones when he crashed into the wall while making a catch in 2006 at Citizens Bank Park.

"There's not a greater man or a guy that you want to go out and leave everything on the field for than Charlie Manuel," Rowand said. "Everybody that's ever played for the man loves him dearly."

Green nevertheless aligned with Manuel's critics. In particular, he thought Manuel was too much of a players' manager and not enough of a, well, hard-ass. Honest as ever, Green expressed that opinion in multiple radio interviews, even though he worked as a Phillies adviser.

Finally, Manuel had enough.

"I just didn't think he had any right to challenge me because I was the manager," said Manuel, who dined with Green after the batting-practice blow-up to hash out their differences more discreetly. "I think it was just straight honesty, just looking each other in the eye, really. I think having a few cocktails probably helped. I always respected Dallas. After that, we were good."

Better than good. They became confidants. On that crowning night in 2008, a reporter asked Green what he thought of the job that Manuel did.

"What the hell? He's going to have a ring on," Green said. "Everybody bitched and moaned about how I did it, but I've got a ring. They can bitch all they want about him, but he's going to have a ring. And we're the only two guys in 126 years that have a ring. I welcome him with open arms because that seat is a tough seat in Philadelphia.

But he has weathered the storm, and he has proven to everybody that he is a pretty damn good baseball man."

After 2008, Manuel said Green would even daydream about how the two Phillies championship clubs would've matched up.

It's a fascinating exercise. The 2008 Phillies featured the best shortstop (Rollins), second baseman (Utley), and first baseman (Howard) in franchise history. The 1980 club had the best third baseman (Mike Schmidt). Both teams had lefty aces (Steve Carlton vs. Cole Hamels), dominant closers (Tug McGraw vs. Brad Lidge), and Gold Glove center fielders (Garry Maddox vs. Shane Victorino).

"Dallas used to tell me they were kind of close in talent," Manuel said. "If you look, both teams had some good pitchers but also we had some weaknesses in our pitching staff. Position players, if you look at them, they were close. That would've been a good series. When I think about it, that could've been a really good series."

Surely, then, it would have come down to the managers.

"I don't know about that," Manuel said, laughing. "The players put us over the top."

11

J-ROLL

Jimmy Rollins sat at a table in the Diamond Club in Citizens Bank Park. Surrounded by reporters at the Phillies' annual winter caravan, the shortstop riffed—as only he could—on barely missing the playoffs again, the offseason additions of pitchers Freddy Garcia and Adam Eaton, and anything else on his mind.

That's when the 13 words spilled out of his mouth.

"I think we are the team to beat in the NL East. Finally."

Now this was 2007, before the ubiquity of iPhones and Twitter and the age of viral videos and the 24-hour news cycle. But it didn't take long for word of Rollins' declaration to spread. It made for great sports-talk radio fodder and back-page tabloid material in New York, where the Mets were fixing to repeat as division champs after falling one game short of going to the World Series in 2006. In time, due largely to Rollins' on-field performance, it would become one of the most prescient quotes in Philadelphia sports history.

But at the moment, in the Phillies' executive offices, it was causing some agita.

"I wasn't sure what to think, to be honest," said Mike Arbuckle, then the team's assistant general manager. "You don't know how it's going to play, especially in a market like New York. My thought was, *I know these players believe it, but I don't know that we really want to come out and say it.*"

General manager Pat Gillick felt similarly. *It's good to be confident,* he thought, *but let your play on the field do the talking.*

Good luck muting James Calvin Rollins, though.

Long before he made three All-Star teams, won four Gold Gloves, set franchise records for at-bats (8,628), hits (2,306), and doubles (479), and became the best shortstop in franchise history, J-Roll oozed confidence and California cool. He grew up in Oakland, raised by a mother who once described herself to *The New York Times* as "a five-tool player" for the Allen Temple Baptist Church women's fast-pitch softball team. His baseball idol: Rickey Henderson, the self-proclaimed "greatest of all time" after breaking the record for stolen bases.

The Phillies drafted Rollins in the second round in 1996, prompting several rival scouting directors to suggest it was a reach to take a 5-foot-7 high school shortstop with the 46th overall pick. But Arbuckle cited one quality that made him certain Rollins would reach the big leagues.

In Philly, it's called *"atty-tude."*

"He had that brashness and confidence that he was going to absolutely maximize every ounce of ability that he had," Arbuckle said. "You could see that in high school, the way he went about playing the game, how confident he was. The mental makeup was the thing that made me say, 'Okay, I'm going to go ahead and take this guy. I don't want to lose this kid.' As it turned out, we were right on with Jimmy."

So, as much as Gillick might have wanted to summon Rollins for a tête-à-tête about the perils of poking the Mets, he failed to see the sense in muzzling a player who derived so much from flapping his gums. Besides, there was something innocent, almost endearing about Rollins' chatter. More often than not, too, he backed it up with his play.

To wit: As a rookie in 2001, Rollins was assigned to take batting practice in a group with veterans Scott Rolen, Bobby Abreu, and Doug Glanville. They were a unique mix. Abreu was the calm, even detached, right fielder; Glanville the Ivy League–educated center fielder; Rolen the hard-nosed third baseman, a throwback in every sense. And Rollins was the cocky motormouth.

"Every time he put the bat on the ball, he was like, 'Dude, did you see that? Backspin. Oooh, yeah, I was looking for that,'" Glanville said. "I found it entertaining. It was harmless. But Scott was like, 'No!' And I get it. Scott was small-town, old-school to the core, and rookies are supposed to keep their mouths shut. One day, Scott pulls me and Bobby aside, trying to get a coalition, and he's like, 'I'd like to kick Jimmy out of the group. He's talking too much. He's acting like he's been here for 10 years.'

"So, Rolen sits him down. It was like talking to a kindergartner. That was the dynamic. He's like, 'Jimmy, we have decided that we're kicking you out of the group. I've made arrangements.' And he told him why. I felt horrible because, quite honestly, I didn't take on Scott. I didn't support him, but I didn't stop him. The thing that's so sad about it is Jimmy didn't talk for days. He just sat there."

Rollins never lost his swagger, though. He led the league with 12 triples and 46 stolen bases and finished third in the Rookie of the Year voting. He brought an energy to the top of the lineup, and the Phillies went from 65 wins in 2000 to 86 in 2001.

It wasn't long before Rollins could hit in any batting practice group that he chose—and talk as much as he wanted.

"When he was finally into his rhythm, he was so funny," Glanville said. "Game against Pittsburgh, he's looking for a slider, he gets the hit, and he comes in and describes it. It was this youthful exuberance

Jimmy Rollins celebrates his walk-off, two-run double in Game 4 of the 2009 NLCS against the Dodgers. (AP Photo / David J. Phillip)

of just loving the game and just wanting to talk to someone about it. It was so infectious. We were so flat and he came up and brought this jolt of energy.

"I joked with Jimmy later that we should've had a promotional item called the 'Jimmy Rollins Talking Bat.' You get a hit and it would just go, 'Oooh, did you see that? Oh my goodness! Wow, that was cool. I was looking for that pitch.' I called him 'Rookie 2.0' because he was like the next generation of player, being able to come up and be free to speak his mind. I thought he was the evolution of our game."

Indeed, Rollins made the Phillies fun again. He viewed baseball as entertainment and saw to it that the fans were properly amused. He seemed to be at his best in the clutch, too, prompting former manager Larry Bowa to dub him a "red-light player." But he couldn't quite get the team over the hump and into the playoffs for the first time since 1993.

The Phillies missed out on the wild-card by one game in 2005, costing general manager Ed Wade his job, and by three games in 2006. Despite a young, homegrown nucleus that included Rollins, Chase Utley, Ryan Howard, and Cole Hamels, fans were beginning to wonder if they were ever going to get a crack at playing in October.

So, Rollins wasn't standing on the sturdiest of limbs with his "team to beat" remark. But Gigi Rollins taught her son to say what he felt, and well, he listened.

"We brought over Freddy Garcia [in a trade], and knowing what he did just a few years earlier in Chicago, I'm like, 'That's the type of pitcher we need,'" Rollins said in 2018 before a 10-year reunion of the Phillies' World Series champs. "I felt we had the offense. We could score with anyone. It was just a matter of keeping the other team from scoring. We bring in some big-name pitchers that had success, and I was like, 'It's our turn.'"

But Garcia made only 11 starts in 2007, none after June 8 in Kansas City when he left with a shoulder ache that required surgery. Eaton posted a 6.29 ERA in 30 starts. The Phillies finished with a 4.73 team ERA that ranked 13th in the NL, and on September 13, they were 7½ games behind the first-place Mets with 17 games remaining.

The team to beat appeared to be beaten.

But the Phillies could mash. They paced the league in runs and on-base plus slugging percentage and were second in homers. And Rollins was the catalyst. He played in all 162 games and led the NL in plate appearances (778), at-bats (716), runs (139), and triples (20). He hit 30 homers and drove in 94 runs out of the leadoff spot, swiped 41 bases, posted an .875 OPS, and edged Colorado's Matt Holliday for the MVP Award.

The Phillies finished on a 13–4 kick, the Mets went 5–12 down the stretch, and on the season's final day, the Phillies overtook them to fulfill Rollins' promise.

"Jimmy likes to throw it out there and say, 'Hey, let's go for it,'" Gillick said. "That's his style, and it works for him. I don't think it hurt us at all. Maybe it even challenged us a bit."

As they celebrated that long-awaited division championship on the field at Citizens Bank Park—the first of five consecutive NL East crowns in a run that included two pennants and a World Series title—Rollins recalled another prediction that he made after getting drafted.

"I told Mom, 'When I get up there, we're going to win,'" Rollins said before his official retirement ceremony in 2019. "That was the only mission I had. All the other stuff came with being healthy and playing every day. If I'm getting there, I'll find a way to have an impact that we'll win. That's what I told my mom the day I got drafted."

As usual, Rollins delivered.

12

A PENNANT COMES TO PHILLY

Stan Baumgartner walked out of the University of Chicago and into the Phillies' home clubhouse at Baker Bowl in late June of 1914.

It didn't take long for the young pitcher to realize that something was rotten.

The Phillies were on their way to a sixth-place finish, only their third losing season in an eight-year span. But this was more than merely a down year. They were the picture of dysfunction. In his book, *The Philadelphia Phillies*, co-authored with Frederick G. Lieb in 1953, Baumgartner detailed a clubhouse divided by age and cultural background, a nasty feud between two outfielders, and a burned-out manager who lacked the energy to pull together a team that was seemingly too talented to play so poorly.

Team president William F. Baker knew that change needed to begin at the top. And so, once the 1914 season ended with the Phillies dropping six of their last eight games and falling to 74–80, Baker replaced manager Red Dooin with Pat Moran, a former catcher who already had the respect of the team's older players because of his role in helping to develop star pitcher Grover Cleveland Alexander and lefty Eppa Rixey.

Moran wasted no time weeding out the problems, beginning with outfielder Sherry Magee. But the offseason trade of Magee to the Boston Braves for a player to be named wasn't universally popular. A high-average hitter with speed and a strong arm, Magee had been the Phillies' most productive player for the previous 11 seasons. And he was at his best in 1914, batting .314 and leading the National League with 171 hits, 39 doubles, 277 total bases, 103 RBI, and a .509 slugging percentage.

As talented as Magee was, though, he could be divisive in the clubhouse. He famously tortured young players, once dropping a laundry bag filled with water on Rixey, Baumgartner, and pitcher Joe Oeschger while they were posing for a picture outside the Metropole Hotel in Cincinnati. Magee and center fielder Dode Paskert loathed one another so much that Magee's two sons once booed so loudly after a Paskert home run that they could be heard in the dugout, according to Baumgartner, an incident that incited a fistfight between the players.

To Moran, trading Magee was addition by subtraction. The Phillies got a productive player in return, too. George "Possum" Whitted played center field for the World Series–winning Braves in 1914 and was known for both his hustle on the field and his good-natured relationship with teammates. Lieb described Whitted as "a funmaker and prankster" and "one of Stan Baumgartner's favorites." In other words, the anti-Magee.

The Phillies made a few other notable moves. Dooin doubled as the backup catcher, but after being stripped of the managerial duties, he couldn't very well play for Moran. He was traded to the Cincinnati Reds for infielder Bert Niehoff, who became the Phillies' everyday second baseman. They also turned to the Pacific Coast League to sign shortstop Dave Bancroft, and the 24-year-old became one of the league's top rookies.

But Moran needed to change the team's collective attitude. It began at spring training in St. Petersburg, Florida. Baumgartner recalled Moran requiring players to walk two to three miles each way from the team's downtown hotel to Coffee Pot Park, its training site on the outskirts of town. When Moran found out that Oeschger and Baumgartner were riding bicycles on part of their route, he added an extra mile to the daily walk.

"From the first day in training, it was evident that Moran was going to run things differently," Baumgartner and Lieb wrote. "He was the boss every minute of the day and night, a stickler for detail. Baumgartner added, 'I also can say that Pat was the smartest manager I ever played for—or observed in action—in my 39 years in baseball.'"

Indeed, Moran instituted a contemporary, relatively advanced system of communication for the pitchers and catchers. The Phillies had three sets of signs and the catcher could switch between them without having to come out to the mound. Baumgartner described Moran as "the most thorough man then in baseball." He was also ahead of his time as far as data collection, keeping a notebook on the tendencies of opposing pitchers.

Moran looked for the slightest edge. He wasn't above directing players to verbally harass opposing managers or umpires if he thought such needling could get under their skin. And opponents often accused the Phillies of going to elaborate means to steal signs, including using binoculars and flashing signs from a clubhouse window in center field at Baker Bowl.

Although Moran encouraged players to have fun in their free time to foster camaraderie, and there were tales of fishing trips in spring training and card games on long train rides, Baumgartner noted that the manager made expectations clear when they arrived for work.

"From the start of the training season Moran reiterated that 'this is not a sixth-place ball club,'" Baumgartner and Lieb wrote. "His favorite speech at meetings which were held before games was: 'This is your bread and butter as well as mine.' And the boys took the advice to heart. But Moran never talked pennant. 'Win this one today,' was all that he ever said."

The 1915 Phillies did a lot of winning. They opened the season with eight consecutive victories and won 11 of their first 12 games. They spent 139 days in first place and never slid more than 4½ games off the pace.

Right fielder Gavvy Cravath, runner-up for National League MVP two years earlier, had the best season of his 11-year career. At age 34, he led the league in runs (89), RBI (115), walks (86), on-base percentage (.393), slugging (.510), total bases (266), and home runs (24), the latter total holding up as the 20th-century record until Babe Ruth blasted 29 in 1919. Cravath went deep 11 more times than the second-best NL slugger, Cy Williams of the Cubs.

First baseman Fred Luderus finished second in the NL batting race with a .315 average, while Whitted batted .281, one point higher than Magee for the Braves. (Magee topped Whitted in nearly every other category, including hits, RBI, and OPS.)

But the Phillies were carried by their pitching. Erskine Mayer (2.36 ERA), Rixey (2.39), and George Chalmers (2.48) all had stellar numbers. The staff was anchored by Alexander, who went 31–10 with a 1.22 ERA, 241 strikeouts, and only 64 walks in 376⅓ innings. He lost more than two starts in a row only once. He posted 12 shutouts and threw four one-hitters, three of which came in an eight-start span.

"Whenever the team started to slip a bit, Grover would step in, win a shutout or low-hit game and start the Phillies off again," Baumgartner and Lieb wrote. "The players admitted they wouldn't have come close without 'old Pete.'"

The Phillies won the National League pennant by seven games over Magee's Braves. And after the crosstown Athletics represented Philadelphia in the World Series in 1910, 1911, and 1913, it was finally the Phillies' turn. Baker built extra box seats in front of the left- and center-field bleachers, a decision that he believed suited the fans' increased ticket demands even if it made it easier for the AL-champion Boston Red Sox to hit the ball out of Baker Bowl.

Phillies catcher Bill Killefer missed most of the World Series because of a sore arm. But the biggest loss came before Game 5. With the Phillies facing elimination, Alexander didn't feel strong enough to start on only one day of rest. Mayer started instead on three days' rest and gave up two runs in 2⅓ innings before giving way to Rixey, who allowed three runs in 6⅔ innings of a 5–4 loss. Baker was roundly criticized after the Red Sox took aim at the shorter fences and hit three homers in the clinching game at Baker Bowl.

But the Phillies lost the series because they scored only 10 runs in the five games. After winning Game 1 at home, they dropped the next four by a combined score of 11–7. Even Cravath was muted, going 2-for-16 without a home run.

Still, for a franchise that had never before been to a World Series, the season represented a smashing success. According to Baumgartner, the Phillies celebrated accordingly.

"The players got pretty high on beer, some of them guzzling it until it came out of their ears," he wrote with Lieb. "Some of them fell into trunks, and Bill Killefer didn't come to until he reached Altoona.

It was a combination of joy and frustration; joy over winning the Phillies' first pennant and frustration over those anemic [batting] averages in the World Series. And the letdown after a season's concentration and rigorous training."

A year later, the Phillies were edged out for the NL pennant by 2½ games. It would be 35 years before they would see a World Series again.

13

OLD PETE

As a journalist, Stan Baumgartner had a duty to maintain objectivity in both his reporting and his writing for the *Philadelphia Inquirer*. But as a former major leaguer, his experience led to inherent biases, especially in his coverage of the Phillies.

Take, for instance, his opinion of Hall of Fame pitcher Grover Cleveland Alexander.

Alexander spent the first seven seasons of his 20-year career, and eight seasons in all, with the Phillies. He set a rookie record with 28 wins in 1911, then put together a four-year peak from 1914 through 1917 in which he went 121–50 with a 1.74 earned-run average and 140 complete games among 170 starts. Considering that his 61 shutouts for the Phillies are nearly twice as many as the next pitcher (Steve Carlton had 39), it's safe to say his franchise record will never be broken. Neither, it seems, will his single-season major-league mark of 16 shutouts set in 1916. As a member of the inaugural Hall of Fame class in 1939, his greatness isn't in dispute.

But to Baumgartner, Alexander left an even more indelible mark. As an impressionable 19-year-old right-hander fresh from the University of Chicago in 1914, Baumgartner considered "Old Pete," as Alexander became known, to be a mentor. And the student paid attention to every move that the teacher made, from the way he changed speeds on his pitches to his particular taste in footwear.

"He wore the same pair of pitching shoes throughout the season," Baumgartner wrote in *The Philadelphia Phillies*, a book that he co-authored with Frederick G. Lieb in 1953, three years after Alexander's death. "When they split, he sewed them and he patched the worn-out places with tape. He would have considered it unlucky to change them."

It was little wonder, then, that Baumgartner "has no hesitancy in saying Alexander is the greatest pitcher he ever saw perform," Lieb wrote. Never mind that the deadball era in which they played was packed with legendary hurlers or that Baumgartner wrote about the early years of Hall of Famer Robin Roberts' career for the *Inquirer*. In his estimation, nobody could touch Alexander.

"'Old Pete' is the greatest of them all—a pitcher as well as a thrower," Baumgartner wrote. "Cy Young, Walter Johnson, Amos Rusie, Rube Waddell, Lefty Grove were throwers, with so much natural ability that they had to do little thinking. Alexander had great natural ability and sharpened it with smartness, as did [Christy] Mathewson."

Objectively, though, Alexander's career—really, his entire life—was marked as much by setbacks as triumphs, with enough highs and lows that Warner Brothers produced a film about him in 1952 titled *The Winning Team*. It seems only fitting that a man named after the sitting United States president was portrayed by future president Ronald Reagan.

Born in 1887, Alexander grew up shucking corn on a farm near St. Paul, Nebraska. He died in a hotel room in 1950, his body ravaged by epilepsy, alcoholism, and finally cancer, which required the amputation of his right ear.

In 1910, the Phillies drafted Alexander from Syracuse of the New York State League for $750, a steal relative to the $3,000 they spent to purchase Scranton pitcher George Chalmers, who went 29–41 with a 3.41 ERA in seven seasons and retired by 1916. One year earlier, though, Alexander got hit on the side of the head by a fastball and suffered a brief spell of double vision that nearly ended his career. Alexander carried the Phillies to their first pennant in 1915. But in 1918 he got shipped off, first to the Chicago Cubs in a fire sale by Phillies owner William F. Baker and then to the European front in World War I, where he lost the hearing in his left ear.

Alexander's baseball tour de force came during that 1915 season. He won 31 of his 49 appearances and led the majors in ERA (1.22), strikeouts (241), and complete games (36). He bookended his season with two of his league-leading 12 shutouts, blanking the Boston Braves on Opening Day at Fenway Park and again on September 29 at Braves Field to clinch the pennant. He also became the only pitcher ever to throw four one-hitters in a single season, including three in the span of one month.

The Phillies had myriad reasons to give Alexander the ball as often as possible, least of which was the briskness with which he pitched. He made quick work of opposing hitters in the most literal sense, seldom pitching a game that lasted longer than 90 minutes, according to Baumgartner and Lieb.

"When [manager] Pat Moran, who had a cottage on the Jersey shore, wanted to make an early train for the resort, he always planned to do so on a day that Aleck was scheduled to pitch," they wrote. "And Grove rarely failed him."

If not for Moran, Alexander might not have gotten an opportunity with the Phillies. The story, as told by Baumgartner and Lieb, goes that manager Red Dooin planned to cut Alexander before the 1911 season began. But Moran, then the Phillies catcher, lobbied to keep him by insisting "he looks better every time out" and pledging to do whatever he could to "help him become a real pitcher." Even then, it wasn't until Alexander shut out the Philadelphia Athletics in an exhibition that he finally won a spot on the team. He went 28–13 with a 2.14 ERA and 37 complete games in 367 innings in 1911, finishing third in MVP voting behind Cubs outfielder Frank Schulte and Mathewson. It still ranks as one of the best rookie seasons ever.

Listed at 6-foot-1 and 185 pounds, Alexander was described by Baumgartner as "a typical son of the Middlewest corn belt, freckled and sandy-haired." From 1912 through 1914, he continued to build his resume as one of the game's top pitchers and became what Baumgartner called "the beacon of the club." Baumgartner credited Alexander for showing him how to "snap a curveball" and described him as "humble, friendly, and helpful."

In 1915, once Moran took over as manager, Alexander was something else, too. He was the Phillies' stopper. He went 16–4 in starts after a loss, which was a big reason the Phillies never dropped more than four games in a row. They finished 90–62, spent 100 days in first place, and were seven games better than the second-place Boston Braves.

"Whenever the team started to slip a bit, Grover would step in, win a shutout or low-hit game, and start the Phillies off again," Baumgartner and Lieb wrote. "The players admitted they wouldn't have come close [to winning the pennant] without 'Old Pete.'"

In the World Series, Alexander pitched the Phillies to a 3–1 victory in Game 1 before 19,343 fans at Baker Bowl. The Red Sox won the next four games, all by a one-run margin, including a 2–1 decision over Alexander in Game 3 in Boston. Facing elimination in Game 5, Moran wanted to start his best pitcher, but with only one day of rest, Alexander was unable to take the ball and apply the exclamation mark to his extraordinary season.

"One of the rare occasions in Grover's long career," Baumgartner and Lieb wrote, "when he complained of an ailing flipper."

Alexander finally won his World Series in 1926, at age 39, with the St. Louis Cardinals, achieving a moment so memorable that it is noted on his Hall of Fame plaque. One day after notching a complete-game victory in Game 6 of the 1926 World Series against the Yankees, he entered in relief with the bases loaded and two out in the seventh inning of Game 7 and struck out Tony Lazzeri. Alexander tossed two more scoreless innings to clinch the championship.

Traded back to the Phillies in 1930, he made nine appearances, didn't record any wins, and retired at age 43 with 373 career victories, tied with Mathewson for third all-time behind Cy Young and Walter Johnson.

The latter years of Alexander's life were marked by tragedy. As Baumgartner wrote, "Aleck was inordinately fond of corn by-product of his native Nebraska, and if Aleck couldn't get corn, well, he wasn't particular. He'd drink anything."

Alcoholism, coupled with epilepsy and other health issues, led to divorce, poverty, and other misfortunes before he passed away in 1950 at age 63. But Alexander left behind a generation of pitchers, notably Baumgartner, to vouch for his greatness.

14

CHASE UTLEY

Chase Utley is a six-time All-Star and a 2008 World Series champion. He is one of the best players in Phillies history and, beginning in 2024, he will get consideration for the Hall of Fame. In the words of late Harry Kalas, Utley is "The Man."

Now, though, he needs a favor: Would anyone mind telling his kids?

"My two sons are at an age where they're sponges. They're taking in so much information," Utley said before his 2019 retirement ceremony at Citizens Bank Park. "I'm helping coach their baseball teams. One thing I can't figure out yet—maybe somebody can help me—they won't listen to me when I try to give them baseball advice. They listen to the other coaches, but for some reason they won't listen to me."

Ba-dum-tshh.

There weren't many jokes around Utley's locker, among not only the media but also many of his teammates, during his 16-year career. It's not that the second baseman was unapproachable. He was just so intense, so laser-focused, even three hours before the game began, that he had little time for jocularity.

But since his retirement at the end of the 2018 season with the Los Angeles Dodgers, and even in the months leading up to it, Utley might as well be accompanied by a laugh track. His sense of humor is dry, his comic delivery decidedly deadpan. It's almost non-stop, though. Nearly everything that Utley says is tinged with sarcasm.

"I told you guys that for years," former Phillies center fielder Aaron Rowand said, chuckling.

Indeed, friends insist they've long seen this side of Utley. But now that he's unshackled from the responsibility of competing every day, he feels freer to show more of his true personality.

There were glimpses over the years.

- Utley had a 35-game hitting streak in 2006, tied for 11th-longest in major-league history, but was too superstitious to discuss it. What ensued was a comical routine in which he would take a question about the streak and answer an entirely different, unasked question, often praising the performance of another teammate.

- In 2008, New York Mets fans roundly booed Utley during the introductions for the All-Star Home Run Derby at Yankee Stadium. His humorous reaction, which was picked up by ESPN's wireless microphones, broadcast on live television, and promptly posted on YouTube: "Boo? [F—k] you!"

- Three months later, Utley addressed the crowd at the Phillies' World Series victory parade. "World champions," he said, pausing a few beats. "World [f—king] champions!" The crowd roared, even if some folks groused about not being able to cover their children's ears in time. Jayson Werth rose from his chair and punched the air with a Hulk fist that he had put on during the parade. It was such an iconic moment that the Phillies chose it as the bobblehead giveaway on Utley's retirement night.

"It has taken on a life of its own," Utley said. "It's what was on my mind at the time. I know some people didn't like it so much. I think we all know how special that day was. So much excitement, so much adrenaline."

But it seemed that Utley finally let down his guard in 2013, three years after his cameo with first baseman Ryan Howard on *It's Always Sunny in Philadelphia* and four years after that half-hour comedy aired an episode in which the character of Mac—played by Philadelphia-native Rob McElhenney—penned a childlike love letter to Utley that began, "I feel like I can call you Chase because we're so much alike," and expressed his desire to have a catch.

In conjunction with MLB Network, Utley narrated his handwritten reply. "I feel like I can call you Mac because you called me Chase," he deadpans before letting Mac down easy by saying that having a catch "sounds like a lot of fun, but I'm really busy playing a lot of baseball for the Phillies."

Cue the laughter. Good thing the video is posted on the internet for posterity, otherwise people might not believe it was really Utley.

"You would catch him at times—on the plane, playing cards, stuff like that, when it wasn't an hour before the game—where he had a dry sense of humor and was willing to talk about other things," former Phillies closer Brad Lidge said. "But he was just someone who was extremely focused on his craft and what he was seeing in the game for 90 percent of the time. It's not like he was ever a guy that was super-talkative."

And if you were an opponent, Utley took a vow of silence, even if you were his friend.

Take Rowand, for instance. In two seasons as teammates, he and Utley grew close. Their wives became friends. Even after Rowand signed as a free agent with the San Francisco Giants in the winter of 2007–08, he and Utley maintained a bond.

But when Rowand wound up on second base after hitting a fifth-inning double against the Phillies on August 1, 2009, he tried to get Utley's attention. He could've set himself on fire and Utley wouldn't have flinched.

"I'll never forget it," Rowand said. "I'm looking at Chase. I know his whole skit. I know what he does and how he will not talk to guys. I started to yell at him, and he just kept getting further and further over towards first base trying to walk away from me. I was yelling all this stuff at him, and I saw the smile on his face and he was shaking his head like, 'I am *not* talking to you.' And then after the game we went out to dinner, and I was laughing to him about it. He said, 'I know what you were doing.'

"But that's just how he is. He's just the ultimate competitor on the field. Any possible thing that could distract him from being the best that he could be, he was unwilling to do it. He wouldn't break the code. If you were playing against him, you were the enemy."

It wasn't always easy for Utley to shut off that intensity when the game ended. Lidge recalls him sitting in the players' dining room, arms crossed, "staring at his dinner like he was angry at it."

"To this day," former outfielder Shane Victorino said, "I'll say he's the most intense athlete that I've ever been around."

Never was Utley's intense focus more evident than in the seventh inning of Game 5 of the 2008 World Series. With the score tied at

Chase Utley leaps over Carl Crawford to complete an eighth-inning double play against the Rays in Game 5 of the 2008 World Series. (Getty Images / Jed Jacobsohn)

3–3, he fielded Akinori Iwamura's grounder up the middle, faked an across-the-body throw to first base, and fired home to cut down Jason Bartlett, who tried to score from second.

It was the signature play in a career that also featured 1,885 hits, 259 home runs, an 87.5 percent success rate on steal attempts, and five homers in the 2009 World Series, tied with Reggie Jackson (1977) and George Springer (2017) for the most in a single Fall Classic.

"I coach college baseball and I probably refer to Chase Utley more than any teammate I ever had," said former backup catcher Chris Coste, who coaches at Concordia College in Moorhead, Minnesota. "There was nobody that was more prepared every single day. He was unconditionally prepared. He watched more video, knew more about our opponents, knew more about his teammates, knew more about that particular game and everybody involved than anybody on that field, both teams combined. The amount of times where I'd be on deck, they'd make a pitching change, we didn't know much about the pitcher, and he would have the random information—'If he gets ahead, he's going to do this; If he falls behind, he's going to do this.' Chase Utley was the single most-prepared major-league baseball player that I ever saw."

How's that for a testimonial for seven-year-old Ben and four-year-old Max Utley?

Utley lives in southern California and pals around with McElhenney, who caught his ceremonial first pitch at the retirement ceremony. (Mac finally got his wish!) Kaitlin Olson, McElhenney's wife and *Always Sunny* co-star, joked on the Phillies' broadcast that night that she would be willing to coach Utley if he wants to give comedy a try.

But Utley, it turns out, is a natural. At the end of his retirement speech, after a highlight video from his career played on Phanavision, he spoke directly to his boys, pausing for a beat that suggested a punchline was near.

"You saw the highlights up there, right?" Utley said. "So, when I'm teaching you a few things... please pay attention."

More laughs for Mr. Intensity, who has ceased getting hits but can't stop being funny.

15

HOLLYWOOD

The bus pulled away from the team hotel in downtown Los Angeles and began the short drive to Dodger Stadium. Mike Arbuckle sat near the front, across the aisle from Cole Hamels, who was slated to pitch in a few hours.

"Are your parents and family and everybody coming up from San Diego?" Arbuckle asked, commencing the small talk.

"Yeah, they're here," Hamels said. "But they're at a different hotel. I didn't see them because I don't want any distractions from what I'm doing."

Arbuckle beamed. At that moment, the longtime assistant general manager realized the Phillies were going to win the 2008 National League pennant.

"Here's this kid that went through some bumps in the road and had to mature, and I just thought, *Okay, this just epitomizes our group,*" Arbuckle said. "From Jimmy Rollins to [Ryan] Howard to Brett Myers, on and on, all these kids that I saw grow from being young high school and first-year players out of college, and now I've got a guy sitting here who was going to become MVP of both the playoffs and the World Series making that comment about the importance of staying focused. I'm thinking, *Boy, this just represents what this whole journey has been for so many of us.*"

For Hamels, in particular. In becoming the Phillies' best homegrown starting pitcher since Robin Roberts more than a half-century earlier, he overcame fits and starts, even a few potholes, some self-inflicted and others beyond his control.

There was the complete fracture of the humerus bone in his left arm in the summer between his sophomore and junior years at Rancho Bernardo High School in San Diego, a devastating injury that left him fearing he would never pitch again. There were the doubts that existed among scouts even after Hamels' arm healed and he had a dominating senior season. There was the elbow strain and later the disc problem in his lower back that cropped up in the minor leagues, limiting him to a total of 10 starts over two seasons in 2004 and 2005 and prompting the Phillies to handle him with extreme care.

And then there was the late-night bar fight. Hamels was leaving Razzel's Lounge, a mile and a half from the Phillies' spring-training facility in Clearwater, Florida, with a group of minor-league teammates on January 29, 2005, when he got into an altercation with a few locals. Hamels claimed he was defending himself. The police report suggested otherwise, indicating that he got out of a car to throw a punch. Regardless, he wound up breaking a bone in his pitching hand and requiring surgery. The Phillies were so disappointed in their top pitching prospect that they disinvited him from major-league spring-training camp in 2005.

But Hamels got called up to start in Cincinnati on May 12, 2006, and never looked back. He went 15–5 with a 3.39 earned-run average in 183⅓ innings and was an All-Star in 2007 and cemented his status as an ace by going 14–10 with a 3.09 ERA in 227⅓ innings in 2008.

And now here he was, preparing to start Game 5 of the NL Championship Series and thinking about nothing other than dominating the Dodgers for seven innings to send the Phillies to the World Series for the first time since 1993.

"When you see an opportunity in front of you dwindling and diminishing because of the way you go about your business—it's not a good feeling," Hamels said in 2006, reflecting on the early career setbacks. "I got off track that first big-league camp. I hurt my elbow and didn't tell anyone. Then I got in the fight. I made a mistake. I learned to walk the other way. It was a wake-up call."

Hamels spent a decade with the Phillies. He was here for each and every one of the five consecutive division titles and the back-to-back World Series appearances in 2008 and 2009. He was here, too, for the downfall that began in 2012. With 114 wins, he ranks sixth on the franchise's all-time list behind Steve Carlton, Roberts, Grover Cleveland Alexander, Chris Short, and Curt Simmons. Only Carlton, Roberts, and Short started more games for the Phillies than Hamels (294); only Carlton and Roberts struck out more batters (1,844).

But only Hamels was a World Series MVP.

If you were going to cast a pitcher in a movie, it would have to be Hamels, aptly nicknamed "Hollywood" by Rollins for his handsome appearance, surfer-dude inflection, and reality-TV-star wife (he married *Survivor* contestant Heidi Strobel in 2006). But he has the substance to back up the style. He's 6-foot-4 and left-handed with a smooth, easy delivery, a bending curveball, and a bat-slowing change-up. Then there's the cool demeanor on the mound. When Hamels is pitching, he never ceases to appear under control.

"When people ask me the question of, 'Who's the guy you most loved to catch in your career?' it was easily Cole Hamels," former Phillies catcher Chris Coste said. "When his change-up was working the way it did, you could tell the hitters it was coming and it didn't matter. He was that guy who was going to throw whatever pitch he wanted. Just let him do his thing and let him dominate. I felt like I was putting down fingers and I couldn't go wrong."

The talent was always evident to Phillies scout Darrell Conner, who filed a report in 2002 in which he labeled Hamels "a No. 1 starter on a major-league club." Scouting director Marti Wolever was on board after watching Hamels in person. So, too, was Arbuckle, who traveled to San Diego to see Hamels make a start before the draft.

But the Phillies didn't pick until No. 17 in 2002. Even in a deep draft that featured top-end pitching talents Zack Greinke, Jeff Francis, Joe Saunders, Scott Kazmir, Jeremy Guthrie, Joe Blanton, and Matt Cain and position-playing prospects B.J. Upton, Prince Fielder, Nick Swisher, Khalil Greene, James Loney, Denard Span, and Jeff Francoeur, the Phillies worried that Hamels wouldn't still be available for them.

"I think he would've gone before where we took him had there been no [broken arm]," Arbuckle said. "I think there's a very good chance we never would have gotten him. But I tip my cap to our medical team, because a lot of teams had either outed Cole or knocked him down as a high-risk guy."

Phillies team physician Michael Ciccotti knew better. He was close friends with Jan Fronek, the orthopedic surgeon who inserted two rods into Hamels' humerus bone. Their sons were classmates at the University of Pennsylvania. Ciccotti felt comfortable asking Fronek about Hamels' case, and Fronek believed strongly that the arm had healed properly. Given that Hamels didn't have shoulder or elbow issues, Fronek didn't view him as a future injury risk. After reviewing Hamels' X-rays and surgical reports, Ciccotti concurred.

"I've got to give Michael Ciccotti credit in a significant way for giving us the comfort level to go out and take Cole in the first round," Arbuckle said. "Michael said, 'I have no reservations about this guy, physically.' He said, 'That arm, the bone is probably going to be stronger than it was before.' That's where the team physician probably should get an award. When Cole got the World Series MVP, Dr. Ciccotti should've been recognized, too."

Hamels was never better than during the 2008 playoffs. He went 4–0 with a 1.80 ERA in six starts, striking out 30 batters and walking only nine. And although the Phillies returned to the World Series a year later in spite of Hamels (7.58 ERA in four playoff starts), he remains one of the best big-game pitchers in franchise history. In nine of his 13 postseason starts for the Phillies, he went at least six innings and gave up no more than three runs.

In the signature move of their rebuild, the Phillies dealt Hamels to the Texas Rangers at the trade deadline in 2015. Six days earlier, on July 25, he made his final start for the team, a 129-pitch, 13-strikeout no-hitter against the Chicago Cubs at Wrigley Field.

Talk about a Hollywood ending for "Hollywood" Hamels.

"You don't ever plan anything to be perfect timing, but it's probably the best going-away party you could ever have," Hamels said a few years later. "It would've been great to be in Philadelphia to do it, but just [with] the group of guys that were still out there with me, Carlos [Ruiz] catching me, it's a great memory."

Not to mention another illustration of how far Hamels came in becoming one of the best pitchers in Phillies history.

16

THE WHEEZE KIDS

L et's talk about the 1983 Phillies.

"Was that the year that Pat Corrales was the manager?" left fielder Gary Matthews said, knowing full well that Corrales got fired midway through that season. "You know we were in first place?"

True story. The Phillies were 43–42, underachieving but nevertheless tied with the St. Louis Cardinals atop the National League East on the morning of July 18, 1983, when they decided to ditch Corrales. For the second time in his tenure as general manager, Paul Owens came down from the front office and skippered the team, which went on a 47–30 tear and won its fifth division title in eight years.

Unusual, right? By itself, though, that doesn't capture the strangeness of the '83 Phillies. Since 1996, in fact, five teams have reached the playoffs after making a midseason managerial change, including the World Series–champion 2003 Florida Marlins. And considering the Phillies featured Mike Schmidt in his prime, eventual NL Cy Young Award winner John Denny, and seven holdovers from the team that won the World Series in 1980, it wasn't as though Owens was inheriting a club that was short on talent. In spring training, he even boasted that it was "the best team I've ever assembled."

No, the weirdness of the '83 Phillies was baked into the roster. Owens and team president Bill Giles acquired 10-time All-Star second baseman Joe Morgan—a Giles favorite from their days together with the Houston Astros—in an offseason trade with the San Francisco Giants. They signed seven-time All-Star first baseman Tony Perez as a free agent. A decade after Morgan, Perez, and Pete Rose played in their first World Series together with Cincinnati's Big Red Machine, they were reunited. And it felt, well, pretty darned good to the Phillies.

"We're in spring training and Wheels [broadcaster Chris Wheeler] and I are watching batting practice," said longtime Phillies public-relations chief Larry Shenk, feigning a batting stance and flapping his back arm to mimic Morgan's signature "chicken wing" motion at the plate. "We just looked at each other and said, 'That's Joe Morgan—in *our* batting cage!'"

Morgan had already cemented his legacy as arguably the greatest second baseman in baseball history. Rose was closing in on 4,000 career hits and eventually Ty Cobb's all-time record. Perez brought 363 home runs to Philadelphia on his way to the Hall of Fame.

Even fellow players were slack-jawed at the iconic ex-Reds. Never mind that reliever Larry Andersen was 30 years old and had already spent a handful of years in the big leagues. When he walked into the Phillies' clubhouse at Veterans Stadium after having his contract purchased from the Seattle Mariners in July, he felt as though he was standing among statues.

"In Seattle I was playing with the likes of—and no disrespect to these guys—Dave Edler, Paul Serna, Bruce Bochte, Joe Simpson, and then I get bought by the Phillies and I walk into Mike Schmidt, Steve Carlton, Tony Perez, Pete Rose, Joe Morgan, Tug McGraw. I'm like, 'Whoa, wait a minute here,'" Andersen said. "Talk about somebody that felt out of place. And I was 30 years old. But to come here and walk into that, I was intimidated. In the baseball world, you shouldn't be intimidated at 30 years old, but I was."

From the start, though, the hodgepodge Phillies lacked an identity. When *Sports Illustrated* came to spring training to do a Phillies photo shoot, Shenk figured they would request Schmidt and Carlton, the faces of the franchise for nearly a decade. Instead, they wanted Rose, Perez, and Morgan, each of whom put on big smiles for the March 14, 1983, cover, appropriately headlined "A ROSY REUNION."

But by then Morgan was 39 years old. Perez was about to turn 41. Rose was going on 42. Reliever Ron Reed was 40. Utilityman Bill Robinson, a member of the "We Are Family" Pittsburgh Pirates in 1979, was 39. Carlton and McGraw were 38. The only under-30 player in the starting lineup was right fielder Von Hayes, dubbed "five-for-one" by Rose because the Phillies traded five players to the Cleveland Indians to acquire him in the winter of 1982–83.

Stan Hochman, the late *Philadelphia Daily News* columnist, called them the "Wheeze Kids," a parody of the 1950 "Whiz Kids." For many of them, it represented the last best chance to add to both their championship-ring collections and their reputations as serial winners. Andersen recalls Rose, in particular, urging on the younger players.

"Pete made sure that the guys in that clubhouse didn't overlook that this might be your last shot," Andersen said. "Pete, for me—and maybe it's just because I was in awe of Pete Rose—he made sure that we were on the same page, that if this is the last shot, let's make the most of it. I think that was definitely the attitude there."

Matthews put it bluntly: "I think all of those guys were concerned about legacies."

But after racing out to a 16–9 start, the Wheeze Kids stumbled. They went 7–17 over the next 24 games, slipping below .500 and into third place. Players began grousing about Corrales' refusal to keep a set lineup. Center field, in particular, became a mishmash of eight-time Gold Glove Award winner Garry Maddox, Bob Dernier, and Hayes, who also split time in right with Rose and Joe Lefebvre. Corrales juggled the batting order, too. Matthews took turns in each of the top six spots. Schmidt was dropped to sixth for two games in July and, according to one account, didn't find out about it until he arrived at the ballpark.

"Nobody knows who the regulars are on this team," Rose told the *Philadelphia Inquirer*.

And if the players had issues with Corrales, the feeling was mutual. In his 2007 memoir, *Pouring Six Beers At A Time*, Giles wrote that Corrales "had become very distant from his players," and would even lament to Giles, "I hate most of these guys."

Finally, after a 5–2 loss at home to the Reds on July 17, Giles and Owens made a change. Under Owens' stewardship, the Phillies remained wildly inconsistent. They'd lose five of seven games, then reel off 12 of the next 15. They dropped nine of 10 games in late August before going 23–8 down the stretch, including an 11-game winning streak.

But Owens was unconcerned about legacies. Rose was benched in favor of younger, more productive Len Matuszek. Hayes lost playing time, too, as Lefebvre took over as the primary right fielder. Owens once used a backup catcher (Ozzie Virgil) to pinch hit for Morgan

(Virgil hit a game-winning grand slam). The Phillies called up 22-year-old second base prospect Juan Samuel in August to provide a spark.

"I think that hurt Pete more than anything, being benched," Matthews said. "Just because of the pride that he had."

Morgan was batting .185 and losing playing time, too, to Larry Milbourne and Kiko Garcia. But he vowed to carry the Phillies into the playoffs if they were close by the beginning of September. He made good on that promise, going 29-for-86 (.337) with seven doubles, five home runs, and a 1.045 on-base plus slugging percentage in the last 24 games. Morgan had three four-hit games during that stretch. In his most memorable Phillies moment, he broke a 6–6 tie with a leadoff homer against Chicago Cubs closer Lee Smith in the eighth inning of a 7–6 victory on September 19 at Veterans Stadium.

"For most of the year, Morgan was awful," Shenk said. "In September, he carried us."

The Phillies won the division with a 90–72 record. And for a team with so many disparate motivations, there wasn't a better NLCS opponent than the Los Angeles Dodgers. Schmidt, Carlton, Maddox and the rest of the longtime Phillies had lost to Los Angeles in back-to-back playoff series in 1977 and '78. Players who were newer to the Phillies were smarting from losing 11 of 12 games to the Dodgers—by a combined margin of 49–15—during the regular season.

Everyone, it seemed, had a score to settle with the Dodgers. And for Matthews, who homered in each of the final three games of the series en route to being named NLCS MVP, the "Beat L.A." chant from the Veterans Stadium crowd still rings in his ears.

"For some of the guys, it was that much sweeter because L.A. beat 'em twice before to get into the World Series," Matthews said. "And they beat us like a drum during the year. To beat L.A. was kind of icing on the cake."

But the Phillies' run ended abruptly in the World Series. They lost in five games to the Baltimore Orioles, who were led by Eddie Murray, Jim Palmer, and a 22-year-old shortstop named Cal Ripken Jr. But it was veteran catcher Rick Dempsey, a .233 career hitter, who went 5-for-13 with four doubles and a home run to cop World Series MVP honors.

"We had no chance," Matthews said.

Giles contends that the Phillies might have if not for a faulty tarp. It rained before Game 3, and the Veterans Stadium tarp had a hole that caused a puddle to form on the left side of the infield. Sure enough, in the seventh inning, Dan Ford's grounder hit the puddle and skidded through shortstop Ivan DeJesus' legs to put the Orioles ahead in a 3–2 victory that gave them a 2–1 lead in the series.

"I still believe that a hole in the tarp could have cost us the entire series," Giles said.

For as quickly as they were dispatched by the Orioles, the Phillies were broken up even faster. Rose and Morgan were released; Perez was sold back to the Reds. Owens stayed on as manager, but the Phillies tried to get younger in 1984. Matuszek and Samuel took over at first and second base, respectively, while Hayes replaced Maddox as the primary center fielder.

Just like that, the Wheeze Kids faded away. They were hardly the Phillies' only pop-up pennant winner. The 1950 and 1993 teams were similarly unable to recapture their magic in future years. But unlike those clubs, the '83 Phillies didn't endure in fans' memories.

"You don't hear hardly anybody talk about that '83 team," said Andersen, who also pitched for the beloved '93 Phillies. "It was almost like they were rebuilding a World Series team throughout the year in '83. It was just unlike anything else. It was really weird."

As weird a pennant winner as you'll ever see.

17

CLIFF LEE AND THE '09 PENNANT

Cliff Lee couldn't have been calmer if he'd gotten shot by a tranquilizer dart.

Acquired two days before the July trade deadline to pitch at this exact moment—Game 1 of the 2009 World Series—Lee delivered a six-hit, 10-strikeout complete game in a 6–1 victory at Yankee Stadium. It was a performance as historic as it was impressive. The lefty became the first pitcher ever—*ever!*—to strike out 10 batters without allowing a walk or an earned run in a World Series game. But when he was through, the new Phillies ace told the world that the whole thing wasn't an especially big deal.

"It's been a long time since I've been nervous playing this game," Lee said, oh so matter of factly, in the postgame press conference. "It's what I've been doing my whole life. You do everything you need to do to prepare, and I try not to leave anything to chance. So what's the point in being nervous?"

Left unsaid, though, was this minor detail: Lee nearly didn't make it to the stadium on time.

True story. And it all began, as some of Lee's former teammates tell it, because the ace left-hander decided against taking the police-escorted team bus from the Phillies' midtown Manhattan hotel to Yankee Stadium. Not wanting to feel rushed, he figured he would hop a taxi for the 8.5-mile ride up the FDR Drive and into the South Bronx. No sweat, right? But Lee didn't plan on hellacious rush-hour traffic, and two hours before the game, he was stuck on the Upper West Side in the kind of New York City gridlock that you only see in movies.

Frank Coppenbarger, the Phillies' longtime director of team travel, was on the field for batting practice when Lee's number popped up on his ringing phone.

"I thought it might've been Cliff saying that he forgot some tickets and could I come and get 'em up to the will call for him," Coppenbarger said. "That wasn't it."

As Coopenbarger recalls, the conversation began something like this:

Lee: "You better tell [manager] Charlie [Manuel] that I might not make it."

Coppenbarger: "Don't be messing around. What are you talking about?"

Lee: "Well, I'm in a cab. And I haven't moved in 20 minutes. I'm not sure if I'm going to get there. What do you think I should do?"

Coppenbarger's first suggestion: *Find a police officer, tell him who you are, and ask for an escort.* Instead, Lee followed a throng of Yankee fans who descended into the subway. He boarded an uptown 4 train to Yankee Stadium.

"I give him some kudos for even thinking that," Coppenbarger said. "I can only imagine. I guess Cliff dressed a little bit country anyway, so most people probably didn't have any idea who it was. If nothing else, it couldn't have been him at that hour of the night."

When Lee got off the train, there was still the matter of finding the players' entrance to the new Yankee Stadium, which was in its inaugural season and still unfamiliar ground. Coppenbarger instructed him to wait outside a McDonald's on 161st Street and sent a clubhouse attendant to find him.

Meanwhile, the Phillies were quietly making contingency plans. The situation never reached DEFCON levels, though, so pitching coach Rich Dubee didn't have to scramble to find a new starting pitcher on the fly. Dubee and Coppenbarger didn't even alert Manuel.

"We never told Charlie," Coppenbarger said. "Charlie didn't know the story until the [10-year] reunion [in 2019]. He goes, 'What are you guys talking about?' I said, 'Something we weren't going to tell you—and Dubee was going to break the news to you, not me!'"

Said Dubee: "Well, we were hoping he was going to get there. We were kind of trying to make secondary plans just in case. But probably of all the guys in our rotation he was the guy that I wasn't too worried about. He didn't have this big, strict routine before he starts. If he got to the ballpark, he'd be fine. I figured he just needed 20 minutes or so to warm up."

Jimmy Rollins and Jayson Werth congratulate Cliff Lee on his 10-strikeout, complete-game victory over the Yankees in Game 1 of the 2009 World Series. (Getty Images / Jed Jacobsohn)

Indeed, Lee's nonchalance was legendary. Nothing seemed to faze him. Dubee recalled a 2009 start at Wrigley Field when catcher Paul Bako's dad interrupted Lee's pregame warm-up and asked him to pose for a picture with his son.

"Here Cliff is trying to get ready to pitch," Dubee said. "He kind of chuckled and was like, 'Here we go,' and took the photo and just moved on. Some guys, you get in the way of their routine and it totally throws them off. Cliff, he's just an easy-going, light-aired guy that wasn't distracted by that type of stuff."

Want to rattle Clifton Phifer Lee? You better come with more than just a traffic jam.

"He comes in, 'Do-do-do-do-do. I'm pitching today. No big deal.' Then he goes out and shoves it up their butt," fellow lefty Jamie Moyer recalled at the 2009 reunion. "Any mortal would be going, 'God, I've had the worst day. I missed the bus. I had to take the train.' It would be an issue."

As the 2009 season unfolded, the biggest issue facing the defending World Series champions was the starting rotation. Cole Hamels, hero of the 2008 postseason, carried a 5.21 earned-run average into June. Moyer was 46 years old. Brett Myers missed most of the summer after hip surgery. Joe Blanton and J.A. Happ were supporting actors, not leading men.

After taking over for semi-retired Pat Gillick in the offseason, first-year general manager Ruben Amaro Jr. didn't make many changes to the World Series–winning roster. The big move was letting longtime left fielder Pat Burrell walk in free agency and signing Raul Ibanez. Otherwise, the same cast of characters returned.

Three months into the season, though, it was clear that the rotation needed to be addressed. Amaro coveted Roy Halladay, but the Toronto Blue Jays were not yet willing to move him. So the Phillies pivoted to Plan B, who happened to be the reigning Cy Young winner in the American League. They pried Lee from the Cleveland Indians for a package of four prospects: pitchers Carlos Carrasco and Jason Knapp, infielder Jason Donald, and catcher Lou Marson.

When Amaro walked through the clubhouse in Arizona after pulling off the trade on July 29, the players gave him a standing ovation.

Lee's addition notwithstanding, there were echoes of 2008 in the Phillies' 2009 run. They remained an offensive juggernaut, leading the league with 820 runs scored. And they dispatched the Los Angeles Dodgers again in the NL Championship Series, winning another tide-turning Game 4 in which Matt Stairs had a key pinch-hit plate appearance against Jonathan Broxton. (This time, Broxton walked Stairs on four pitches before Jimmy Rollins lined a game-winning, two-run double—the biggest hit of his 17-year career—to cap a 5–4 walkoff victory.)

But unlike in 2007 and 2008, when the Phillies had to rally in September to clinch the division title in the season's final days, they pulled away from the field in 2009. They went 20–7 in July and built a seven-game lead in the NL East.

And that was before they added Lee and Pedro Martinez.

Martinez signed with the Phillies on July 15 and made his first start 28 days later. He went 5–1 with a 3.63 ERA in nine regular-season starts in what amounted to the swan song of his Hall of Fame career. And as necessary as Lee proved to be to the 2009 Phillies' success, Martinez was almost as central. The team went 8–1 in his starts. He threw seven shutout innings in Game 2 of the NL Championship Series at Dodger Stadium. He even started two games in the World Series at Yankee Stadium.

"I don't know if you realize this, but because of you [media], in some ways I might be at times the most influential player that ever stepped in Yankee Stadium," the former Boston Red Sox ace said in a memorable press conference before Game 2. "I can honestly say that."

Ruth. Gehrig. DiMaggio. Mantle. Reggie. Mattingly. Jeter. Pedro?

"For some reason with all the hype and different players that have passed by, maybe because I played for the Red Sox is probably why you guys made it such a big deal every time I came in," Martinez said. "But I have a good bond with the people."

Martinez wasn't able to make one last Yankee Stadium memory. He gave up three runs in six innings of a 3–1 loss in Game 2, then allowed four runs in four innings of a 7–3 loss in the Yankees' clinching Game 6. After 371 days as champions, the Phillies were dethroned.

Six weeks later, inconceivable as it was, Lee got traded to Seattle for three prospects, a move designed to replenish the farm system after Amaro emptied it out to finally acquire Halladay. Lee returned after the 2010 season, signing a five-year, $120 million contract as a free agent and joining Halladay, Hamels, and Roy Oswalt in a star-studded rotation.

"When you have the opportunity to have that kind of rotation," Amaro recalled in 2017, "that's kind of a once-in-a-lifetime situation."

But Lee's impact in 2009 was his enduring Phillies legacy.

Even if he nearly missed his biggest moment.

18

THE COLLAPSE OF 1964

As a rookie public-relations director in 1964, Larry Shenk created the Phillies' first media guide, an 8"x4" horizontal booklet bound by hole punches and paper fasteners. The cover design was the sketch of a cap that Shenk's wife, Julie, colored with red magic marker on all 360 copies. It was rudimentary, but somehow it fit an organization that had neither won a pennant nor finished better than third place since 1950.

"I didn't know what I was doing the first year," Shenk said. "I was a fan."

And there was plenty to cheer about. Dick Allen hit 29 home runs and was named National League Rookie of the Year. Jim Bunning twirled a no-hitter on Father's Day. Johnny Callison slugged a walkoff home run to win the All-Star Game. Everything that manager Gene Mauch tried—sacrifice bunts and squeeze plays in the first inning, moving sure-handed shortstop Ruben Amaro to first base in the ninth, using pinch-hitters and making double switches—worked like a charm.

The Phillies built a 7½-game lead in the National League by the final week of August. By the time September rolled around, there was cause to begin planning for the World Series, an event that Philadelphians witnessed only slightly more often than Halley's Comet. It was such a rare occurrence, in fact, and the Phillies were so confident even after losing first baseman Frank Thomas to a broken thumb, that catcher Gus Triandos began to call 1964 "the year of the blue snow."

But Connie Mack Stadium couldn't accommodate all of the media that covers a World Series, so plans were made for an auxiliary press box and broadcast booth. Credentials needed to be printed, along with a World Series program.

Then there was the matter of hosting Major League Baseball's annual gala on the eve of the World Series. The Phillies needed a venue, so Shenk and director of sales Frank Powell went to the posh Warwick Hotel on 17th Street in Rittenhouse Square. When they were told that the ballroom was booked for a wedding reception, Powell asked to speak to Frank Mann, the hotel's owner, who was vacationing in Paris.

"[Powell] says, 'Well, get him on the phone then,'" Shenk recalled. "The general manager of the hotel calls and says, 'I'm with Frank Powell and he says they need the ballroom.' They say, 'Okay, we'll bounce the wedding and give you the ballroom.' I couldn't believe it."

What happened next, though, left Shenk even more incredulous.

On September 20, the Phillies led the St. Louis Cardinals and Cincinnati Reds by 6½ games with 12 games left and were about to begin a seven-game homestand that felt more like a coronation.

Then they lost 10 in a row.

"It's hard to explain how that all came about," shortstop Bobby Wine said. "I just look back on those 10 days and everything that could happen went wrong."

Start with an ill-advised steal of home.

In the sixth inning of a scoreless game on September 21, Reds rookie Chico Ruiz broke for the plate even though Hall of Fame slugger Frank Robinson was batting with two out. Reds manager George Sisler later said that Ruiz could have kept running all the way to the team's Triple-A affiliate in San Diego if he hadn't been safe.

But Ruiz's mad dash surprised nobody quite so much as Phillies pitcher Art Mahaffey. The lanky right-hander was pitching from the windup rather than the stretch, and when he saw Ruiz take off, well, he winged the ball wide of catcher Clay Dalrymple's target.

"He panicked," Dalrymple said. "I don't know what the hell went through his head. You don't throw the ball outside. It never should have happened."

Ruiz's run was the only one that was scored that night, and it set off the 10-game skid. Consider some of what happened during that collapse:

- Left-hander Chris Short allowed six runs in a 9–2 loss to the Reds on September 22, marking the only time in 42 outings that year that he gave up more than four runs in a game.
- Callison caught the flu but insisted on playing. He hit a game-tying homer in the eighth inning on September 25 and bashed

three homers two days later. The Phillies lost both games. He finally came out of the lineup on September 29 in St. Louis, and after notching a pinch-hit single, he asked for a jacket at first base but was too sick to zip it.

• The Phillies blew a 4–3 lead in the ninth inning against the Braves when Rico Carty's three-run triple hit the chalk line in right field. "If that goes foul..." Shenk said, his voice trailing off.

Through it all, Wine remembers Mauch being calm, which couldn't have been more out of character for a manager that Shenk describes as "an animated monster." Mauch was so intense, in fact, that he once enforced curfew in spring training by giving a ball to the bellman at the Jack Tar Hotel in downtown Clearwater and ordering him to get the autograph of every player he saw after midnight. The next day, Mauch fined four players.

But as the losses piled up, Mauch didn't overturn any tables in the clubhouse or even deliver a rousing speech.

"Up until probably the last two to three weeks of the season he was always on us," Wine said. "We could've got beat 2–1, he'd come in and yell about some play or some situation that happened or whatever. And during that 10 days he was really mellow. He was probably eating himself alive, but he was pretty level and mild. He'd come through the clubhouse and say, 'We'll get 'em tomorrow. Keep your head up. We'll get 'em.' It was like he didn't want to show panic."

Not outwardly. Through his actions, though, it was clear that Mauch was freaking out.

Mahaffey made only one more start after the Chico Ruiz game. Dennis Bennett made just two starts down the stretch. Rick Wise, an 18-year-old rookie who appeared in 25 games, got into only three games, all in relief, after September 17. Ray Culp started 19 games for the Phillies in 1964, none after August 15.

Instead, with the season spiraling away, Mauch leaned on Bunning and Short. Bunning started on two days' rest twice and came back for the regular-season finale on only one day of rest; Short started twice on two days' rest.

"That was stupid," Dalrymple said. "You had a couple of guys on the bench that could pitch. Ray Culp had good stuff, man. He was a good pitcher and Mauch wouldn't pitch him because he gained 10 pounds. He got a little fat and it pissed [Mauch] off. I think Gene Mauch has to take a lot of the blame for what we had going down that drive.

"And no one would dare say a word to Mauch because he knew how to scare the s—t out of guys. He had an attitude toward the players, and he made you shut up so you didn't say anything against him. But boy, I couldn't believe watching some of the decisions he made those last 10 days. They weren't what I would expect a manager to do."

Wine takes a more forgiving view, especially because Bunning was rested enough after getting knocked out early on September 27 and September 29.

"Mauch gets blamed for pitching Bunning and Short, Bunning and Short, Bunning and Short. Well, who was our best two pitchers? Bunning and Short," Wine said. "Now you look back and say, 'I wish he wouldn't have done that.' But neither one of them couldn't come back or wouldn't come back. Bunning would've taken the ball every day if you would've given it to him. I can't say if Mahaffey was hurt. I can't say if Culp was hurt. I can't say if Bennett was hurt. I don't really know, except he thought Bunning and Short were going to win a game."

The Phillies finally won, 4–3, in the season's penultimate game with four runs in the eighth inning against the Reds. They won the season finale, too, with Bunning tossing a six-hit shutout in Cincinnati. But the Cardinals rallied to defeat the San Francisco Giants and won the pennant by one game.

Just in case, the Phillies had a bulldozer standing by to add field-level seats next to both dugouts. Team employees were told to be prepared to come into work on October 3 to sell tickets for the World Series or a potential tie-breaker. Shenk designed a World Series program.

"Two years later we used it as the yearbook cover," he said. "Nobody knew that."

For years, everybody held up the 1964 Phillies as the quintessential late-season collapse. Mauch, who died in 2005, got tired of talking about it. Former utiliyman Cookie Rojas once told Shenk to stop giving out his phone number to reporters who were writing about September folds.

But Wine chooses to look at it differently.

"That year was a magical year," he said. "I don't think anybody ever figured we'd be where we were. We had a perfect game by one of our pitchers. We had three triple plays. We had a guy hit a home run in the All-Star Game. And we were leading the league. Who ever thought all of that was going to happen? And then, at the end, we just didn't get the job done."

19

THE COMEBACK OF 2007

When did you start to believe? When did you think it might really be possible? When did it feel as though another seemingly lost season for the Phillies would wind up as one of the most triumphant in their history?

Chris Coste has it narrowed down to an exact date and time.

It was August 30, 2007, 5:08 PM Eastern. Chase Utley had just singled through the right side of the infield in the bottom of the ninth inning to cap a game-winning rally against New York Mets closer Billy Wagner and complete the Phillies' four-game sweep at Citizens Bank Park. Tadahito Iguchi slid across home plate and jumped into the waiting arms of Pat Burrell. Shane Victorino jumped on Burrell's back. A boisterous celebration ensued on the field as Mets catcher Paul Lo Duca trudged back to the visiting dugout, mask in hand, solemn expression on his face.

A few minutes later, Lo Duca opened his mouth.

"They're dancing around the field now," he told reporters in the Mets' clubhouse, "but we'll see what happens when the time comes."

Say no more.

"Lo Duca made that comment in the paper, and it was like, to us, we were excited, we won the game, but also it was a realization that the Mets don't think that we're in this," Coste said. "I just remember that was a conversation in the clubhouse. It probably made the board. A lot of people kind of forget about that, but that's one thing I'll never forget because it was a motivating factor for us."

If Lo Duca's words didn't seem particularly inflammatory to the general populace, it was because the Phillies weren't much of a threat to the division-leading Mets. At least not until that four-game sweep. Even then, they were two games behind the Mets' pace, and within two weeks, the deficit stretched back to seven games.

For a team that was supposed to be running a pennant race, the Phillies looked more like dead men walking.

But what happened next, over a period of 17 days in September, changed the course of franchise history.

"I think '07 was pretty damn important for us winning it all in '08," said general manager Pat Gillick.

Coste added, "I'm not sure '08 happens quite the same way without '07."

It all began with yet another sweep of the Mets, a three-game wipeout on September 14–16 in New York that kickstarted a roll in which the Phillies won six games in a row, nine out of 10, and 12 out of 16. The Mets, meanwhile, dropped five straight, six out of seven, and 11 out of 16. Going into the season finale, the rivals were tied atop the National League East, but the arrow was pointing in decidedly one direction.

If the Phillies are being honest, though, most would agree that it didn't feel like an epic comeback while they were going through it.

"I've seen so many September races through the years and seen the crazy things that can happen, so I never—until just the last few days—felt like we really, really had a leg up on this thing," then–assistant general manager Mike Arbuckle said. "Too many things can happen, going all the way back to '64 with the Phillies."

Indeed, there were echoes of that monumental collapse, which began when the Phillies had a 6½-game lead with 12 games remaining. This, though, seemed like some sort of cosmic makeup call, the Phillies rallying to wipe out the Mets' seven-game lead with 17 left to play.

And even before the Phillies took the field for the season finale, a 1:35 PM home game against the Washington Nationals, the right-field scoreboard showed that the Mets were losing again, 7–1 to the Florida Marlins in a game that began a half-hour earlier in New York.

"I'm thinking, *There's no way that's possible. Tom Glavine is pitching. Somebody up there is messing with us*," left fielder Pat Burrell recalled in the *Philadelphia Inquirer's* 2017 oral history of the 2007 finale. "I just couldn't believe it. I ran inside. It was on inside somewhere, one of the video rooms. Oh my God."

The sellout crowd of 44,865 was roaring as Jamie Moyer threw his warmup pitches in the bullpen and kept right on going through Ryan Howard's two-run single in the third inning, Jimmy Rollins' RBI triple in the sixth, Howard's solo homer in the seventh, and closer Brett Myers' called third strike against Wily Mo Pena that sealed a 6–1 victory.

If only Gene Mauch had been there to see it. Surely this would have been sweet relief for the maligned '64 Phillies manager, who died two years earlier.

"I think I threw my glove into the air, my hat, everything. I wanted to strip naked," Myers told the *Inquirer*. "I didn't know what I was doing. I was just so excited. I jumped into the stands. I poured beer all over me, and I don't like wasting beer. I was a crazy idiot. Yeah, we went a little crazy. We partied like we won the World Series, and we just made the playoffs."

The Phillies were entitled. In addition to completing a most improbable comeback, it marked the franchise's first postseason appearance since 1993. Oh, and it also made good on Rollins' January boast that the Phillies, not the Mets, were the "team to beat" in the division.

It was the Phillies' modest version of Joe Namath's Super Bowl guarantee, and it generated back-page headlines in both Philadelphia and New York when Rollins made the statement in the offseason and doubled down on it in spring training.

"I think when he said that," manager Charlie Manuel said, "he helped get us going."

Rollins' bravado made him a bigger New York villain than King Kong. But when the Phillies started out 4–11, a stretch that included three losses in four games against the Mets, Rollins ran the risk of becoming something 10 times worse: irrelevant.

"I don't think a lot of us thought that it was going to be that big of a deal in the first place," Coste said. "I think a lot of us thought it maybe got blown up a little bit more than what even Jimmy might've meant. But it was more of a spring-training kind of thing and we had forgotten about it for a while until the last month. That's when it came back again."

It only added to the narrative that Rollins batted .346 with six homers in 18 games against the Mets, part of a season in which he was named NL most valuable player. He led the league in plate appearances (778), at-bats (716), runs (139), and triples (20). He hit 30 home runs, drove in 94 runs, and batted .296 with a career-high .875 on-base plus slugging percentage. Down the stretch, Rollins went 25-for-81 (.309) with three doubles, three triples, three homers, and an .864 OPS.

When the Phillies' comeback was complete, the back page of the *New York Daily News* featured a picture of Rollins spraying champagne and the headline "I TOLD YOU SO!"

"Jimmy took it personally that year," Coste said.

Rollins wasn't alone. Howard, the reigning NL MVP from 2006, hit nine home runs in the final 16 games. Center fielder Aaron Rowand hit four homers. Utley had 10 extra-base hits and scored 15 runs. Even the pitching got it together. The Phillies posted a 4.73 team ERA, 13th in the 15-team National League, but Kyle Kendrick won two games down the stretch, Brett Myers notched six saves, and setup men J.C. Romero and Tom Gordon combined to allow two runs in 22 innings.

"That group of guys, we were a very close-knit team," said Rowand. "It was a great season, a fun season. I cherish that year as much as I do the years that I ended up winning a World Series [with the Chicago White Sox in 2005 and the San Francisco Giants in 2010] because of how close that group was. To this day, they're still some of my best friends. We were just tight."

But if the Phillies' comeback was a bolt from the blue, their postseason ouster was even more shockingly abrupt.

The Colorado Rockies surged into the playoffs with 14 wins in 15 games, including a one-game play-in against the San Diego Padres. In the best-of-five division series, they kept right on rolling, sweeping the Phillies in three games.

"We were feeling on top of the world, and then we get punched in the nose by the Rockies," Coste said. "When our '07 season ended, it hurt. We were so excited and then all of a sudden, five days later, we're home. We went to spring training that next year with a lot to prove. The pain that we all felt, that disappointment of letting down the city and ourselves, it all made '08 a hugely motivational year."

And it doesn't happen without 2007.

20

TUG & LIDGE

If not for his ability to throw such a nasty slider, Brad Lidge could have been the real-life Indiana Jones.

As it is, Lidge is a certified archaeologist. Seriously. The former All-Star closer has a master's degree in archaeology and ancient history from the University of Leicester in England, and since his retirement from baseball, he has taken annual trips to work on excavation sites throughout Italy.

Leave it to Lidge, then, to always be on the lookout for artifacts linking the Phillies' two World Series titles.

One of his favorites is a picture that can probably be dug up in a few sports memorabilia shops in the Delaware Valley. It features mirror images of Tug McGraw and Lidge—the only pitchers ever to record the final out of a World Series for the Phillies—leaping in the air at the clinching moment. Look closer, though, and you will see an even deeper connection.

"He was No. 45. I was 54," Lidge said. "There was [the years] '80 and '08. He was a lefty, I'm a righty. It's just kind of a weird, crazy reverse image thing that I think is super cool."

And it makes Lidge feel a kinship with McGraw, even though they never met.

McGraw, who died in 2004 from a brain tumor, was one of the game's all-time characters. His given name was Frank, but as McGraw once explained, his mother nicknamed him Tug because of the aggressive way that he nursed. He signed with the Mets for $7,000 in 1964 and was in the big leagues a year later at age 20. In his third career start, on August 26, 1965, he outdueled Sandy Koufax in a 5–2 victory at Shea Stadium in New York. Surely he was bound for instant stardom.

Cue the sound of screeching tires.

Ineffectiveness and injuries slowed McGraw over the next two years, even landing him on the Mets' Florida Instructional League roster in the fall of 1966. It was there that he met Ralph Terry, a 23-game winner for the New York Yankees in 1962 who was nevertheless known for giving up Bill Mazeroski's World Series–ending home run in 1960. Terry was trying to extend his career with the Mets, but his biggest contribution to the team proved to be teaching McGraw to throw the screwball, a pitch that darted in on right-handed batters and away from lefties.

Armed with the new pitch, McGraw returned to the big leagues in 1969 and was soon given a new role, too. Mets manager Gil Hodges convinced him that he could be most effective out of the bullpen. And with McGraw posting a 1.47 earned-run average in 38 relief appearances, the "Miracle Mets" went 38–11 down the stretch and overcame a 10-game deficit to win the division, then swept the Atlanta Braves in the National League Championship Series and defeated the heavily favored Baltimore Orioles to win the World Series.

Four years later, having cemented his status as an elite reliever, he went 5–0 with a 0.88 ERA and 12 saves over his last 19 appearances and shouted the rallying cry "Ya Gotta Believe" to lead the Mets to another stunning NL East title.

But McGraw developed shoulder trouble in 1974, and the Mets unloaded him in a six-player trade with the Phillies, who gave up outfielder Del Unser and touted catching prospect John Stearns. And for the next 10 years, he anchored a bullpen that featured horses such as Ron Reed and Gene Garber and homegrown Warren Brusstar, Kevin Saucier, and Dickie Noles.

It wasn't merely McGraw's body of work (a 3.10 ERA and 94 saves in 463 appearances) that made him a star with the Phillies. It was his free-spirited, carefree attitude that lightened the mood for a young team that tended to be uptight in big situations.

To wit: McGraw named his pitches. There was "Cutty Sark... because it would sail," he said, "Bo Derek, which had a nice little tail to it, and the John Jameson was hard and straight, just like the Irish whiskey."

"As flamboyant as he was, he loved life. He loved to have fun," Noles said. "The greatest thing about Tug was that he was a great friend. If you had a bad game, he was right there—'Let's go get something to eat; let's go have a drink; let's go out and talk.' You'd get a little baseball and a lot of other stuff, and the next day you'd be all right. Tug was probably the best teammate I ever had. I loved that man dearly."

Phillies fans fell hard for McGraw in 1980. He posted a 1.46 ERA, with 75 strikeouts and 20 saves in 25 chances, and finished fifth in the NL Cy Young Award voting. In the final game of the season, he struck out fastball-mashing Montreal Expos slugger Larry Parrish on three heaters in a row to clinch the NL East title.

Then, in the postseason, McGraw appeared in nine of the Phillies' 11 games and recorded one win and four saves with a 2.87 ERA in 15⅔ innings. He embodied the cuticle-chomping closeness of many of those games. Pitching with a one-run lead in the ninth inning of Game 5 of the World Series, he allowed a long foul ball down the left-field line by Hal McRae and clapped his chest as he received a new ball from the umpire.

"Tug was a fun guy to watch," Noles said. "He's the only pitcher I ever saw that in pressure situations would play around on the mound at times. He'd be pumping his heart like, 'Oh, lord of mercy.' A guy would throw his bat and he'd take it back to him, punch him in the stomach with it. He had a lot of heart on the mound. He wasn't scared of anything, and he knew how to get the job done."

Nobody got it done quite like Lidge in 2008.

Although converted starter Brett Myers pitched well as the closer down the stretch in 2007 to help the Phillies overtake the Mets for the division title, general manager Pat Gillick believed he could strengthen the pitching staff in multiple areas by returning Myers to the rotation and acquiring a closer. Lidge had been outstanding for the Houston Astros, but after hanging a slider to Albert Pujols in the 2005 NLCS, he faltered badly in 2006. He pitched better in 2007, but the Astros suspected his confidence was still bruised from giving up the titanic homer.

Veteran Phillies scout Charlie Kerfeld didn't share those concerns.

"Charlie strongly recommended Lidge to us even though Lidge had not had a particularly great year," Gillick said. "Charlie was very strong in saying that he was going to bounce back, and we thought we needed somebody that could close on a consistent basis. I think Lidge, the way he performed in 2008, it was unbelievable."

That's one word for it. Here's another: perfect.

Lidge went 41-for-41 in save opportunities during the regular season. He posted a 1.95 ERA and struck out 92 batters in 69⅓ innings. And the postseason wasn't any different. Lidge appeared in nine of the Phillies' 14 games, recorded a 0.96 ERA, and went 7-for-7 in save chances.

Where McGraw succeeded with his screwball as the offset to his fastball, Lidge did the same with his dirt-diving slider. And while Lidge was more stone-faced than demonstrative on the mound, he had a few light moments, too, none more so than Game 5 of the 2008 World Series with two outs and the tying run on second base. As pinch-hitter Eric Hinske walked to the plate, pitching coach Rich Dubee made a trip to the mound. As Lidge recalls, the conversation went something like this.

Dubee: "Hey, do we know what we're going to do here?"

Lidge: "Well, last time I faced him, I threw him a fastball."

Dubee: "How'd that work out?"

Lidge: "He waffled me."

At that point, the five teammates who had gathered on the mound erupted in laughter, and catcher Carlos Ruiz said, "Okay, we just throw sliders."

Lidge struck out Hinske on a slider, of course, just as McGraw had whiffed Willie Wilson to end the 1980 World Series.

And that's when they struck their iconic poses that are frozen for eternity.

Having hunted down the photo like so many of the archaeological remains that he tracks in his spare time, Lidge is hoping to eventually meet McGraw's son, Tim, the country music star and actor. Good luck finding a baseball player who appreciates history more than Lidge or better understands his place in it alongside Tug McGraw.

"If I'm able to meet Tim, I want to tell him how cool it is to be on that picture and what an honor it is to be on it with his dad," Lidge said. "I know Tug McGraw was so well respected and was such an amazing guy. To be on it with him is a really cool thing. I'm real proud to be able to have done that in the same way that he did."

In Phillies lore, they are two of a kind.

21

CHARLIE HUSTLE

In the fall of 1976, as the Big Red Machine chugged towards its third pennant in five years, Pete Rose paused to consider the vanquished.

"That team's got talent," Rose said of the Phillies, winners of 101 games but swept by the Reds in the NL Championship Series. "All's they need is a leader."

Two years later, Rose kept coming back to that thought.

After 16 seasons in his hometown of Cincinnati, he was a free agent. He had forged a legacy there. It was where he established his all-out, no-holds-barred playing style. It was where he reached 3,000 career hits en route to eventually becoming the majors' all-time hits leader. It was the site of his greatest triumphs, and years later, the setting for the demise that led to his banishment from baseball in 1989.

But as Rose braced to leave the Reds after the 1978 season, he set out to make an imprint in another city. And he did exactly that in only four seasons with the Phillies. Not only was he the most high-profile free-agent signing in franchise history, at least until Bryce Harper came along 40 years later, but he backed up the hype by helping the Phillies win the 1980 World Series.

"He had a cockiness, a swagger about him," catcher Bob Boone said. "I think that's something we needed."

Rose's road to Philadelphia wasn't absent twists and turns. After a meeting with Phillies owner Ruly Carpenter, who told Rose and agent Reuven Katz that he wouldn't increase an offer that was inferior to other suitors' bids, there was reason to believe a deal wouldn't happen at all.

At age 37, Rose was one of baseball's most recognizable stars. He worked with Katz on a short highlight video that they showed to owners of interested teams. But his resume spoke for itself: 3,164 hits, .379 on-base percentage, 1963 NL Rookie of the Year, 13-time All-Star,

1973 NL Most Valuable Player, five postseason appearances in the previous nine years, and two World Series rings.

To nobody's surprise, Rose received several desirable proposals, most of which went beyond merely a six-figure salary that would've made him the highest-paid player in baseball. St. Louis Cardinals owner August Busch Jr. offered a Budweiser beer distributorship. From Pittsburgh Pirates owner John Galbraith, there were top-flight racehorses. Kansas City Royals owner Ewing Kauffman would have given Rose a four-year, $4 million contract, plus stock in his pharmaceutical company.

"[Ted] Turner offered me $1 million a year for four years," Rose said, referring to the Atlanta Braves owner and cable television mogul. "When he found out I was negotiating with the other guys, he came back and said, 'I'll give you the same $1 million guarantee, but I'll give you $100,000 a year every year after you retire until you die.'"

For Turner, like many other owners, the notion to sign Rose went beyond winning baseball games. Star players put fans in the seats. They boost TV ratings. They build the brand.

"When [Turner] talked to me, he was very honest," Rose said. "He said, 'Listen, I know how you can play baseball. I want you to help me sell TV.'"

Rose had other ideas. He didn't care about driving viewership. He enjoyed betting on horses but wasn't itching to own one. The Royals were a powerhouse, but at his age, Rose didn't feel like switching leagues. And with the money he was going to make, he'd be able to buy all the Budweiser that he could drink. All he wanted was to win another World Series before he retired. The Phillies couldn't pay him as much as, say, the Cardinals or Braves, but they were closer to being a championship club.

Led by the homegrown core of third baseman Mike Schmidt, shortstop Larry Bowa, left fielder Greg Luzinski, and Boone—as well as the trade acquisitions of Gold Glove center fielder Garry Maddox and ace pitcher Steve Carlton—the Phillies had won three consecutive NL East titles. But they followed the 1976 sweep by the Reds with NLCS defeats to the Los Angeles Dodgers in 1977 and 1978. As the offseason began, Carpenter, club president Bill Giles, and general manager Paul

Pete Rose and manager Dallas Green celebrate the 1980 World Series victory.
(Getty Images / Bettmann / Contributor)

Owens were looking for the missing piece that could finally help put the team over the top.

Rose believed he had the answer.

"My philosophy was that the Phillies' problem in the '70s wasn't the Phillies. It was the Reds," he said. "If I leave the Reds and go to the Phillies, we don't have the same problem."

Phillies officials concurred, but their initial overture was only three years, $2.1 million. Giles convinced WPHL-TV, which aired Phillies games, that Rose would improve their ratings and asked them for an additional $200,000 per year in rights fees. The station agreed, the Phillies upped their offer, and on December 5, 1978, Rose agreed to a four-year, $3.2 million contract.

If you can't beat 'em, sign 'em.

"Bill understood that Rose had an aura about him," said Dennis Lehman, a longtime Cleveland Indians executive who worked in the Phillies' front office at the time. "He was a front-page kind of guy. It drove television ratings and radio ratings as well. The impact was historic in a lot of ways."

In the 30 days that followed Rose's arrival, the Phillies sold $3 million worth of tickets, according to Giles' 2007 book, *Pouring Six Beers at a Time*. Attendance at Veterans Stadium spiked from 2.5 million in 1978 to 2.7 million in 1979. The buzz over "Charlie Hustle," as Rose was known, was palpable.

But there were still unanswered questions, including which position he would play. Primarily a third baseman for the previous four years with the Reds, Rose wasn't about to unseat Schmidt. The Phillies settled on moving Rose to first base and traded incumbent Richie Hebner to the New York Mets in spring training for right-handed pitcher Nino Espinosa. Never mind that Rose had played a grand total of 16 innings in his career at first base. He reported to spring training and went to work with Triple-A manager Lee Elia on getting comfortable at his new position.

"Every day for the first 2½ weeks, Lee Elia took me down to the complex and all's we did is we worked on first base," Rose said. "Short hops, footwork. Short hops, footwork. This, that. This, that. I don't think I ever got the credit for the job I did at first base. What's the sense in having Schmidt and Bowa, Gold Glove infielders, if you have a guy at first base who can't catch the f—ing ball? And I really worked at first base. I really thought I was a good first baseman—I think Schmidt and Bowa would tell you—and it's because I worked hard because I wanted to help the team when I had a glove on my hand."

Rose helped out in every way in 1979. He batted .331, stole 20 bases, notched 208 hits, and led the league with a .418 on-base percentage. But the Phillies went 84–78 and finished in fourth place.

With hard-driving manager Dallas Green at the helm in 1980, the Phillies had a better regular season but still didn't clinch the NL East title until the season's final weekend. Rose's numbers dipped to .284, 12 steals, 185 hits, and a .352 on-base percentage. But he had a firmer grasp on the leadership void that seemingly existed when he arrived one year earlier.

"As far as I was concerned, Bowa respected Schmidt, Schmidt respected Luzinski, Luzinski respected Maddox, Maddox respected Bowa and Boone. But they were all about the same age," Rose said. "And when you're all about the same age and you came up through the same organization, it's hard for one to become a team leader. They don't look up to each other. Bowa, he loved Schmidt, but he wasn't going to look up to Mike. Mike wasn't going to look up to Luzinski.

"When I walked in the clubhouse for the '79 season, I already had 3,000 hits. I had World Series championships. I had all the individual awards you could have. But I didn't walk in that clubhouse and say, 'Okay guys, I'm here and I'm your leader. Let's go.' Because all Bowa and Luzinski and Maddox and Schmidt and all those guys knew about me is what they saw 12 times a year when we played the Phillies. Now, after watching me play every day for the '79 season, I didn't set out to do it, but I kind of became a team leader."

Schmidt conceded that the Phillies needed a veteran leader. He recalled that Rose commanded respect because of what he had accomplished in Cincinnati. But Rose also infused his younger teammates with confidence by telling them they were "right at the doorstep" of winning a World Series. Specifically, he used positive reinforcement to build up Schmidt.

Rose had his moments on the field, too. In Game 4 of the epic 1980 NLCS against the Astros, for example, he jammed his forearm into catcher Bruce Bochy's jaw as the ball bounced away to score the go-ahead run from first base on Greg Luzinski's single in the 10th inning. Rose went 8-for-20 with five walks in that series.

In Game 6 of the World Series, with the Phillies two outs from clinching the title and the Kansas City Royals threatening, Rose caught a foul pop that ricocheted off Boone's glove.

"Charlie Hustle, my ass," Boone said, cackling. "He always says, 'Well, I caught it, didn't I?' I say, 'Yeah, because I let you catch it.' The way that play goes, as a catcher, you don't call it. It's a much easier play for the first baseman. So I'm waiting for Pete to call me off. It's his ball all the way. I don't hear him. I keep getting closer, and all's I'm thinking is, *We're really close to that dugout. If I go for this, he's going to hit me and we're both going in the dugout.* After a while, I thought, *Well, I've got to go get this.* I know I can outrebound him, so I went up for the ball, and the whole time I'm going, 'Where is Pete?'

"When it bounced out of my glove, I was so teed off at Pete, I wanted to kill him. All of a sudden, I saw his glove go right in front of my face and catch it, and I wanted to kiss him."

Phillies fans felt the same way during the 1980 World Series parade. Rose had delivered on the expectations that followed him to town. He left his mark on Philadelphia.

22

THE SIGNING OF JIM THOME

Jim Thome still has the hat.

It isn't much to look at, just a white baseball cap with a black brim and "PHILADELPHIA WANTS JIM THOME" in red lettering across the front. It was hastily made at KO Sporting Goods, an old shop on Moyamensing Avenue in the heart of South Philly. And it was given to Thome by one of the electricians from the IBEW Local 98 who lined up on Darien Street near the construction site that would eventually become Citizens Bank Park on that cold November day in 2002.

Know this, though: That hat had almost as much to do with Thome joining the Phillies as the six-year, $85 million contract offer.

"I've always felt so honored that Philadelphia recruited me and really poured their heart out," Thome said. "They're passionate people. That city, they will embrace you if you just give it everything you've got and you're accountable. Those electricians, man, they were my introduction to that."

Thome played only about 15 percent of his 22-year Hall of Fame career in Philadelphia. He's best known for slugging home runs for the Cleveland Indians. But for a sliver of time he had a profound impact on how the Phillies were perceived across baseball.

Not only did Thome lead the majors with 47 homers, drive in 131 runs, and post a .958 on-base plus slugging percentage in 2003 to live up to the hype that came with signing the largest free-agent deal in club history until Cliff Lee's five-year, $120 million pact in 2010, he also became the Phillies' centerprice as they bridged the gap between the final year in Veterans Stadium (2003) and the first season at Citizens Bank Park (2004).

Oh, and then there was this: Thome restored credibility to a franchise that had only one winning season in nine years prior to his arrival.

Never mind that Thome was long gone, traded to the Chicago White Sox, by the time the Phillies reached the playoffs again in 2007 and won the World Series in 2008. Without him as a symbol for an organization on the rise, it might have taken longer for the Phillies to enjoy those successes.

"Those of us working in the organization, we knew that we were getting better. We knew we had players coming," former assistant general manager Mike Arbuckle said. "But you have to get the rest of the world to believe that. [Thome] gave us legitimacy again. Once you get that, it gives the general manager the opportunity to go out and get Player B and Player C because now you're viewed by agents and players as a legitimate franchise that has a chance to win. Jimmy did exactly that for us."

But as badly as the Phillies wanted Thome, they were far from confident that they would actually get him.

Born and raised in Peoria, Illinois, Thome is Midwest to the core. He's meat-and-potatoes, blue-collar, the youngest of five, and down to earth as it gets, qualities that he probably gets from his late father, Chuck, who built bulldozers for Caterpillar and taught his children the value of a hard day's work.

When Thome reached free agency after the 2002 season, he didn't lack for suitors. At age 32, he was coming off seven consecutive seasons with at least 30 homers. The Baltimore Orioles, Chicago Cubs, and Los Angeles Dodgers wanted to plug him into the middle of their orders. But the most serious threat to the Phillies came from the Indians, who made a five-year, $60 million offer to retain Thome and agreed to add a vesting option for a sixth season.

"We knew his makeup and ability, and from that end absolutely he fit for us," Arbuckle said. "But I don't think we knew whether we truly fit for him. He was just this guy from Peoria, and we were trying to sell him on a Philly market—big city, bright lights. There was a lot to overcome to convince him that he was the right fit with our organization and that we were the right fit for him."

It helped that the Phillies had a close relationship with Thome's agent, Pat Rooney. It also helped that a year earlier they hired Charlie Manuel as a special assistant. Manuel was Thome's hitting coach in the minor leagues and later with the Indians, and they developed such a close bond that the slugging first baseman refers to Manuel as his "baseball father." In a well-told story, Thome was struggling in Triple-A when, before a game in Scranton, Pennsylvania, Manuel suggested that he point his bat toward the pitcher as a pre-pitch timing mechanism, a la Roy Hobbs in *The Natural*.

"Charlie took a scrappy, young kid who was anxious to hit a million home runs and actually encouraged those crazy dreams," Thome said in his Hall of Fame speech in 2018. "He told me that I could hit as many home runs as I wanted to. From day one in that dugout, he always believed in me."

But the Indians were the only team that Thome had ever known, so when the Phillies invited him to town for a recruiting visit, they put on a show. Thome toured the city, including a trip to the famous "Rocky steps" at the Philadelphia Museum of Art. He got a glimpse of the new ballpark's construction site. He went to a Flyers game and received a standing ovation. And team president David Montgomery and general manager Ed Wade outlined their vision for the franchise's direction.

"I remember their honesty. They were straightforward," Thome said. "I really noticed how excited and hungry they were. They had a game plan. They truly laid it out. I felt really good about where they were going. I even said to my wife, 'I think over this contract that we could possibly win one or two World Series.'"

The electricians from IBEW Local 98 weren't part of the Phillies' sales pitch. They were working on the construction of the new park and read in the newspaper that Thome would be in town. So they made banners and signs and awaited Thome's arrival.

Sure enough, a white limousine carrying Thome and team executives made the turn onto Darien Street. Thome asked to stop the car. He got out, shook hands with the electricians and signed autographs for about 15 minutes. They gave him the hat; he offered his appreciation for their support.

Wade closed the deal a few weeks later. In an email to Thome and his wife, Andrea, he outlined reasons why he believed Philadelphia would be the best fit for them. It was a heartfelt note that proved to be the perfect touch. Thome still credits Wade with reassuring him that he was making the right move.

Thome's every step was chronicled in spring training of 2003. He homered in his first Grapefruit League at-bat, then tripled in his first at-bat of the final home-opener at the Vet, and helped the Phillies close the old place with a spectacular season in which he finished fourth in the NL MVP voting. A year later, he played a starring role in ushering in Citizens Bank Park. He hit 42 homers, including the 400th of his career, drove in 105 runs, and instantly fell in love with the hitter-friendly ballpark.

"When you sign with a team, you want to really have a good year to let the fans know and justify why they brought you in," Thome said. "It's natural for the player to want to do really well. I was very fortunate to do that."

After being hampered by a back problem in previous seasons, Thome benefited from a program designed for him by then-Phillies athletic trainer Jeff Cooper. But injuries caught up with Thome in 2005. He had two stints on the disabled list and underwent season-ending elbow surgery in August.

Uncertainty over Thome's health, coupled with the rise of slugging first baseman Ryan Howard, created a quandary for the Phillies. They tried to turn Howard into a left fielder, but it didn't take. Ultimately, they traded Thome after the 2005 season, shipping him to the White Sox for center fielder Aaron Rowand, who became an instant fan favorite in Philadelphia in 2006 when he broke his nose and fractured orbital bones by crashing face-first into the outfield wall to make a catch.

The trade was a blessing for Thome, too. His mother had passed away less than a year earlier and playing for the White Sox enabled him to be closer to home. But that didn't mean he stopped daydreaming about teaming up with Howard in the middle of the Phillies' batting order.

"Who wouldn't?" Thome said. "Here was a guy, a young player, that emerged into an MVP. Ryno tried to go out to left field. The selfish side of you wishes he could've learned to play the outfield because to hit around him in the lineup would've been amazing. To have two guys in the middle of the lineup that could hit home runs, drive in runs, get on base, and then you add [Bobby] Abreu and [Pat] Burrell and [Chase] Utley and [Jimmy] Rollins, I mean, what a lineup. Charlie and I still talk about it like, man, what could that have been like?"

The Phillies re-signed Thome in 2012, and during spring training, Utley spoke to the team about wanting to win a World Series for him. By then, though, Thome was a part-time player, even with Howard missing half the season while recovering from a torn Achilles tendon. With the Phillies headed for a third-place finish, they traded him to the Orioles on the final day of June.

Thome retired at the end of that season, finishing with 612 home runs, eighth on the all-time list. Of those, only 101 were hit with the Phillies.

But whenever he looks at that hat, which is displayed in his hunting lodge in Illinois, he's reminded of a time, however fleeting, when he was the biggest star in a city that began to fall for baseball again.

"It was a moment for me that was like, 'Wow, these guys really, really care, and they really want me to come here,'" Thome said. "I felt that vibe of love. It was a really good feeling."

23

THE BRYCE IS RIGHT

For 3½ months in the winter of 2018–19, the baseball conversation in the Delaware Valley centered on two free agents. Their strengths and flaws were analyzed ad nauseum. Debates raged over how much money they would get, which rival teams might be interested, and which superstar would represent the better buy.

Manny Machado or Bryce Harper?

Bryce Harper or Manny Machado?

The Phillies were sure to sign one of them. For years, they targeted this free-agent class as the opportunity to acquire their next franchise player, and after improving from 66 wins in 2017 to 80 wins in 2018, the time was right to chase a marquee name. Besides, owner John Middleton all but telegraphed the club's intentions at the beginning of the offseason when he told *USA Today* that the Phillies were ready to spend money and would "maybe even be a little bit stupid about it."

But November turned into December, and December into January, without either player coming close to signing. The Phillies hosted Machado at Citizens Bank Park on December 20. They visited Harper in Las Vegas on January 11. Then they waited. And waited. Spring training began, and they waited some more.

Finally, on February 19, Machado agreed to terms on a 10-year, $300 million contract with the San Diego Padres. By total value, it was the richest contract ever given to a free agent and the second-richest overall behind Giancarlo Stanton's $325 million extension with the Miami Marlins in 2014. By average annual value, it was the most money for a free-agent position player and tied for the third-most for any free agent.

The bar was now set for Harper. The Phillies no longer could play Machado's agent, Dan Lozano, against Harper's agent, Scott Boras. Suddenly it was Harper or bust for Team Stupid Money.

And Middleton knew what he needed to do.

While almost all agents deal mostly with general managers, Boras' modus operandi is to appeal directly to owners. As front offices have become increasingly driven by analytics—and consequently, more conservative in their decision-making on free agents—Boras understands that owners tend to be more emotional. They also control the purse strings.

Middleton's thirst for winning once prompted Phillies shortstop Jimmy Rollins to dub him "Steinbrenner South," a nod to late Yankees owner George Steinbrenner. It's a comparison that Middleton embraces. He made his money in his family's tobacco business and bought a 15-percent stake in the Phillies for $18 million in 1994. He owns slightly less than 50 percent of the team now and assumed a more visible role in 2014. In a 2017 interview with 94-WIP, the Phillies' flagship radio station, he said, "We're going to get that [World Series] trophy back somehow—or I'm going to die trying."

Boras and Middleton came together on a three-year, $75 million deal for pitcher Jake Arrieta in March 2018. Ten months later, the billionaire owner was part of the Phillies' contingent that traveled to Vegas to meet with Harper and his wife, Kayla. Now, late in the afternoon of February 20—one day after Machado's agreement—Boras texted Middleton, who replied that he was prepared to begin the first serious negotiation for Harper.

"We were getting ready to talk about specifics about the offer, and Scott says, 'Look, here's what I want: I think it's really important for you to come back out—just by yourself, not with [team president] Andy [MacPhail] and [GM] Matt [Klentak] and [manager] Gabe [Kapler] and [assistant GM] Ned [Rice]—and just sit down with Bryce and Kayla and talk. They got to know you a little bit in January, but I think it would be really helpful,'" Middleton recalled. "And as we talked about that and I understood what he wanted, I said, 'How would you feel about Leigh coming out, too?' And immediately he said, 'That would be great.' Right away I called my wife and I said, 'Our plans have changed. We're flying to Las Vegas.'"

Let it be said, then, that the Phillies' courtship of Harper truly got serious at a table for five at Carbone, an Italian restaurant in the ARIA resort and casino on the Las Vegas strip.

It was February 22, a Friday night. Dinner lasted for almost four hours, and not once, according to Middleton, did the sides discuss contract terms. Instead, Bryce and Kayla Harper got to know John and Leigh Middleton.

"We're going on 41 years of marriage," Middleton said. "They were curious as to how that kind of career marriage arc works, what are the ups and downs that you face and how do you work through those kinds of issues. It was a really personal conversation."

Boras, never at a loss for words, sat there like Charlie Chaplin.

"I didn't say a word," he said. "They talked about everything."

And when they finally rose from the table, the Middletons called an audible. Rather than returning to Clearwater, Florida, on their private jet the next morning, as scheduled, they pushed back their flight. Middleton had a four-hour breakfast meeting with Boras, then

John Middleton shakes hands with Bryce Harper as GM Matt Klentak looks on during the press conference to introduce Harper as a member of the Philadelphia Phillies on Saturday March 2, 2019, at Spectrum Field in Clearwater, Florida. (Getty Images / Mike Carlson/MLB)

rejoined his wife and met the Harpers for lunch. That's when the owner ratcheted up his sales pitch. With Kayla expecting the Harpers' first child (Krew, a 7-pound, 9-ounce baby boy, was born in August), Middleton boasted about the quality of the schools, hospitals, and restaurants in the Philadelphia area.

Still, though, there wasn't much contract talk. What there was, quite clearly, was a bond between an owner and a star player.

"When I met with the Middleton family, I felt that commitment," said Harper, who had a close relationship with Washington Nationals owner Ted Lerner. "Me and my wife walked away [thinking], *Wow, we're blown away by these amazing people.* They really understand where we're coming from, understand the family aspect of our life. John wants to win more than anybody, and I saw that passion, I saw that fire. He talked about wrestling in college and the commitment he made to that. I mean, it was just amazing to hear."

A day later, after the Middletons had left town, a group of Dodgers officials, including manager Dave Roberts, touched down in Vegas. They offered an annual salary that topped pitcher Zack Greinke's free-agent record of $34.4 million with the Arizona Diamondbacks, but weren't willing to go longer than four or five years. A few days after that, the San Francisco Giants arrived with a 12-year offer for about $310 million.

Harper and Boras wanted top Stanton's $325 million. Harper was emphatic, too, about securing a contract long enough that it could be his last. At age 26, that meant more than 10 years, a commitment that eliminated the Dodgers. The length of the deal meant so much to Harper, in fact, that he had no interest in the opt-out provision that Boras has gotten for so many clients since Alex Rodriguez's 10-year, $252 million deal with the Texas Rangers in 2000.

"At the beginning of the process, I told [Boras] I want to be able to dig my roots somewhere," Harper said. "That was through the good and the bad, through the ups and downs of a team and an organization."

Middleton was willing to go to $330 million. That left Klentak and Boras to haggle over the years. Negotiations went back and forth, and when Klentak went to sleep on February 27, he was pessimistic that the sides would reach an accord. But Boras reached out again the next morning. The talks had gotten so frantic that Klentak opted to work from his Clearwater Beach condo rather than going to his spring-training office at Spectrum Field.

At last, Klentak called Middleton. They had the parameters of a deal: 13 years, $330 million. All Middleton had to do was give the okay.

Was there any doubt?

"One of the things you have to learn to do when you're working on deals your whole life is not allow yourself to get too high and never let yourself get too low," Middleton said. "You have to understand that there's ebbs and flows to these things."

Once news of the agreement broke on February 28, the magnitude of the deal became clear. It was the Phillies' biggest signing since at least Cliff Lee in 2010 and ranked with the signings of Jim Thome in 2002 and Pete Rose in 1979 as the most buzz-worthy free-agent moves in franchise history. The Phillies sold roughly 100,000 tickets on February 28, according to senior vice president of ticket operations John Weber. They sold another 80,000 the next day. Harper's jersey—he chose No. 3—flew off the shelves, too. According to Fanatics, it was the top-selling jersey of all time for any player in any sport within 24 hours of being released.

Harper made an impact on the field, too, particularly during the second half of his first season with the Phillies. In the most electric moment at Citizens Bank Park since at least 2011, he crushed a grand slam to bring the Phillies back from a 5–3 deficit in a 7–5 victory over the Chicago Cubs on August 15. He also became the first Phillies player since Ryan Howard in 2011 and the first Phillies outfielder since Pat Burrell in 2005 to hit 30 homers and drive in 100 runs in a season. He finished with 35 homers, 114 RBI, and a .510 slugging percentage despite striking out a career-high 178 times, and was a first-time finalist for the Gold Glove in right field.

"Every time he comes up," Phillies pitcher Drew Smyly said, "I think everybody in the park expects him to do something great."

That's why Middleton wanted him. Now Harper has until 2032 to get back what Middleton *really* wants: the World Series trophy.

24

JIM BUNNING

In pulling off a four-player trade with the Detroit Tigers during the winter meetings at the El Cortez Hotel in San Diego in December 1963, Phillies general manager John Quinn accomplished more than acquiring an All-Star pitcher to anchor the team's starting rotation.

Like it or not, he gave voice to the players.

Before Jim Bunning came along, Phillies players weren't granted free parking at Connie Mack Stadium, where garage space was scarce and cars on the street were frequently broken into. They couldn't bring their wives on road trips. When the Los Angeles Dodgers and San Francisco Giants came to town, players weren't allowed to leave tickets for their family and friends because management expected to draw larger-than-usual crowds.

Bunning changed all that. The slender 6-foot-3 right-hander had been the Tigers' representative in the players' association, and upon being traded to the Phillies, his new teammates selected him to take over those duties from pitcher Dallas Green. In the ensuing years, he played a central role in the hiring of executive director Marvin Miller, who helped turn the MLBPA into one of the strongest labor forces in the country. And it wasn't long before Bunning began to speak out against what he believed to be the mistreatment of players.

"One day he came over and said, 'What does that sign [in the clubhouse] mean?' We said, 'Well, we're not allowed to leave tickets for the Giants and Dodgers series coming up,'" former Phillies shortstop Bobby Wine recalled. "He said, 'Wrong! Illegal!' And he went upstairs to John Quinn and read him the rules and regulations. A little while later he came down and said, 'Here's your pass list, boys.' Jim got things done. Let's put it that way."

It wasn't any wonder, then, that the late Bunning spent his post-baseball career in politics. He served in the United States Congress for

24 years, including two terms as the Republican junior Senator from Kentucky, a seat that is presently occupied by Rand Paul.

But for as much as Bunning advocated on his teammates' behalf during a 17-year playing career, he made his teams stronger simply by taking the mound. He won 224 games, posted a 3.27 earned-run average, and recorded 2,855 strikeouts, 19th-most all-time. He also threw no-hitters in both leagues, including a perfect game for the Phillies on Father's Day in 1964.

Bunning spent only six seasons with the Phillies, but they were the most dominant of his career. From 1964 to '67, the first of his two stints with the club, he led the majors in strikeouts (992), innings (1,191⅔), and shutouts (23), and ranked third in wins (74), fifth in complete games (60), and tied for ninth in ERA (2.48).

"He had the running slider, which looked like a fastball but it just kept moving across the plate," said Clay Dalrymple, who caught more of Bunning's starts (102) than any catcher. "He had a nice roundhouse curveball and he had a hard slider and a fastball. He could hit the corners, and if you wanted a pitch high, he'd throw a pitch high. Jim had a variety of pitches that he could work with that were good."

And they all came out of a funky sidearm delivery. Bunning would also fall off the mound toward the first-base side in his follow-through, a wrinkle that made his pitches appear even more deceptive to opposing hitters.

The Phillies won 87 games in 1963 despite having one of the youngest pitching staffs in baseball. Chris Short, Art Mahaffey, Dennis Bennett, and Ray Culp were in their early- to mid–twenties, and although each had flashed potential, manager Gane Mauch wanted a more accomplished and experienced pitcher to lead the group.

Bunning checked both boxes. At age 32, he was in his prime after averaging 16 wins, 34 starts, 252 innings, and 191 strikeouts in the previous seven seasons with the Tigers.

Before there were exhaustive scouting reports and statistical breakdowns to detail every little tendency of an opposing hitter, the Phillies had Bunning. Mauch would ask the ace to sit in on pregame scouting meetings even when he wasn't scheduled to pitch, according to Wine, and the manager often asked, "Okay, what do you want to do, Jim, about this guy?"

"It really took a lot of the pressure off all the infielders because if he said, 'Play 'em up the middle,' then we didn't worry about the hole or the other end," Wine said. "If they hit it there, it was a mistake. And that didn't happen very often with Jim."

Ferguson Jenkins, the Hall of Fame pitcher who broke in with the Phillies in 1965 before getting traded a year later to the Chicago Cubs, recalls lockering next to Bunning in spring training. He took note of Bunning's breaking ball, admired his durability, and pressed him about his approach to different hitters in specific instances in a game.

After all, who better to learn from than a nine-time All-Star at the peak of his powers?

"I would try to pick his brain sometimes—'What do you do in this situation? How does this guy not hit you?'" Jenkins said. "And we'd just talk about the game of baseball. He stayed ahead of the hitter. He was a workhorse. He didn't miss starts. He had a fabulous career."

Bunning was willing to share what he knew. He also set an example for younger pitchers with how he prepared for a start and executed a game plan.

"He would say, 'How come you're only running five [laps]? It wouldn't hurt you to do two more,'" Wine said. "And then people would start following what he was doing. He would kind of set the standard. If he was out doing it, some of the other guys started falling in line and saying, 'Well, I better do it.' There was no clowning around with Jim."

Except, ironically, in the middle of the best game that he ever pitched.

It was June 21, 1964, Father's Day, and Bunning was scheduled to face the New York Mets in the first game of a doubleheader at Shea Stadium. He was a father of seven at the time, and his wife, Mary, and daughter Barbara were at the game on a 90-degree day.

From the beginning, Bunning had the stuff to dominate. He got through the first three innings by setting down nine consecutive Mets hitters on only 27 pitches, getting weak contact and never going to a three-ball count. But while other pitchers would be superstitious in the midst of such a performance, Bunning was the opposite.

"It was a hot day, so he kept telling our trainer, 'Give me that [new] shirt and give me that shirt and give me that shirt,'" Wine said. "He had 'em hanging up in the runway. You know how no one ever likes to talk about no-hitters and guys sit in the same spot and all that kind of stuff? He was going, 'Hey guys, they don't have any hits yet. Don't forget now. We're getting closer.'"

In his 1998 autobiography, *Jim Bunning: Baseball and Beyond*, Bunning explained that he was trying to keep himself relaxed by being so chatty. "The other guys thought I was crazy," he wrote, "but I didn't want anyone tightening up. Most of all, I didn't want to tighten up myself. I started thinking about it around the fifth inning. By then, you know you have a chance."

Especially after you benefit from a hit-stealing play. With one out in the fifth inning, Phillies second baseman Tony Taylor knocked down a Jesse Gonder line drive, crawled after the ball, and threw out Gonder at first base. It was the Mets' best chance at a hit.

The Phillies stretched the lead to 6–0 in the sixth inning on a leadoff homer by Johnny Callison and two-out RBI hits by catcher Gus Triandos and Bunning. Then Bunning mowed down the top of the Mets' order in the seventh, striking out Jim Hickman on three pitches, getting Ron Hunt to ground out, and fanning Ed Kranepool.

Bunning had thrown a no-hitter earlier in his career with the Tigers on July 20, 1958, at Fenway Park in Boston. Now, though, as he returned to the dugout after each inning, Bunning was audibly counting down the number of outs remaining.

"It was so funny," Wine said. "[Superstition] never entered into it. He just knew when he went out there for that given inning exactly what he wanted to do. Jim was a perfectionist."

Literally. Bunning got Charley Smith to pop out to Wine for the first out of the ninth inning, and as pinch-hitter George Altman came to the plate, Bunning asked to speak with Triandos.

"He calls me out and says I should tell him a joke or something, just to give him a breather," Triandos said at the time. "I couldn't think of any. I just laughed at him."

Bunning struck out Altman, then fanned pinch-hitter John Stephenson on a curveball—only his 89th pitch of the game—to record the seventh perfect game in baseball history. Bunning also joined Cy Young and Addie Joss as the only three pitchers to throw a no-hitter and a perfect game. That club has grown to include Sandy Koufax, Randy Johnson, Mark Buehrle, and Roy Halladay, who threw his perfect game and a playoff no-hitter for the Phillies in 2010.

Despite all of his accolades, Bunning wasn't elected to the Hall of Fame by the writers, falling a few votes shy in 1988 and dropping off the ballot in 1991. Five years later, he was selected for induction by the Veterans Committee.

"I never really thought about the Hall of Fame for him," Dalrymple said. "All I thought about was, *If I think like Jim Bunning and I call a game according to how he would want the game called, he's going to enjoy pitching to me*. He'd yell hard at me a couple times because he was so competitive. I'd say, 'Jim, I'm on the same team you're on.' But he had a great personality. Bunning never got in trouble because he knew how to pitch. It was really fun to catch Bunning. He was a good guy to have on your side."

For reasons that weren't limited to pitching.

25

SCHILL

Before he became a 20-game winner and a World Series champion, before the 300-strikeout seasons and the Bloody Sock, before his video-game company went belly up and ESPN fired him, before he issued a Twitter endorsement of violence against journalists and turned into a right-wing pariah, Curt Schilling was a cocky, young pitcher walking through the door of the Phillies' clubhouse at Veterans Stadium in April 1992.

"He walked in with Brian Bosworth hair and that walk that looks like a strut," former first baseman John Kruk told the *Philadelphia Inquirer* in 2018. "It came across like, 'This guy is either going to be the greatest pitcher who ever lived, or the biggest jackass.'"

It was never that clear cut, of course. Schilling's legacy, as a pitcher and in his post-baseball life, is too complex to be so neatly compartmentalized. Let seven years' worth of Hall of Fame voting serve as a referendum on just what a polarizing figure he has become.

Here, though, is one thing that Schilling's supporters and detractors agree on: He ranks among the best big-game pitchers of all time.

It's there for everyone to see, without any shades of gray. In 19 career postseason starts, he has an 11–2 record and a 2.23 earned-run average. He has two complete games and four shutouts. He has started a Game 7 and won three elimination games and two clinchers.

"He was fearless. I mean, *fearless*," former Phillies center fielder Doug Glanville said. "He wanted the ball. He wanted to go deep in the game. He wanted to take on the best players. He loved the bragging rights. And he loved competing. He was always fighting for the team's life every day. He loved for it to be on his shoulders."

Schilling cemented his big-game reputation with the Arizona Diamondbacks in 2001, going 4–0 with a 1.12 ERA in six postseason starts and being named most valuable player of the World Series. He will be forever remembered for starting Game 6 of the 2004 American League Championship Series on a sutured right ankle that bled through his sanitary hose. It was the signature moment in the Boston Red Sox's comeback from a three games-to-none deficit against the Yankees and their run to a Curse-breaking World Series championship that brought so much joy to New Englanders after 86 years of torture.

But while Schilling is most often associated with those franchises—he did, after all, win one World Series ring with Arizona and two with Boston—he actually pitched for the Phillies (8½ years) longer than he did for the Dbacks (3½ years) and Sox (four years) combined. He ranks fifth on the franchise all-time list in strikeouts (1,554), seventh in wins (101) and walks/hits per inning pitched (1.120), and ninth in innings (1,659⅓). And he established himself as a money pitcher in the 1993 postseason. His 147-pitch, five-hit shutout of the Toronto Blue Jays in Game 5 of the World Series ranks with the best games ever pitched in Phillies history.

But because Schilling spent so much of the last few years of his Phillies tenure angling to get shipped out of town—and maybe because the Phillies lost the 1993 World Series—it's easy to overlook his successes here and focus instead on the self-serving things that he often did, from calling 94-WIP to spar with sports-talk radio host Angelo Cataldi to placing a towel over his head to shield his eyes when white-knuckle closer Mitch Williams was on the mound in the ninth inning.

Former Phillies general manager Ed Wade offered the best summary of life with Schilling with this memorable quip: "Every fifth day Curt's our horse. The other four days he's our horse's ass."

"I think if we won the World Series that it would've changed the narrative here for Schill," former Phillies third baseman Dave Hollins said. "All's I know is that when he pitched, that was a fun game to play. When he was out there, you knew we could beat anybody."

The Phillies acquired Schilling from the Houston Astros on April 2, 1992, in what must be considered one of the best trades in franchise history, an even-up swap for right-handed journeyman Jason Grimsley. He began the season in the bullpen, moved to the rotation in mid-May, and posted a 2.27 ERA and 10 complete games and four shutouts in 26 starts.

Schilling returned as the Phillies' ace in 1993 and made his first star turn in the playoffs. But it wasn't until 1996, at age 29, that he really

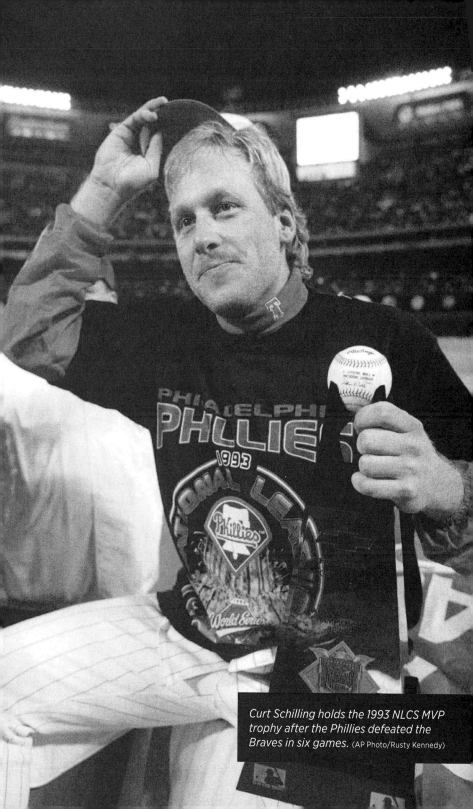

Curt Schilling holds the 1993 NLCS MVP trophy after the Phillies defeated the Braves in six games. (AP Photo/Rusty Kennedy)

reached his peak. He led the league with 319 strikeouts in 1997 and 300 in 1998. From 1996 to '99, he ranked sixth among NL starters with a 3.22 ERA, trailing Kevin Brown (2.50), Greg Maddux (2.66), Pedro Martinez (2.75), John Smoltz (3.01), and Tom Glavine (3.14).

"We were completely confident in him," former Phillies second baseman Mickey Morandini said. "We knew what kind of pitcher he was. We knew how he prepared."

Indeed, Schilling's preparation was legendary. Glanville recalls the ace studying scouting reports to uncover patterns for how to attack specific hitters. Schilling was also willing to listen and learn. He became a devoted pupil of pitching coach Johnny Podres, who transformed his career by instructing him to grip the ball across four seams and unleash a power fastball rather than the two-seam sinker that he threw with the Astros.

"Outside of the Lord, my wife, and my father, there was no person who impacted my life more than Johnny Podres," Schilling wrote on his blog, "38 Pitches," when Podres died in 2008. "He asked everything of me and always got everything I had. He made me realize the only limits in my life were self-imposed."

Schilling's tour de force with the Phillies came on October 21, 1993. One night earlier, in Game 4 of the World Series, they blew a 14–9 lead in the eighth inning of a 15–14 crusher. Now, facing elimination against a Blue Jays team that featured three Hall of Famers (Rickey Henderson, Roberto Alomar, and Paul Molitor), Schilling saved the season in a 2–0 victory that sent the Series back to Toronto.

"He came out and shut out a f—ing All-Star team," Hollins said. "I'll never forget that. Schilling was just dominant. You love to have a teammate like that."

Tell that to Williams, who has questioned Schilling's Hall of Fame credentials on Twitter and said in 2014 that he "never forgave" him for putting the towel over his head. Old grudges die hard, it seems.

"I, personally, didn't have a problem with Schill at all until the towel incident," former reliever Larry Andersen said. "It's like you're calling out your teammate. We didn't do that. That bothered me a lot. I still look back at it and just think of how wrong it was. And then when he saw the attention that he was getting with that, he was like, 'Well,

I can get more attention if I keep doing it.' It was just wrong. It was something you don't do. Obviously, Mitch didn't like it, but I think the players on the team didn't like it."

In time, though, they chalked it up to Schilling being Schilling.

Glanville bonded with Schilling over their shared video-game hobby. They played EverQuest, an online version of Dungeons & Dragons in which they inhabited characters who would travel to the Butcherblock Mountains to kill Aviak birds.

"We literally sounded like we were from another planet," Glanville said, laughing. "I got along well with Curt. We had that common interest, and we had a good enough relationship that we kept in touch even after we both were retired."

But as the Phillies regressed from a pennant-winning club in 1993 to 75-, 95-, 94-, 87-, and 85-loss seasons from 1995 to '99, Schilling aimed his arrows at ownership for not spending enough money to build a contender. In 1999, when the Phillies opened the season with a $28 million payroll, he challenged the owners to step up or sell the team. Two years earlier, when president Bill Clinton—and his massive Secret Service detail—visited the Phillies' clubhouse before a game at Camden Yards in Baltimore, Schilling joked, "You'll have to excuse me if I seem a little nervous, Mr. President. I'm not used to being in my uniform in front of this many people."

Schill being Schill.

Eventually, Schilling got his wish, forcing a trade to Arizona and having so much success that his Phillies years receded into the background. He has only become more outspoken in retirement, and if you want to hear his thoughts on almost anything, he spews them daily in an online radio show for the far-right Breitbart News.

"He gained a lot of confidence in himself here [with the Phillies], and I think that might have spurred him on to do things that maybe weren't as acceptable to us as a whole," Andersen said. "But I'll tell you what: You talk about a guy that comes in and pitches big games, and he was right there. He was the guy you wanted on the mound."

And that's one opinion—probably the only one—about Schilling that's universal.

26

DOC

s Cliff Lee mowed down batter after batter in Game 1 of the 2009 World Series, Roy Halladay tortured himself at home in Florida.

"Turn that darn TV off," his wife, Brandy, said.

Sorry, but Halladay could neither look away nor stop thinking that it should have been him on that mound at Yankee Stadium. At 32, he overcame an early career demotion to the minors and was a six-time All-Star. He twice won 20 games, to say nothing of a Cy Young Award. His competitiveness was fierce, his preparation exhaustive, his reputation as one of the top two or three pitchers in baseball universal.

There was only one thing he hadn't done in 12 big-league seasons: start a playoff game.

Halladay made 320 career starts, in fact, before appearing in the postseason, more than any active pitcher at that time. But 2009 was supposed to be the year. He was sure that the rebuilding Toronto Blue Jays were going to trade him. Heck, general manager J.P. Ricciardi even called him before spring training to brace him for the possibility.

"Doc," as Halladay was nicknamed early in his career by Jays broadcaster Tom Cheek, would have bet that he'd wind up with the Phillies. The defending World Series champs lusted after him for years, first under general manager Pat Gillick and then his successor Ruben Amaro Jr. Rival scouts even joked that Halladay was Amaro's white whale. It seemed like a fait accompli.

But on July 29, two days before the trade deadline, the Phillies acquired Lee from the Cleveland Indians. Halladay, against both the odds and his wishes, stayed in Toronto.

In a scheduling coincidence that only the baseball gods could arrange, the Blue Jays were playing in Oakland on July 31 and staying at the Westin St. Francis in San Francisco, the same hotel that the Phillies were occupying for a series against the Giants in which Lee made his debut. In the lobby, Halladay bumped into Phillies director of travel Frank Coppenbarger, who expressed surprise that a trade with Toronto didn't materialize. Halladay, despondent as ever, didn't say much. At least Coppenbarger didn't tell him that the Phillies had a No. 34 jersey with his name on it stashed at the bottom of an equipment trunk.

So, yes, Halladay could be excused for feeling like Lee's shining moment against the Yankees should have belonged to him.

A year later, though, it was at last Halladay's turn. In December 2009, two months after losing in the World Series, the Phillies sent three prospects, including touted right-hander Kyle Drabek, to the Blue Jays, signed Halladay to a contract extension, and presented him that No. 34 that had been earmarked for him but given to Lee instead. Amaro then attempted to replenish the farm system by shipping Lee to the Seattle Mariners.

Halladay had an even better season in 2010 than the Phillies expected. Pitching coach Rich Dubee introduced the 6-foot-6 right-hander to a new pitch—a split-changeup, they called it, which incorporated elements of a split-finger fastball—and he went 21–10 with a 2.44 earned-run average, 219 strikeouts, and 30 walks in 250⅔ innings. He threw a 115-pitch perfect game on May 29 in Miami—the 20th of 23 perfect games in history, after which he gifted $4,000 watches to teammates and members of the Phillies' support staff—and copped another Cy Young Award. And on October 6, he was set for his long-awaited postseason debut in Game 1 of the Division Series against the Cincinnati Reds at Citizens Bank Park.

"We were all just excited for everyone in the world to see him throw a playoff game," closer Brad Lidge said. "He'd been waiting for that opportunity for so long. I think we all knew he was going to have a great game because he had done it the entire season. But with more on the line, you expected him to do amazing things."

But the second no-hitter in postseason history?

"Yeah, we didn't know it was going to end like that," Lidge said, chuckling.

Lidge watched Halladay ever since they played against each other for rival Denver-area high schools. He would love to tell you that there was something different about Doc in the days and hours leading to the start of his life. But before tossing the first postseason no-hitter since Don Larsen's perfect game for the Yankees in the 1956 World Series, Halladay did everything the same way that he always did.

In life, Halladay was a thrill-seeker. He once belly-flopped into the Amazon River—and goaded his close friend, former St. Louis Cardinals

Carlos Ruiz and Roy Halladay celebrate Halladay's playoff no-hitter in the moments before the entire Phillies team mobs them. (Getty Images / Chris Trotman)

pitcher Chris Carpenter, to do so, too—just so that he could tell people that he did it. After retiring in 2013, he became a licensed pilot and bought a single-engine ICON A5 light sports aircraft. He died tragically in 2017 when he crashed that plane into the Gulf of Mexico.

But in baseball, Halladay never left anything to chance. On the day before his first playoff start, he ran alone on the warning track (in a downpour, no less) before slipping into what he called "isolation mode," a state of complete concentration in which he would envision every pitch he planned to throw. A slave to routine, he adhered to his usual program, right down to the 42 warmup pitches in the bullpen.

"He was clockwork," Dubee said. "I don't know if he was any more locked in because he was always locked in and focused. I know how long he waited to pitch in the playoffs, but I can't say that a playoff game took his focus and attention to detail higher because every game was like a playoff game with Roy."

Halladay dismissed any questions about how he would handle the pressure of the postseason by throwing 10 pitches in the first inning, 12 in the second, nine in the third, and 12 in the fourth. He struck out Scott Rolen and Jonny Gomes to open the fifth inning before walking Jay Bruce on a full-count pitch.

Bruce was the first—and last—batter to reach base.

"You knew after about six hitters or so," Dubee said. "Just the way they were swinging at him and trying to approach him, you had a feeling that he could dominate."

The Phillies had a 4–0 lead by the eighth inning, when Halladay struck out Gomes on three pitches, got Bruce to tap a first pitch in front of the mound, and fanned Drew Stubbs on three pitches.

Quite simply, the Reds had no chance.

"You can try as many tricks of the trade as you want—ruin his rhythm, step out, call time, whatever," Gomes told reporters after the game. "But when a guy's pounding the zone like that and is in the zone like that, none of that really works."

Most historic pitching performances feature at least one dazzling defensive assist. Halladay scarcely required help. The closest call came with two out in the ninth inning on, of all things, a dribbler by Phillips in front of home plate. It wouldn't have been a big deal except that the ball nicked Phillips' bat in the dirt. Catcher Carlos Ruiz dropped to his knee to make sure the ball didn't skip away, then made an on-target throw to first base.

Halladay was swarmed by Ruiz. The rest of the Phillies followed. When the relievers ran in from the bullpen, it marked the first time all night they stirred.

"His pitch count was low enough [104] that you knew he was going to take it all the way no matter what," Lidge said. "Honestly, even if he was at 140 pitches, he was going for it. That was his ballgame. You were just hoping that nobody gets a broken-bat hit on a great pitch and it accidentally gets broken up. But he was not going to let that happen. It was like he was going to will a no-hitter."

It was the 11th of 13 no-hitters in Phillies history. Halladay is the only Phillies pitcher with two of his own. Cole Hamels combined on a no-hitter in 2014 before completing one of his own in 2015. The rest of the club: Charlie Ferguson (1885), Red Donahue (1898), Chick Fraser (1903), Johnny Lush (1906), Jim Bunning (1964), Rick Wise (1971), Terry Mulholland (1990), Tommy Greene (1991), and Kevin Milwood (2003).

Halladay had more big moments in his career, though nothing came close to matching his postseason no-no. The Phillies re-signed Lee and put together the "Four Aces" rotation in 2011. Halladay was still the best of the bunch, going 19–6 with a 2.35 ERA and 220 strikeouts in 233⅔ innings. But despite winning a franchise-record 102 games, the Phillies were ousted in the Division Series by the St. Louis Cardinals.

Injuries, including shoulder problems, curtailed Halladay's career in 2013. He was posthumously inducted into the Hall of Fame in 2019.

Let it be said, though, that Halladay lived to pitch in the postseason. And wouldn't you know it, he made the most memorable playoff debut ever.

How's that for a legacy?

"It still crushes me that he's gone," Amaro told the *Philadelphia Inquirer*. "I think about him every day not just because of the impact he had on the Phillies as an organization, but also because of the impact he had on me."

27

AN "EXTRA"-SPECIAL SERIES

Quick, what's the best postseason series you have ever seen? It's tough to beat the Boston Red Sox's rally from three games down to vanquish the New York Yankees in the 2004 American League Championship Series, or the seven-game thriller in 2016 that gave the Chicago Cubs their first World Series triumph in 108 years, or the 2001 World Series that began amid the backdrop of 9/11 and ended seven games later with Luis Gonzalez's flare off the great Mariano Rivera. Fans of a certain age will recall Jack Morris pitching the Minnesota Twins to a 10-inning victory in Game 7 in the 1991 World Series, the 1986 National League Championship Series between the New York Mets and Houston Astros, and the Big Red Machine outlasting Carlton Fisk and the Red Sox in 1975.

But we're talking about the Phillies, and for edge-of-your-seat, cuticle-chomping drama, no series in the history of the franchise—and only a select few in baseball lore—can match the 1980 NLCS against the Astros.

"Most exciting five-game series ever," Pete Rose said flatly.

"Four one-run games and four extra-inning games?" Bob Boone said. "Us coming back to beat Nolan Ryan, which virtually had been undoable? It has to be one of the best series in the history of the game."

"Every game was extra innings except one," said Larry Bowa. "Tough to beat that."

And when you consider how much was riding on those five games for the Phillies, the stakes couldn't have been any higher, the tension any more extreme.

The Phillies won the NL East crown in 1976 and were defeated in the NLCS by the defending-champion Cincinnati Reds at the height of their 1970s dominance. They won the division in 1977 and 1978, too, but fell to the Dodgers in the NLCS both years. After missing the playoffs in 1979 and feuding with manager Dallas Green for most of the 1980 season, they pulled it together to clinch the NL East on the penultimate day of the season and finished with a 91–71 record.

But if they didn't get past the Astros—a 93-win team that had to win a play-in game at Dodger Stadium to clinch the NL West—in the best-of-five League Championship Series this time, well, everyone knew what would've happened.

"I think that would've been our last hurrah, to be honest with you," said Greg Luzinski, a staple of the Phillies' homegrown core who already seemed likely to be shipped out. "They definitely would've broken us up."

No pressure, right?

The Phillies were 0–6 at home in the three previous NLCS losses, so optimism was scarce across the city. As Ray Didinger wrote in the *Philadelphia Daily News*, "For the Phillies, October isn't a month. It's a padded cell waiting to slam shut on them."

But Steve Carlton gave the Phillies seven strong innings in Game 1, a 3–1 victory powered by Luzinski's two-run homer in the sixth inning against Astros starter Ken Forsch. They dropped the second game, though, 7–4, when the Astros scored four runs in the 10th inning against reliever Ron Reed.

The Phillies knew all along that the series would be decided at the Astrodome, where the Astros had never before played a postseason game and the atmosphere was straight out of *Friday Night Lights*.

"That's the loudest place I ever played in my entire life," Luzinski said. "Now I know why Steve Carlton used to put cotton in his ears. But we went to Houston knowing—and we talked about it a little bit—that we always got good-pitched games there. Our pitchers always kept us in. We thought we had a chance, even if a lot of other people didn't."

Game 3 was scoreless until the 11th inning, when Joe Morgan led off with a triple against Phillies closer Tug McGraw. And after back-to-back intentional walks loaded the bases, Denny Walling lifted a sacrifice fly to score pinch-runner Rafael Landestoy with the winning run.

The Phillies were on the brink of elimination. Again.

"Things start going through your mind," Luzinski said. "It's like, 'Oh, not again,' especially to the rainbow-clad Houston Astros in that crazy dome. It can't happen like that."

Game 4 was marked by controversial calls and late-inning lead changes. The Phillies nearly hit into a triple play in the fourth inning, but after a furious argument from Green in which Bowa and Rose went ballistic, the umpires changed the call to a double play.

The Phillies were trailing 2–0 in the eighth inning, their scoreless drought having reached 18 innings, when they tied the game on back-to-back RBI singles by Rose and Mike Schmidt. Although they took the lead two batters later, a missed call by Bruce Froemming—the same umpire who achieved infamy on "Black Friday" in 1977—prevented the rally from continuing. Manny Trillo's drive to right field was caught on a short hop by Jeffrey Leonard, but Froemming ruled that it was caught on the fly. Rose tagged and scored from third base, but Schmidt was doubled off first and the Phillies had to settle for a 3–2 lead.

It loomed large when the Astros tied it in the ninth inning on an RBI single by Phillies-nemesis Terry Puhl—"Every time we'd get a lead, he'd come back and do something," Bowa recalled, his voice still tinged with frustration—and pushed the game into extra innings again.

But with one out in the 10th, after Rose singled off reliever Joe Sambito, Luzinski came up as a pinch-hitter and lined a double into the left-field corner. Jose Cruz played the ball cleanly off the wall and hit the cutoff man. Rose roared around third base and charged to home plate like a crazed bull in Pamplona. Bracing for impact, Astros catcher Bruce Bochy bobbled a short-hop throw, then took a forearm shiver to the jaw as Rose plowed ahead for the go-ahead run in what turned out to be a 5–3 victory.

"I was hell bent on scoring," Rose said. "I was like, 'I'm going to score this run right here.' I figured, if he hits the ball down the left-field line, I'm on first, I've got to be able to score, especially in the Astrodome."

After the game, Tug McGraw told reporters, "There has never been a game to compare with that one. It was like going through an art museum on a motorcycle. You don't remember all of the pictures you saw because there were so many and they came so fast."

Little did McGraw know, Game 5 would top it.

The Phillies trailed 5–2 in the eighth inning against Ryan, a death sentence for most teams. But Rose, by now the Phillies' unequivocal leader, knew better.

"Pete came up to me and says, 'Bow, if you get on, we're going to win this game,'" Bowa said. "Now, go look at Nolan Ryan's numbers when he had a lead that year. But we felt we were in the game."

Sure enough, Bowa led off with a single and Boone singled off Ryan's glove, a ball that might have been turned for a double play if Ryan had fielded it cleanly. Greg Gross dropped a perfect bunt to load the bases to bring none other than Rose to the plate. Rose worked a walk to force in a run and knock Ryan out of the game.

"Everybody wonders why they didn't have anybody up. Well, it happened like that," Bowa said, snapping his fingers. "Our attitude was good the whole series. Let's face it, we had to fight for every game. Why would the last game be any different?"

Keith Moreland grounded out to drive in another run. And after Mike Schmidt struck out, pinch-hitting Del Unser singled in the tying run and Manny Trillo notched a two-run triple to give the Phillies a 7–5 lead.

The Astros tied it back up in the eighth on back-to-back RBI singles against McGraw. The game lurched into extra innings, of course, and Del Unser lined a one-out double and scored on Garry Maddox's follow-up double.

Dick Ruthven retired the side in the 10th inning, and the Phillies had the most cathartic win in franchise history in the most riveting series you will ever see.

"It was like somebody put a pin in a balloon," Bowa said. "I'm not going to lie to you, that Houston series—and in that Dome you couldn't hear anything—I mean, it was pressure. To win that, I exhaled. I said, 'We got here.'"

"We burst the bubble," Luzinski added. "The bubble was gone. It blew up."

So, what's the greatest playoff series that you've ever seen?

PHILADELPHIA PHILLIES

The 1980 NLCS defied belief to such an extent that former Phillies reliever Dickie Noles, recovering from a hip replacement a few years ago, had to rewatch it just to make sure that it actually happened.

"I watched every game, every play," Noles said. "How do you beat Nolan Ryan? One of the greatest pitchers in the history of the game, probably the most theatrical pitcher ever. He was bigger than life. Game 5, you're almost a spectator watching him blow fastball after fastball against major-league hitters and they don't have a chance. We're down 5–2 and we come back? Against him? Get out of here. It was the most exciting, most heart-wrenching, most up-and-down series. I think it was the greatest ever."

Hard to argue.

28

THE WAITING GAME

Under normal circumstances, Brad Lidge wouldn't have gotten much sleep on the night before a potential clinching game of the World Series.

But these were hardly normal circumstances.

Since 1903, when Major League Baseball decided its champion with a best-of-nine series between the Pittsburgh Pirates and the Boston Americans, there have been 672 World Series games played over 115 years. Many were packed with as much drama as any episodic television series. But nothing in World Series history bears a resemblance to Game 5 in 2008.

It began at 8:30 PM on Monday, October 27, the Phillies needing one victory to close out the Tampa Bay Rays. It didn't end until 9:59 PM on Wednesday, October 29. In between there was rain. A lot of rain. So much rain, in fact, that field conditions at Citizens Bank Park deteriorated from slick to soggy, water-logged to underwater, and finally to unplayable, leaving commissioner Bud Selig no choice but to suspend the game in the middle of the sixth inning with the score tied 2–2.

The rain didn't stop for almost two days. So the Phillies waited. The Rays, holed up in a hotel in Wilmington, Delaware, waited, too. And the waiting, as the late Tom Petty sang, was definitely the hardest part.

"That [Tuesday] felt like forever," Phillies center fielder Shane Victorino said. "You wanted the game to happen now. Seeing the weather being as bad as it was, you were just anxious. It's like you're so close but yet so far."

But it had barely started drizzling when Lidge arrived at the ballpark on October 27. The Phillies closer heard the forecast but knew there was a chance it could be wrong. After going 41-for-41 in save opportunities during the regular season and converting his six chances in the postseason, he could conceivably end the night on the mound, delivering the pitch that clinched the second World Series title in franchise history. He considered that scenario in his mind. The anticipation made it almost impossible to think about anything else.

Now, imagine feeling that way for three days.

"I didn't really sleep before Game 5, just knowing how close we were," Lidge said. "Then, on [Monday] night, I was assuming we were going to play the next day, so I didn't really sleep at all that night. And then knowing it was going to be like a shotgun start [once play resumed], it was impossible to sleep the night after we had the rain delay. For me, just the amount of adrenaline that was exerted over those three days was crazy. It was not something where you're going to sleep soundly at night. You just want to play the dang game."

The weather caused nightmares for MLB, too. Phillies manager Charlie Manuel was livid that Selig and the umpiring crew allowed the teams to start the sixth inning. With the rain getting heavier and the infield turning to mud, the Rays took advantage and tied the game. Manuel contended that the game should've been stopped sooner or the Phillies should've been allowed to bat in similar conditions in the bottom of the sixth.

Crew chief Tim Welke saw Manuel's point, even agreeing with it, but as he told the *Philadelphia Inquirer* [in 2018], "the field was gone. We lost the integrity of the mound and the plate. It was unplayable. It wasn't safe." Selig couldn't take the Rays' run off the board, but the game couldn't continue either.

There were logistical problems, too. With if-necessary Game 6 set to be played at Tampa Bay, the Rays checked out of their downtown Philadelphia hotel. When Game 5 was halted, traveling secretary Jeff Ziegler had to find rooms for 170 people. The best he could do on short notice was the Hotel Du Pont in Wilmington, Delaware, 26 miles away.

Lidge lived in Haddonfield, New Jersey, a 15-minute drive from Citizens Bank Park. His daughter, Avery, was four years old. His wife, Lindsay, was pregnant with their son, Rowan. He had recently started taking online classes in religious archaeology from Regis University, a Jesuit school in his native Denver. He had plenty to keep him occupied.

But Lidge, as much as any Phillies player, was consumed by Game 5 and what it could mean for the franchise and himself. He had pitched in previous postseasons, even reaching the World Series in 2005 with the Houston Astros, but watched as Chicago White Sox closer Bobby Jenks recorded the championship-clinching out.

Even if Lidge had gotten that chance, there was doubt about his ability to finish off an opponent. The questions stemmed from Game 5 of the 2005 National League Championship Series. One out from winning the pennant, Lidge gave up a single, a walk, and a titanic three-run home run to St. Louis Cardinals star Albert Pujols, a blow that haunted him.

Brad Lidge drops to his knees as Carlos Ruiz rushes to celebrate after the final out of the 2008 World Series. (AP Photo / Charles Krupa)

At last, Lidge was nearing a chance for redemption. If only it would stop raining.

It rained all day on October 28, prompting MLB to announce before lunchtime that play wouldn't resume until the following night. Lidge went to the ballpark anyway and did some light throwing. He returned home and tried to focus on his studies. He took his family for a quiet dinner near their house. Nothing could take his mind off of baseball.

"I probably watched as many movies as I possibly could that had nothing to do with it," Lidge said. "I had started school, going back and trying to finish up my degree, so I remember trying to do more of that. But it's one of those deals where you read a sentence and you can't concentrate after that."

The sky finally cleared on Wednesday, and with the game set to resume in the bottom of the sixth inning, there were decisions to be made. Manuel needed to choose a pinch-hitter for pitcher Cole Hamels. Rays manager Joe Maddon had to select a pitcher. Would he stick with right-hander Grant Balfour, who had come on in the bottom of the fifth inning? Or would he pick someone else? Perhaps he would go with David Price, the rookie phenom who had been a weapon out of the bullpen since getting called up late in the regular season.

It didn't take long for the Phillies to get the lead. Pinch hitter Geoff Jenkins doubled off Balfour, went to third on Jimmy Rollins' sacrifice bunt, and scored on Jayson Werth's bloop single. The Rays tied it again in the seventh inning on Rocco Baldelli's solo home run and thought they were about to score the go-ahead run, but Chase Utley backhanded a grounder to second base, faked a throw to first, and threw a one-hopper to catcher Carlos Ruiz to cut down Jason Bartlett at the plate in a signature play by the second baseman.

"As I'm running to catch it, my time clock is telling me this is going to be a tough play," Utley told the *Inquirer* in 2018. "I caught it and I decided it was more important to keep that runner from scoring than it was to get that runner at first base. So at that point, I faked it and lucky for us, Bartlett kept going, which actually from a baserunning standpoint was not a bad play. I probably would have done the same thing. The stars aligned on that play."

Pat Burrell opened the bottom of the seventh with a double, and Pedro Feliz gave the Phillies a 4–3 lead with a one-out RBI single.

Lidge was going to get his chance, after all.

"I tried not to let it feel any different, but your body knows, everybody knows," Lidge said. "I took the exact same eight warm-up pitches. I did my normal sequence—two fastballs, four sliders, two fastballs, and go. I didn't want to do anything different at that moment than I had done the whole year. But your brain knows what's on the line."

Lidge allowed a one-out single to Dioner Navarro. Pinch runner Fernando Perez stole second before Ben Zobrist hit a screaming liner that Werth caught in right field. As pinch-hitter Eric Hinske walked to the plate, Lidge recalled a previous matchup in which Hinske crushed a fastball.

One out from a championship, Lidge decided to throw only sliders.

Hinske fouled off the first one, then swung through the second. Lidge uncorked one more dirt-diving slider, and Hinske had no chance. Lidge dropped to his knees, put his arms in the air, and screamed along with the announced crowd of 45,940. For all that time that he spent thinking about his championship moment—even during that torturous 46-hour rain delay—he never considered choreographing what he would do if it actually arrived.

"In 2005 I let myself think about clinching that game and the fans roaring and how cool that would be, and the moment came but not with me on the mound," Lidge said. "The last thing I was going to let myself do was think ahead of the hitter. On the off day, no matter what, I would not let myself think of anything beyond that."

That's fine. Lidge lived out the reality—and it was worth the wait.

29

BIG PIECE

Spend almost 40 years beating the bushes for baseball talent and you accumulate more than just airline miles and hotel nights. Do the job long enough and you build a network of contacts. And sometimes, every now and then, one of those contacts passes along a tip that pays off.

That's how Jerry Lafferty discovered Ryan Howard.

Lafferty probably would have heard about Howard anyway. After all, any player who slugs 19 home runs as a college freshman isn't exactly a secret. But three years before Howard broke through at Missouri State, Corey Smith whispered in Lafferty's ear about a sophomore at Lafayette High School in suburban St. Louis.

"You better come see this guy," said Smith, a former 49th-round pick of the Phillies who played only nine minor-league games in 1987.

Lafferty obliged. Then, he promised Smith and Howard not to forget what he saw.

"Just grow up, son," Lafferty said, "and we'll try to get you when it's time."

Howard's 13-year big-league career—spent entirely with the Phillies—was many things. His rise was meteoric. From 2006 to '09, "Big Piece," as manager Charlie Manuel called him, hit 58, 47, 48, and 45 home runs and racked up a National League Most Valuable Player Award and three other top-five finishes. His exploits were straight out of tall tales, like that time he hit three home runs against Atlanta Braves star Tim Hudson (September 3, 2006) or when he came off the bench in Cincinnati to hit the game-tying and go-ahead homers despite being weakened by the flu (May 14, 2006). He hit two homers in Game 4 of the 2008 World Series and told his teammates, "Get me to the plate, boys," before delivering a game-tying two-run double in a Division Series–clinching three-run ninth inning in 2009 in Colorado.

But his downfall was precipitous. He tore the Achilles tendon in his left leg on the final out of the Phillies' 2011 Division Series loss to

Ryan Howard takes a bottle of champagne on a walk around Citizens Bank Park on September 30, 2007, as the team and fans celebrated the Phillies winning the NL East.
(Getty Images / Chris Gardner)

the St. Louis Cardinals and didn't hit more than 25 homers in any of his final five seasons, during which he made $125 million, a contract extension that is regarded as one of the worst in baseball history. He also endured an ugly and very public legal battle with his parents and twin brother over his finances.

Howard's legacy: it's complicated.

But whatever you might have thought of Howard, there's no denying that his career was a triumph for every level of the Phillies' scouting department.

It began, as it always does, with the area scout. Lafferty, in this case, followed the tip from Smith. He kept tabs on Howard, getting to know him as more than merely a big, strong kid with what old-timey scouts call "double-plus" power. He learned that Howard came from a middle-class family, played football and also trombone in the marching band, was on the small side before a growth spurt, and wanted to go to college, which wasn't a tough decision considering he went undrafted out of high school.

Lafferty tracked Howard at Missouri State. He witnessed that eye-opening freshman year and the 18 homers that Howard hit as a sophomore in the school's new, bigger ballpark. He was also there when Howard hit only 13 homers as a junior, causing his draft stock to slide.

"I've always been of this philosophy: Give 'em a chance to prove me wrong," Lafferty said through a Johnny Cash twang. "The toughest thing in scouting is, when you see a quality prospect, the reason you're there to see him is the amount of success that he's had. But how's he going to handle adversity? If his early-season performance isn't good, good. Let's see how he does with adversity."

That's basically what Lafferty told the Phillies' cross-checkers who read his reports on Howard and came in to get their own glimpse. When he sensed their waning interest, he told tales of what he had witnessed over the years.

There was that time, for instance, when Howard took extra batting practice while one of his friends, pitcher Andrew Jefferson, cracked jokes and carried on behind the cage.

"Ryan put down the bat, walked back to him, and said, 'Blankety, blank. I'm trying to work here,'" Lafferty recalled. "That told me how serious he was about working hard and being successful."

But Howard fell out of the first four rounds of the 2001 Draft. Lafferty wasn't in the war room. He can't even recall if he was able to follow along in real time. But when the Phillies' turn came up in the fifth round, after 139 players had already been selected, Lafferty's words were still ringing in the heads of amateur scouting director Marti Wolever and assistant general manager Mike Arbuckle.

"Jerry, in our final meeting, kept saying, 'I want this guy. Let's take this guy. Get this guy for me,'" Arbuckle said. "For me, the first two to three rounds, I have to have guys that have been producers. I don't want to roll the dice. But starting fourth round on, we were always looking for guys with a big tool that maybe hadn't produced up to the level that draft year. It happened that Marti, he was the one that said, 'Okay, Howard. He's got that double-plus power. It's time. Let's take him, regardless of the [junior year] numbers.'"

Howard quickly made the Phillies look smart. He hit 19 homers at low-A Lakewood in 2002, 23 at high-A Clearwater in 2003, 37 at double-A Reading in 2004, and nine in 111 at-bats after getting promoted to triple-A Scranton/Wilkes-Barre later that season. He was a September call-up in 2004 and NL Rookie of the Year in 2005.

The Phillies traded Jim Thome after the '05 season to open first base for Howard, and from 2006 to 2010, Howard led the majors in homers (229) and runs batted in (680) and ranked second in slugging percentage (.573) behind only Albert Pujols (.628). It was a five-year stretch that ranked with any slugger in Phillies history, including Dick Allen's 145-homer/.552-slugging run from 1964 to '68, Chuck Klein's 180/.636 surge from 1929 to 1933, Greg Luzinksi's 147/.517 tear from 1975 to '79, and even Mike Schmidt's 190/.571 peak from 1980 to '84.

But Lafferty wasn't about to boast. And he certainly wasn't going to take credit for Howard's success. That isn't what scouts do.

"On the day I signed him, I made a statement to him where I said, 'I'm probably not going to see you except maybe when you come to Busch Stadium in St. Louis and you hit home runs against them dreaded Cardinals,'" Lafferty said. "But I says, 'The real thing I'll do is I'll be at Cooperstown when your 20-year career is over and you go into the Hall of Fame. I will be there for that. I don't care how old I am. I'll be there.' And we both chuckled a little bit."

If anything, though, Lafferty's promise only amplifies the ultimate "what-if" of Howard's career: What if he hadn't crumbled to the ground after hitting that Division Series–ending grounder to second base against Cardinals starter Chris Carpenter in Game 5 in 2011?

"Man, I'm going to tell you," Howard said before his official retirement ceremony in 2019, "if it was going to blow, it was going to blow. Game 5, Game 1 of the NLCS, whatever, my Achilles was probably going to blow regardless."

Howard played his last major-league game on October 2, 2016, after which Dr. Jill Biden, wife of the vice president, tweeted, *"This is not a goodbye, @ryanhoward, but a thank you for being such an inspiration for so long to so many in my hometown."* Howard tried to make it with the Atlanta Braves and later the Colorado Rockies in 2017 but never got out of Triple-A and called it quits.

He retired with 382 home runs, second-most in Phillies history behind Mike Schmidt (548) and 68th all-time. He had 1,475 hits, 1,194 RBI, and a .515 slugging percentage. Solid numbers, sure, and a career that most players would envy. But Cooperstown-worthy? Doubtful, which is disappointing if only because of his trajectory through his first half-dozen seasons.

"To me, Ryan Howard is a Hall of Famer," Lafferty said. "His career was cut short. But Mr. Howard has rewarded me. I've got a World Series ring, National League championship rings. I'm deeply appreciative for things like that. It's my legacy for my children and my grandchildren."

And that's a legacy that can't be denied.

30

CRASH

Say what you like about Dick Allen, and Lord knows, most people old enough to remember him certainly have. When it comes to the most controversial player in Phillies history, there are no shortage of opinions.

Mark Carfagno has only ever known Allen as a friend.

Not just any old friend, either. Allen is the kind of friend who stuffs $100 in your locker so you can take your family to the Jersey Shore for a day. He's the kind of friend who says, upon meeting you after getting traded back to the Phillies in 1975, "If you ever need anything and you don't ask me, I'm going to whoop your butt."

"Dick likes to look out for people," Carfagno said. "That's just the way he is."

Most people would do anything for a friend like that. So when Allen's son, Richard Jr., phoned Carfagno in 2013 and asked a favor, it was as good as granted.

"He says, 'Frog,'" Carfagno recalled, using the nickname that everyone calls him, "'It's my dad. I want to get him in the Hall of Fame. But number two, I want to clear his image.'"

Carfagno was already hard at work on the first part. Years earlier, he began lobbying—nay, crusading—for Allen to be voted into the Hall of Fame by the then–Golden Era Committee, a 16-person group that met every three years to consider candidates who played from 1947 to 1972 and weren't elected by the Baseball Writers' Association of America. Despite receiving neither help nor cooperation from Allen, Carfagno launched a full-scale campaign that would've made a presidential candidate blush. He wasn't stopping.

But that second request? Well, there wasn't much that even Carfagno could do. It seems that not even Mr. Clean can wipe away the stains on Allen's image.

"I'm very surprised," Carfagno said, "because people tend to forget as time goes on. But this guy, 50 years and they haven't forgiven him yet. It's very frustrating to me. He's such a nice guy and so misunderstood."

Allen played 15 seasons in the majors, nine with the Phillies. His career preceded nightly *SportsCenter* highlights, so tales of his 351 home runs, many of which were moonshots, are just that, stories locked in someone's memory.

"He had awesome, awesome power," former Phillies shortstop Bobby Wine said. "I would love to have known where some of his home runs landed in Connie Mack [Stadium]. He hit 'em over the roof, over the billboards, out of sight."

Allen also played at the height of the Civil Rights Movement. As difficult as it is for a 21-year-old from a rural town in western Pennsylvania to reach the big leagues, imagine how much tougher it must be if he can't use the same bathrooms or stay in the same hotels as white players. Allen once put a meatball sandwich on a lamp to show Carfagno how he would heat up takeout that then–equipment manager Pete Cera smuggled from restaurants that refused to serve African Americans.

The Phillies also had a deplorable history with race relations. Under Bob Carpenter's ownership, they didn't sign a black player until 1957, a decade after Jackie Robinson's major-league debut. Robinson was treated appallingly by the Phillies. General manager Herb Pennock opposed integration and threatened to boycott a game in 1947 if the Dodgers brought Robinson to Shibe Park. Manager Ben Chapman taunted and insulted Robinson during games.

Allen was the Phillies' first black star. He broke in late in the 1963 season and was named Rookie of the Year in 1964, batting .318 with 29 home runs and 91 RBI and leading the National League in runs (125) and triples (13). He hit 20 or more homers in 10 seasons, topped 30 homers in six seasons, and even hit 40 once. He led the league in slugging three times and on-base plus slugging four times. His 156 career adjusted-OPS is tied for sixth among all players with at least 3,000 plate appearances since 1947. The only players ahead of him: Ted Williams, Barry Bonds, Mike Trout, Mickey Mantle, and Mark McGwire.

But many people made up their minds about Allen after a 1965 fight with Phillies first baseman Frank Thomas. Never mind that at least two teammates reported that Thomas baited Allen by using the phrase "Muhammad Clay" and swung a bat at him. When the Phillies reacted to the incident by releasing Thomas, many of the team's white fans turned on Allen.

So it began that Allen got booed before at-bats, even at home. He felt compelled to wear a batting helmet in the field to protect against projectiles, a look that led wisecracking catcher Bob Uecker to dub him "Crash," as in crash helmet.

"He was like a rebel," Carfagno said. "His mother told him, 'As soon as you leave [his hometown of Wampum, Pennsylvania], your life's gonna change.' And as soon as he got off that plane in Tampa—restrooms, white chair, black chair, the restaurants that wouldn't serve him—it all changed."

It didn't help that Allen could be standoffish, even confrontational with the media. He never cared to tell his side of any story. Instead, he was accused of drinking alcohol before games and staying out late at the track. He missed time in 1967 after cutting two tendons and severing a nerve in his right hand while trying to push his 1950 Ford up the driveway and got suspended two years later after missing a team flight to St. Louis and reporting late for a doubleheader against the Mets in New York.

Things got so bad that Allen took to writing "BOO" and other messages in the dirt around first base. Eventually, after the 1969 season, the Phillies granted his wish to leave the team by trading him to the St. Louis Cardinals.

"I know he had some contract problems with [general manager] John Quinn, and after whatever happened there he started drifting away from the press and whatever else," Wine said. "But for a teammate, you wouldn't want anybody better. He was a great guy, a great teammate. He gave management headaches, yes. But when that game started, I wanted him on my team."

Three years later, after pocketing an American League MVP Award with the Chicago White Sox, Allen returned to the Phillies in a midseason swap. That was when he got to know Carfagno, a groundskeeper at Veterans Stadium. Allen preferred hanging out with the grounds crew rather than talking to the media in the clubhouse, and Cera mentioned to Allen that Carfagno's father died when he was 10, his mother when he was 17.

"Dick liked to look out for people like that," Carfagno said. "We established a tremendous friendship."

To Allen and Carfagno, it meant that they had one another's back. If Allen did an interview that was dragging on, he flashed a signal to Carfagno, who interrupted by saying, 'Dick, you've got a phone call.' Their families got together often at Allen's farm in Wampum.

Allen retired after the 1977 season. Five years later, when his name appeared on the writers' ballot for the Hall of Fame, he received only 3.7 percent of the votes. He topped out at 18.9 percent in 1996, never getting within sight of the 75 percent required for election.

Bill James' criticism was particularly harmful. In his 1995 book *Whatever Happened to the Hall of Fame*, the noted baseball historian wrote of Allen: "He did more to keep his teams from winning than anyone else who ever played major league baseball. And if that's a Hall of Famer, I'm a lug nut."

Allen doesn't believe in self-promotion. Never has. He considers stumping for himself as a Hall of Fame candidate to be inelegant. But once Allen's Hall of Fame chances were turned over to the Veterans Committee, later redefined as the Golden Era Committee and then subdivided further, Carfagno went into campaign mode. He wrote letters to Allen's peers in the Hall of Fame: Mike Schmidt, Hank Aaron, Willie Mays, Nolan Ryan, and others.

In 2008, Allen got on the Veterans Committee ballot but received only seven votes. Then came the call from Richard Jr.

Allen's grandson, Richard III, was playing baseball for St. John Neumann Regional Academy, a private catholic high school in Williamsport, Pennsylvania, when he got heckled running to first base.

"He's telling me that people were yelling, 'You're just like your grandfather. You're lazy. You'll probably turn out to be nothing,'" Carfagno said. "Then his friends are telling him afterwards, 'Yeah, we heard your grandpa was a helluva player, but he was an ass—.'"

Say no more. Carfagno launched a website (www.dickallenbelongs. wordpress.com) with a snappy slogan ("He Won't Campaign, So Let

Us Explain") and started a Facebook page. He reached out to local politicians.

In 2014, Allen appeared on the Golden Era ballot again. The committee included former Phillies teammates Jim Bunning and Ferguson Jenkins. Momentum was building, especially within the sabermetric community. Carfagno even booked a ticket to San Diego, where the results would be announced on the first day of the winter meetings. If you don't think the Hall of Fame means anything to Allen, consider this: On the eve of the 2014 Golden Era announcement, Allen called Frog in the hotel in San Diego.

"He was practically crying on the phone, just filling up," Carfagno said. "He was reminiscing about all of the people who were part of his journey."

Allen needed 12 votes. He got 11.

So, Carfagno presses on. The Golden Days Committee will meet again in December 2020. After that, Allen would have to wait until 2022.

"Look, was he a saint? No. But he was nowhere near like the way he was being depicted," Carfagno said. "He was a shy person. He didn't like to talk, period. If he spoke to the media, he always felt that he was misquoted. That's all I could tell you. So, I just continue to beat the drum."

Relentlessly, like any friend would.

31

BOWA & VUKE

They were the toughest SOBs in baseball. Dutch and Dude. Krukkie and the Wild Thing. Mikey and Inky and Big Schill. They wore beards and had permanent dirt and tobacco stains on their red-pinstriped uniforms. They didn't take crap from anybody.

But when Larry Bowa and John Vukovich walked in the room, well, even the Macho Row gang knew it was best to sit down and listen up.

"If we played a horseshit game, we would go back into the training room and Dutch [catcher Darren Daulton] would say something like, 'Uh oh. They're both pissed off,'" Bowa said, bursting into laughter at the mere thought of it. "He'd go and say, 'You guys mad at us? We don't want to get you guys mad at us.' It was kidding, you know? But I think they were a little bit serious, too."

Bowa, the third-base coach for those 1993 Phillies, was a hard-nosed former shortstop and a World Series champion with the Phillies in 1980. He won two Gold Glove Awards, played in five All-Star games, finished third in the National League Most Valuable Player race in 1978, and notched 2,191 career hits. But he also got cut three years in a row from the baseball team at C.K. McClatchy High School in Sacramento, California, and went undrafted out of college. The chip on his shoulder weighed about as much as he did when he was 18 (140 pounds). His temper was fierce. When the Phillies sent area scout Eddie Bockman to a doubleheader at Sacramento City College, Bowa got ejected from both games.

"He took a lot from people, from the press that said he would never be a hitter, blah, blah, blah," former Phillies slugger Greg Luzinski said. "You look back at Larry Bowa's career, he had over 2,000 hits. For somebody that couldn't hit, he had a pretty damn good career."

But if Bowa scrapped for everything he got in baseball, Vukovich fought harder than Rocky. How else do you explain a .161 career hitter with a total of 21 extra-base hits playing 10 seasons in the big leagues?

Among non-pitchers with at least 600 plate appearances since 1900, Vukovich had the second-lowest on-base plus slugging percentage (.425), trailing only turn-of-the-20th-century catcher Bill Bergen (.395). Yet he stuck around for a decade, even playing 49 games for the 1980 Phillies, then had a long coaching career that included serving as manager Jim Fregosi's bench coach with the '93 team. He might still be working in the game, too, if a brain tumor hadn't killed him in 2007 at age 59.

"He was a great fielder. I mean, a great fielder. He just couldn't hit," Bowa said. "But I know what baseball meant to Vuke. He was my best buddy."

They practically grew up together, Bowa in Sacramento and Vukovich 45 miles to the east in Sutter Creek. They met as opponents in American Legion ball. A few years later, they were teammates in the minor leagues. Bowa, almost two years older, played shortstop for the Phillies' instructional league team in Florida; Vukovich played third base. In the offseasons they would go back home and work out together for hours on an empty field.

Bowa made his major-league debut in April 1970; Vukovich five months later. They comprised the left side of the Phillies' infield for the majority of the 1971 season before Vukovich got dealt to the Milwaukee Brewers as part of a seven-player trade in 1972. Three years later, they were reunited when the Phillies brought Vukovich back from the Cincinnati Reds.

But Bowa and Vukovich bonded over more than merely their northern California roots and positional proximity. They were cut from the same mold. Feisty and passionate, sticklers for working hard and paying attention to detail, fiercely loyal to the organization for which they were working (usually the Phillies), they didn't hold back when it came to pushing themselves or others. Tales of their intensity were legendary.

To wit: Bowa got ejected in the third inning of an August 30, 1972, game in Houston for arguing a called third strike. In protest, he stood frozen in the batter's box and wouldn't move. Phillies manager Danny Ozark directed Luzinksi to go to home plate and retrieve Bowa.

"As I went up there to go get him, he turned around and he takes the bat like he's going to take a swing at me," Luzinski said. "I put mine up there to block it."

Bowa finally left the field. When the game ended, the rest of the Phillies headed back to the clubhouse, too, only they couldn't see where they were going because Bowa had shattered all of the light bulbs in the tunnel that led from the dugout.

And then there's this gem: Bowa, Vukovich, and Luzinski were instructional league teammates in 1968 when Luzinski ribbed Bowa for not being able to turn a double play after a runner slid hard into second base during a game at Al Lang Stadium in St. Petersburg, Florida.

"He used to jabber all the time, so I said, 'What are you, afraid of contact?'" Luzinski recalled. "Well, he thinks I'm talking about hitting because he was 0-for-2 or something. So he fires back at me and I go back at him."

The back and forth continued on the bus on the way back to the Ramada Hotel in Clearwater, where the players were staying. Luzinski had been asked to change rooms and was placed with Bowa.

"I get in the room and Vuke comes in the room, and Bowa's still chirping, chirping, chirping," Luzinski said. "I didn't know him that well yet, but he just aggravated the hell out of me. Finally I jumped up, grabbed his T-shirt, tore his T-shirt, and I went to swing. Vuke jumped in there and I hit Vuke. Well, Vuke kind of hit the wall a little bit, and the next thing we heard was somebody knocking at the door and it was [coach] Bob Wellman saying, 'Everything all right in this room?' I just knew after that, that's just the way Bowa's going to be."

When Bowa got his first managerial job with the San Diego Padres in 1987, Vukovich discussed his friend's temperament as a younger player by telling the *Los Angeles Times*, "If I went five days without an argument [with Bowa], something was wrong. He felt everybody was against him. Well, he fought everybody and ended up winning. I think he realized his size saved his life 100 times. Nobody wanted to beat the s—t out of him because he was so small. But he was an antagonistic little guy."

Here's the thing, though: Beneath the gruff exterior, Bowa is really a softie. The same went for Vukovich. As a rookie in 1971, Vukovich befriended Bonnie Loughran, a Phillies usherette from Olney, Pennsylvania, who was part of the "Hot Pants Patrol" at brand-new Veterans Stadium. He invited her to a party thrown by pitcher Chris Short and fell cap over spikes.

"Cancel your dates for the rest of the summer," Vukovich told Loughran, according to his obituary in the *Philadelphia Inquirer*.

They were married the following year.

Bowa and Vukovich poured their passion into coaching. Bowa managed the Padres for a year and a half and the Phillies for four seasons. He also coached for about 20 seasons with the Phillies, Anaheim Angels, Seattle Mariners, New York Yankees, and Los Angeles Dodgers. Vukovich spent more than two decades as a coach, first with the Chicago Cubs and then with the Phillies. He was an interim manager twice and could have managed full time, but he was considered too valuable as an instructor to be moved off a coaching staff.

"Bo and Vuke were my two favorite big-league coaches," said Mickey Morandini, the 1993 Phillies' second baseman. "They took losses worse than players sometimes. I liked them because they were always pushing me to improve and always were in teaching mode, no matter how good you were or how many years in the big leagues you played."

In 1993, Fregosi entrusted Bowa and Vukovich with keeping the Phillies' motley crew in line. It was a much easier job than anybody thought. For as colorful and outspoken as Lenny Dykstra, John Kruk, Mitch Williams, Curt Schilling, and the others could be, they fell in line behind Daulton, a leader with a firm hold on the clubhouse.

"Dutch held everything together," Bowa said. "We had three guys that, I don't want to say we were pricks, but we weren't afraid to get in somebody's face. I'm not talking about making an error. I'm talking about going through the motions, giving in, not playing 27 outs. We took care of all that, and Vuke was very much a part of that. He was a tough-love guy. He wouldn't be afraid to say, 'You stink. You need to f—ing pick it up.' We sort of had the same personality."

It's little wonder, then, that Vukovich spent 24 seasons in a Phillies uniform, seven as a player and 17 as a coach.

The only person with greater Phillies longevity: Bowa, of course, who wore the red pinstripes for 28 seasons, 12 as a player, four as a manager, and 12 over two stints as a coach.

"I'm just glad that we got to the World Series in '93," Bowa said. "He was part of our team in '80, but there were some bad years after that. I mean, there were some bad teams. To have him be a part of that, to be able to go through it with him, after we played against each other all those years before back in Sacramento, it was special. It was a great time."

32

BLACK FRIDAY

Never mind the 1976 division champions who broke a 26-year postseason drought or even the conquering heroes of 1980. The best team from the first golden era in Phillies history—a run of four National League East crowns in five years—was the 1977 club. But don't take our word for it. Ask around.

"No doubt about it," shortstop Larry Bowa said.

"There's no question," added slugger Greg Luzinski. "That was a great ballclub."

"We were good in 1980," catcher Bob Boone said, "but that [1977] team, I'd probably say we were better."

The 1977 Phillies won 101 games, matching the total from a year earlier. They had the best record in the NL and were one game behind the Kansas City Royals for the best in baseball. They scored 847 runs and allowed 668 for the league's second-best run differential behind the NL West champion Los Angeles Dodgers. They won 60 of 81 games at Veterans Stadium during the regular season, the best home record in baseball.

They were led once again by the NL Cy Young Award winner (Steve Carlton). Luzinski was the MVP runner-up to George Foster of the Cincinnati Reds. Mike Schmidt overcame a slow start (.182 in April) and put up his usual numbers: 38 home runs, 101 runs batted in, and a .967 on-base plus slugging percentage. The bullpen was deep and talented, featuring Tug McGraw, Ron Reed, sidearming Gene Garber, and Warren Brusstar.

But the most impressive part of the '77 Phillies was their depth. Backup catcher Tim McCarver had a .936 OPS, including a .410 on-base percentage. Righty-hitting first baseman Davey Johnson hit eight homers and slugged .545. Utilityman Tommy Hutton had a .394 on-base percentage.

"A lot of us hit .300 off the bench," said McCarver, who batted .320. "When you can compile that kind of talent, even the older guys [feel like they] are playing a lot younger. I know I was playing a lot younger at the time. It was a hell of a team. Some of the great times of my life."

At this point, we know what you're thinking: If the '77 Phillies were so good, how come they didn't win it all? How come they didn't even get to the World Series?

For that, you have to go back to Game 3 of the NL Championship Series at Veterans Stadium. Top of the ninth inning, to be even more precise. It was October 7, 1977, but the locals know it as "Black Friday." And it ranks right up there with Games 4 and 6 of the 1993 World Series and Game 5 of the 2011 Division Series on the list of the Phillies' all-time most gut-wrenching postseason defeats.

"Black Friday," Luzinski said, "will always probably be remembered in a negative way in Phillies history."

The best-of-five series was tied 1–1, and the Phillies were leading 5–3 with Carlton lined up to start Game 4 at the Vet the next night. McGraw was available to close out the game, but manager Danny Ozark stuck with Garber, who recorded six consecutive groundouts to set the side down in order in the seventh and eighth innings. The bottom half of the Dodgers' order was due to bat.

Garber got two more quick groundouts, from Dusty Baker and Rick Monday, to put the Phillies one out from victory when pinch-hitting Vic Davalillo beat out a perfectly placed drag bunt.

But there was still no overwhelming reason for Phillies fans to fret. Well, except that Ozark strayed from his usual practice of using Jerry Martin to replace lumbering Luzinski in the late innings when the Phillies had the lead.

Trouble? Naturally.

Garber froze Mota with a changeup and got him to swing through a slider. One strike from the victory, with an announced crowd of 63,719 on its feet and roaring, Mota hit a fly ball to deep left field that bounced out of the glove of leaping Luzinski and hit the wall. Harried, Luzinski missed the cutoff man and the ball skipped away from second baseman Ted Sizemore, enabling Davalillo to score and Mota to reach third base.

"I threw it into second. That hurt us more than anything," Luzinski said. "The ball hit the seam [in the turf] and it got by Sizemore. That hurt."

Ozark later explained that he kept Luzinski in the game because his spot in the order was due to come up in the bottom of the ninth. It amounted to an admission that he was more worried about losing the lead than he was about protecting it.

"Bull shouldn't have been in left field. He'll be the first to tell you," Bowa said. "Jerry Martin catches that ball in his back pocket."

Be that as it may, the Phillies were still one out away from winning, and Garber got another ground ball. But Davey Lopes' smash to third base caromed off Schmidt's mitt and was barehanded at shortstop by Bowa, who fired a dart to first base. Lopes was called safe by umpire Bruce Froemming, prompting a furious argument by Ozark and first baseman Richie Hebner, who drop-kicked his cap in protest. Mota scored from third, and the game was tied.

"Froemming gave them the game," Luzinski said, although the play was so close that even the use of expanded instant replay, which wouldn't be introduced for 37 years, might not have proved conclusive enough to overturn the call. "When have you seen a first baseman throw his hat down, kick it over the umpire's head, and stay in the game? He knew right then and there after he made that call that he was wrong. He anticipated [Lopes' speed] and didn't anticipate Bowa making probably one of the best plays ever. If he's out, that's a play that's talked about for a lifetime."

Instead, it lives only in infamy. Lopes took second on an errant pickoff throw by Garber, who got two strikes on Bill Russell before giving up a go-ahead single up the middle, another play that easily could have gone differently. As Garber noted in August 2019 as a guest on *Bull Session*, the weekly radio show on WBCB–1490 AM in Bucks County, Pennsylvania, that Luzinski co-hosts with longtime public-address announcer Dan Baker, the ball went "right back between my legs. If I catch that ball," Garber added, "the game's over right there."

"Garber brought that up and I didn't remember it," Luzinski said. "I told him, 'Well, you're off the hook.'"

The Phillies didn't score in the bottom of the ninth, and one night later, Tommy John outdueled Carlton, 4–1, in the rain at the Vet to stun the Phillies and end their season. The Dodgers moved on to the World Series and lost to the New York Yankees in six games, with Reggie Jackson slugging three home runs in Game 6 at Yankee Stadium.

A year later, the Phillies and Dodgers met again in the NLCS, and the Dodgers won again in four games. That series featured more strangeness, including eight-time Gold Glove Award–winning center fielder Garry Maddox dropping a two-out fly ball in the 10th inning of Game 4. One batter later, Bill Russell singled home Ron Cey with the winning run against Tug McGraw.

"If you look at some of those games against the Dodgers, weird s— happened," Bowa said. "Garry Maddox never drops a fly ball. It wasn't like we got blown out in every one of those games. We were in 'em, but something weird would always happen."

And the best teams don't always win. Sometimes they're even forgotten. History can be cruel that way.

"I have all these films and everything. That's the game that, once a winter, I always look at it," Bowa said. "That will live forever for me. I think that was our best team. I think we would have had another ring, maybe. Or at least a chance to win another."

Maybe the 1977 Phillies would have won the World Series. Maybe Ozark wouldn't have gotten fired two years later and Dallas Green wouldn't have become the manager. Maybe 1980 would've gone differently.

Even after 101 victories, the '77 Phillies will know never know.

33

JOE FREAKIN' CARTER

Dave Hollins will never forget the noise.

"Loudest sound," he said, "that I ever heard in my life."

It wasn't just the crack of the bat, although that certainly was what started it all. Hollins can still see the pitch, a 2-2 fastball down and in to a hitter who loved the ball down and in. He can still see the swing, a short right-handed stroke that almost got cut off as it sliced through the strike zone. And he can still hear the crowd—52,195 strong at SkyDome in downtown Toronto—roaring in delirium.

"The crowd, the noise, everything was in slow motion for about 10 seconds," said Hollins, the former Phillies third baseman. "It's something you try to block out, but you never really get rid of it. You never really forget that moment."

It happened at precisely 11:37 PM on Saturday, October 23, 1993, and it marked only the second time ever that a World Series ended on a home run.

Joe Freakin' Carter.

Mitch Freakin' Williams.

Until the moment that the ball disappeared over the left-field wall, the 1993 Phillies believed they would come back and be crowned champions. Heck, they were doubted all year, right from the preseason projections that branded them a last-place team, and they kept coming back. Even now, in the sixth game of the World Series, this rag-tag bunch of bearded brawlers with mullets and dirt-stained uniforms rallied from a 5–1 deficit in the sixth inning and was two outs away from forcing a Game 7. *Whatever it takes, dude.* That was their mantra, their credo, and damn if they didn't live by it.

But here was Carter, jumping for joy as he rounded the bases, and Williams, making the slow trudge back to the dugout after throwing the pitch—the one pitch out of the nearly 9,000 that he unleashed in an 11-year big-league career that he would take back.

It was a home run that ranked with any in baseball history. Bobby Thomson's shot heard 'round the world off Ralph Branca to give the New York Giants the pennant in 1951. Bucky Bleeping Dent taking Mike Torrez deep over the Green Monster in 1978. Kirk Gibson vs. Dennis Eckersley in 1988. And, of course, Bill Mazeroski homering off Ralph Terry in Game 7 to win the 1960 World Series for the Pittsburgh Pirates.

How does a pitcher get over that? How does a team move on? After playing all-out, every single day for seven months, what do you do next?

You close ranks.

"We rallied behind Mitch," second baseman Mickey Morandini said. "Nobody blamed him. A lot of guys went up to him and said, 'It's not your fault.' We're not there without Mitch. We're not even close to being in the World Series without Mitch and the year he had for us."

When it came to defending Williams, the Phillies had a lot of practice. White-knuckle saves were the specialty of "Wild Thing," as Williams became known for being the real-life pitching embodiment of Charlie Sheen's character in *Major League*. As late Phillies manager Jim Fregosi often joked with longtime public-relations honcho Larry Shenk, "Mitch is the reason I'm still smoking, Baron. I'd quit, but then I have to bring him in."

In Game 6, Fregosi brought in Williams to face the top of the Blue Jays' order with the Phillies leading 6–5. Rickey Henderson drew a four-pitch leadoff walk, never a promising start for a pitcher. After getting Devon White to fly out, Williams gave up a single to Paul Molitor to put the tying run in scoring position.

Up stepped Carter, 0-for-4 to that point in his career against Williams. The first two pitches were balls. Carter took a fastball right down the middle, then swung over a breaking pitch to even the count. Catcher Darren Daulton called for a fastball down and away. Williams sped up his delivery with a slide-step, a move that he rarely used to hold runners, and yanked the pitch inside.

"One of the things he regrets most was that he did a slide step on that pitch," Hollins said. "He doesn't know why he did it, but he did. It was late in the year, his arm was not the same, he was tired, and he threw a cookie down and in."

It was the ultimate gut-punch, not that the feeling was foreign to Williams. Only three nights earlier, in fact, back in Philadelphia, he imploded in a six-run eighth inning that turned a 14–9 lead into a 15–14 crusher.

Looking back now, more than two decades later, many of the '93 Phillies agree that Game 4 was even more difficult to swallow. For one thing, it was the pendulum that swung the series in the Blue Jays' favor. If only they had safeguarded a five-run lead with six outs to go, the Phillies would have squared the series at 2–2 with their ace, Curt Schilling, slated to start Game 5 at home.

Instead, they needed Schilling to beat the Jays just to send everyone back to Toronto—and he did, 2–0, in a 147-pitch complete game that stands as the first of his many postseason heroics.

"There were just so many, myself included, below-par outings [in Game 4]," said former Phillies reliever Larry Andersen, who gave up three of the eighth-inning runs before Williams allowed three more. "There were so many things that happened. It was a game that we had in hand—or we should have, anyway—and we didn't, and that was hard. That was really tough."

To Hollins, the postgame scene in the clubhouse is as frozen in time as Game 6.

"I mean, you could hear a pin drop for at least an hour after that 15–14 bulls—," he said. "A game like that, it just eats away at you."

If 15–14 ripped out the Phillies' hearts, Joe Carter left them feeling numb. As the roof nearly blew off SkyDome, they retreated to the visiting clubhouse, where some of them remained until 6:30 in the morning, commiserating over beer as they often did after games that season. First, though, they had to meet the media.

"You're the PR guy and you're supposed to open the clubhouse right after the game, right? Well, I just couldn't," Shenk recalled. "I dragged my feet. I stalled as long as I could. But Mitch Williams was a man. He was at his locker answering wave after wave, the same questions. I was going to go bail him out out there, and just then Terry Mulholland grabbed him and took him in the trainer's room. Mitch was a man. I'll always respect him for that."

Mitch Williams didn't hide from reporters after giving up Carter's walk-off home run. (AP Photo / Rusty Kennedy)

Indeed, Williams sat at his locker and lamented letting his teammates down. After a while, a few teammates tried to lighten the mood. Daulton, the consummate leader, told Williams, "All year I've been telling hitters what's coming, and wouldn't you know, in a World Series someone finally believed me."

Not all of the Phillies were as compassionate. According to historian Bill Kashatus, who in 2017 authored *Macho Row: The '93 Phillies and Baseball's Unwritten Code*, Lenny Dykstra jogged in from center field after Carter's home run, passed by Williams and said, "I guess there's not going to be a Game 7." In 2015, Dykstra and Williams got into an obscene argument on stage at a Philadelphia sports roast.

But in the moment, Williams maintained perspective amid his intense disappointment. He vowed he would overcome the home run, telling reporters that he was "not going to go home and commit suicide or anything like that." It didn't stop him from getting death threats, though. After Game 4, in particular, he returned at 2:00 AM to the house that he and his then-fiancée were renting in Moorestown, New Jersey, and found a police officer waiting by the driveway.

"I'm like, 'What are you doing here?'" Williams said in a 2014 interview on *The Dan Patrick Show*. "And he said, 'They didn't tell you?' I said, 'Tell me what?' He said, 'Well, you've had a number of death threats.' I said, 'I've got my gun in my hand right now. I guess I won't put it in my truck. I guess I'll take it in the house.' He said, 'Well, don't shoot me,' and I said, 'Don't come in the house.'"

Williams received permission to fly home to Texas after the World Series rather than returning to Philadelphia with his teammates. The Phillies traded him 40 days after the World Series because, well, they didn't have much choice. He was never going to live down two blown saves in one World Series, to say nothing of getting walked off in the deciding game. Not in Philly. And not with his frayed relationships with Dykstra and Schilling, who would cover his head with a towel when Williams entered a game because he couldn't bear to watch. So, they shipped him off to the Houston Astros for pitchers Doug Jones and Jeff Juden.

For years after he retired in 1997, Williams didn't want to return for the Phillies' annual Alumni Weekend, fearing that he would get booed off the field—or worse. Eventually he did come back and received an ovation, although he declined an invitation to the '93 Phillies' 25th reunion weekend in 2018.

"The aftermath of what Mitch received from a lot of Phillie fans," Morandini said, "it's just really disappointing."

But as deplorable as the treatment that Williams received was, something happened in the Phillies' clubhouse about an hour after Carter's home run that was equally uplifting. A few Blue Jays players, including Molitor and pitchers Dave Stewart and Duane Ward, came over to congratulate the Phillies on a hard-fought series and a memorable season, a scene that Andersen still describes as "surreal."

"It showed a lot of respect to our team for those guys to come over and do that," Andersen said. "But it also made you see how special that team was. Here they just won a World Series, and they wanted to come over and see *us*."

"They just wanted to say, 'Hey, what a great playoff. You guys played your asses off,'" Hollins said. "I never had that happen before where guys from the other team came into our clubhouse. But I guess they felt like they needed to come over and just, man-to-man, let us know how they felt about us as a competitor. I remember shaking their hands. It was a classy move. That doesn't normally happen."

What better way to end a night unlike almost any that baseball had ever seen than with a gesture like no other?

34

END OF THE ROAD

As Brad Lidge walked, his mind raced.

It wasn't supposed to end like this, he thought. Not for the 2011 Phillies, who set a club record with 102 wins during the regular season. They had a star-studded starting rotation that then–general manager Ruben Amaro Jr. still calls "a once-in-a-lifetime situation" and even grander ambitions. They counted on playing long into October. Anything less than the franchise's third World Series championship would be a disappointment. What, then, was a five-game ouster in the Division Series against a St. Louis Cardinals team that barely scraped into the playoffs with 90 wins?

That's how fickle the playoffs can be. One lousy week can undo six glorious months. One team-wide batting slump—the Phillies scored six runs over the series' final three games—can counteract even the "Four Aces" or the "Fab Four" or whatever moniker you preferred for the supposedly indomitable foursome of Roy Halladay, Cliff Lee, Cole Hamels, and Roy Oswalt.

Lidge tried to process all of that as he walked out the door to the bullpen and across the outfield grass and down the dugout steps and up the tunnel and into the clubhouse. The closer looked around at the stunned, sad faces in the crowd at Citizens Bank Park. He saw the Cardinals exulting on the mound around triumphant pitcher Chris Carpenter. *Was this really happening? Surely this was some sort of twisted nightmare.* And he wondered what his future held after an injury-marred season and with free agency looming.

"There was a lot of things swirling around in my head," Lidge said. "You think about the fact that we won the World Series [in 2008], that we got there and lost [in 2009], then we were in the NLCS and lost [in 2010] and now the Division Series and lost. There's obviously a backward trend going on there that nobody wanted to see. But it was there and it was unavoidable. There was just a lot of things going on."

So many things, in fact, that Lidge almost didn't notice Ryan Howard writhing in pain on the grass 30 feet from home plate.

For the record, the Phillies' dynasty—if you will permit the slight overstatement—fell along with Howard at 11:06 PM on October 7, 2011. Nothing was ever the same again. Howard ruptured his left Achilles tendon and underwent surgery, and although he played for another five years, he never again hit 30 homers or drove in 100 runs after averaging 44 and 133 from 2006 to 2011. Just the same, a run of five consecutive division titles, two National League pennants, and one World Series crown—the second-longest sustained period of prosperity in the Phillies' tortured history—devolved into an 81–81 season in 2012 and six consecutive losing seasons after that. The Phillies lost 627 games from 2012 to '18. Only the Miami Marlins (634) and Chicago White Sox (630) lost more.

It's difficult, then, to look at what happened on that Friday night in South Philadelphia and not classify it as one of the darkest nights in franchise history. It's right there, in fact, with Black Friday—34 years earlier, to the day—and Game 6 of the 1993 World Series on the short list of doomsday defeats.

"Sometimes the best team doesn't always win," shortstop Jimmy Rollins said in 2019. "You come against a team that's hot, especially in that first series, five-game series, a team can get out on you and it's hard to make up those games. Everyone that played on those teams I think would say we should've gotten three rings. Shoulda, coulda, woulda."

In 2009, the Phillies came within two wins of another ring but lost to the New York Yankees in the World Series. That's the one that sticks with Lidge, who allowed three runs in the ninth inning of a 7–4 loss in Game 4 at Citizens Bank Park. Win that game and the series would've been tied at 2–2 with Lee on the mound at home in Game 5. Instead, Johnny Damon worked a nine-pitch walk and executed a double steal before Alex Rodriguez lined a go-ahead RBI double and Jorge Posada stroked a two-run single.

"A-Rod had a great World Series run," Lidge said. "I think we know now that he was on PEDs. He's literally said that. I throw him a fastball and he turns on it. I think there's some things that are irritating about that."

Charlie Manuel still thinks back to the 2010 NL Championship Series—Game 6, to be exact—and Juan Uribe's go-ahead homer in the eighth inning against reliever Ryan Madson to lift the San Francisco Giants to a 3–2 victory and the pennant. To the former manager, that loss is as painful as any during the Phillies' run.

But there was something epic about Game 5 of the 2011 Division Series. Maybe it was the pitching matchup—Carpenter vs. Halladay, fierce competitors and close friends who went toe-to-toe in one of the best duals that you will ever see.

Halladay gave up a leadoff triple to Rafael Furcal and an RBI double to Skip Schumaker in the first inning. After that, though, he allowed only four hits over the next seven scoreless frames. A one-run deficit should've been easily overcome by an aging Phillies offense that nevertheless was still loaded with former All-Stars, from Rollins and Howard to Chase Utley, Raul Ibanez, Shane Victorino, Placido Polanco, and Hunter Pence.

But Carpenter held the Phillies to three hits by unleashing a barrage of curveballs and change-ups. As Manuel recalls, the Phillies kept trying to muscle up for home runs. Instead, they rolled 18 groundouts.

"I don't know if it was the sixth or seventh inning, but I'll tell you, there was kind of a collective discomfort in our bullpen just because Carpenter just had this look about him," Lidge said. "We had seen our offense come back so many times and do such great stuff even against great pitchers. But in the same way that Mariano Rivera gets down there and it just doesn't matter how good you are, Carpenter had that look like he was on another planet that night. That was tough to watch."

The Phillies didn't have a hit after Utley's one-out single in the sixth inning. Utley flew out to deep center field to open the ninth before Carpenter finished it off by getting Pence and Howard to ground out. Howard stumbled as soon as he accelerated out of the batter's box. He struggled to his feet, took three hops, and crumpled to the ground, where he lay while the Cardinals celebrated. He was carried off the field by third-base coach Juan Samuel, assistant athletic trainer Mark Andersen, and Victorino.

"When Howard went down, the game's over and we're kind of walking out of the bullpen," Lidge said. "I remember being like, 'Is Howie okay? What the heck is going on?' For me it felt like a little bit of an ending. Not necessarily for the Phillies, but at least for me."

In the funereal clubhouse, Halladay sat alone, in full uniform, and stared into his locker. Victorino ripped up a pair of World Series tickets and threw them in the trash. Ibanez and others answered questions about the future.

"At times, I'm like, 'How did we only win one World Series?'" said Lidge, who played one more season with the Washington Nationals before retiring. "Because I did feel like we were the best team in baseball for about four in there."

Howard chooses not to look back. He doesn't ask, "What if?" Why play that game, he says, when it won't change anything?

"If you want to look at a crystal ball and try to see the best-case scenario, yeah, if my ankle doesn't go out maybe it goes to the opportunity where instead of David Freese hitting the triple, maybe that's me hitting the triple and we go on to win," Howard said, referring to Freese's two-out, two-run heroics for the Cardinals in the ninth inning of Game 6 of the 2011 World Series. "But you can't go back again. I think we all felt we should've won more than just one, but nothing's guaranteed in this game. Take what you can get, because there's a lot of guys that played numerous years that haven't won a championship. I think it's about what you do with the opportunity when you get it."

The Phillies had one last perfect opportunity in 2011.

And then everything changed.

35

CHUCK KLEIN

Uncle Chuck had been gone 14 years by the fall of 1972, and it often felt as though nobody outside the family even noticed. There was no Hall of Fame plaque in Cooperstown, New York, no number-retirement ceremony in Philadelphia. There was only a small, rectangular stone in the ground at an Indianapolis cemetery to mark the final resting place of a man who, according to the obituary that ran in most newspapers across the country, "died in obscurity."

But then the letter from 1600 Pennsylvania Avenue arrived in Bob Klein's mailbox.

It was printed on White House stationery and it came with a thick gold pamphlet bearing the presidential seal. It was pulled together by government staffers and hand-signed by Richard Nixon. And it amounted to a declaration—by the leader of the free world, no less—of what everyone seemed to forget across the previous two decades: Chuck Klein, for at least five years, ranked with the greatest sluggers in baseball history.

Nothing obscure about that, is there?

"I was amazed," said Bob Klein, Chuck's nephew and oldest surviving relative. "I knew that President Nixon was a baseball fan, but I didn't know that he was that much into it. I didn't know that he would take the time to do that and send me a letter. I was just amazed."

For a half-dozen seasons during the Great Depression, Chuck Klein amazed Philadelphia baseball fans with his prodigious power. He made his major-league debut on July 30, 1928, with a pinch-hit appearance against the St. Louis Cardinals and batted .360 with 11 home runs over the next two months. He hit 43 dingers in 1929 and 40 in 1930 and led the National League in slugging in 1931, '32, and '33. He was crowned NL MVP in 1932, and that was merely a prelude to a 1933 season in which he won the Triple Crown with a .368 batting average, 28 homers, and 120 RBI.

PHILADELPHIA PHILLIES

From 1929 to 1933, Klein's age-24 to age-28 seasons, he had more hits (1,118) and doubles (232) than any player in baseball. He ranked second in runs (658), fourth in homers (180) and slugging percentage (.636), and fifth in RBI (693). The only players with an on-base plus slugging percentage of at least 1.000: Babe Ruth (1.148), Jimmie Foxx (1.099), Lou Gehrig (1.084), Klein (1.050), and Rogers Hornsby (1.030).

Klein's peak was both short and undeniably aided by the Phillies' home ballpark. Baker Bowl was only 280 feet down the right-field line with a 60-foot high wall that made Fenway Park's left-field Green Monster appear small by comparison. Klein possessed brute strength that he attributed to years of tossing 200-pound blocks into a furnace at the Chapman-Prico Steel Mill in Indianapolis. But a left-handed hitter didn't have to flex much muscle to pepper that wall for doubles or clear it with towering home runs.

Nevertheless, Klein's numbers during that five-year stretch were so overwhelming that President Nixon couldn't fathom excluding him from his list of the greatest players of all time, an idea that came about in the midst of his reelection campaign in 1972.

It all began when a reporter asked Nixon to name his favorite baseball players, then followed up by wondering if he would be willing to pick his all-time team. A few weeks later, during a retreat to Camp David, Nixon dove into the statistics and decided to choose 20-player teams for both the American and National leagues in the pre- and post-1945 eras. And while Paul Waner, Mel Ott, and Hack Wilson represented Nixon's starting outfield for the pre-1945 NL team, Klein, Edd Roush, and Joe Medwick were on the roster as reserves.

Nixon's picks didn't go unnoticed. White House press secretary Ron Ziegler distributed them to the Associated Press, which published a story. And after Ted Williams, Hank Aaron, and other players publicly expressed their gratitude for being chosen, Nixon decided to write letters to every player or next of kin and directed his staff to put together a packet to commemorate the project. That's how a note from the president wound up at Bob Klein's home in Greenwood, Indiana.

"No team would be complete," Nixon wrote, "without your uncle's name."

Bob Klein watched Uncle Chuck play in person twice, both times in Cincinnati in the waning years of his career. But he was born too late to witness the glory days. He missed the home run titles, the 170-RBI season, the four-homer game against Pittsburgh in 1936, the 1933 All-Star Game when Uncle Chuck started in right field for the National League, and the 1934 game when he came off the bench and delivered an RBI single.

And Chuck was far too modest to regale his young nephew with tales of his exploits on the field. He never boasted of his .320 career batting average or his 300 homers, seventh-most of any player at the time of his retirement in 1944. He never mentioned that he has the highest slugging percentage (.553) and OPS (.935) in Phillies history or that he ranks fifth in both home runs (243) and RBI (983) and seventh in hits (1,705) and doubles (336).

Besides, he was in rough shape by the time he returned to Indianapolis in 1947. He was an alcoholic, his body so ravaged by all the booze and a debilitating stroke that he walked with a cane at age 43. He separated from his wife and lost the bar that he owned in the Kensington section of Philadelphia.

"He came home with literally nothing except for what he had sent home to his mom, my grandmother," Bob Klein said. "He sent a lot home to her, money-wise. But he came home and he never touched a drink from that day on. He came a long way before he passed away. We were proud of him from that standpoint."

Uncle Chuck moved in with his mother. His brother and sister-in-law, Ed and Florence, lived next door. Florence was "a pretty stern lady," according to Bob, and she watched over Chuck, helping him sober up and get healthy.

It was then that Bob Klein grew close to his uncle. They would walk half a mile to Lake Shore Country Club two or three times a week and meander the course together. Uncle Chuck would sneak Bob into the clubhouse or even the bar to mingle with fellow members. And yes, they would go to baseball games, occasionally making the two-hour drive to Cincinnati but often staying closer to home to see the minor-league Indianapolis Indians at Victory Field.

Bob became the son that Chuck never had, and Chuck was a father figure to Bob, who lost his dad when he was five.

"We were really pretty close," Bob said. "I asked him a lot of questions about people that he played with and things like that. He would talk a lot about when he was still playing amateur ball here in Indianapolis. He probably talked more about that. But he was humble. He was a quiet man. He never really relished thinking about what he'd done from a baseball standpoint."

That was okay. Somehow young Bob knew. He could look up all the numbers. He knew what they meant. He understood there wasn't a better hitter on the planet than Uncle Chuck for those five years. And he didn't need Hall of Fame voters to validate that legacy.

Chuck Klein's name was on the writers' ballot for 14 years. He never garnered more than 22.8 percent of the vote before dying of a cerebral hemorrhage in 1958 at age 53. His highest vote total came in 1964, his final year of eligibility, when he finished at 27.9 percent, nowhere close to the 75 percent required for Hall of Fame enshrinement.

But then came the recognition from President Nixon. Seven years later, the Hall of Fame's Veterans Committee took up Klein's case for induction. And one year after that, in 1980, he was elected to the Hall of Fame.

Bob Klein delivered an acceptance speech that was written by his wife, Barbara. He still remembers shaking hands with then-commissioner Bowie Kuhn and sitting on the stage alongside 1980 inductees Al Kaline, Duke Snider, and former Boston Red Sox owner Tom Yawkey. His daughter had an hour-long conversation with Sandy Koufax. To this day, he has no earthly idea what they talked about.

"It was a moment," said Bob, who worked as a sales manager for Pitney Bowes and officiated high school football, basketball, and softball in Indiana for 40 years. "You get around players that you saw play—Kaline, I saw him play—and it's just amazing to be up there with those people. It was an amazing weekend that we spent up there. The four days were just unbelievable. It was quite an honor."

If Uncle Chuck died in obscurity, he achieved a sort of posthumous immortality. His plaque in Cooperstown notes that he was the "only player in the 20th century to collect 200 or more hits in each of his first five full major league seasons." The Phillies added him to their Wall of Fame in 1980. Seventy-five years after he played his last game, folks know his name.

Bob Klein came to that humbling realization several years ago. He was traveling to Jeffersonville, Indiana, when he decided to make a stop at the factory where Hillerich & Bradsby Company produces Louisville Slugger bats. He asked the receptionist if there were any relics of old bats that might have been used by his uncle.

"She said, 'What was his name?'" Bob Klein recalled. "I said, 'Chuck Klein.' She said, 'Wait a minute,' and she called to the back. This little bitty Italian guy who must have been 85 years old comes running out. He's kind of got broken English, and he's got my uncle's nameplate and he says, 'I made the bats for your uncle!'

"Well, two months later, I get two bats in the mail, two bats that they had made. It was the same bat that he made for my uncle, and he sent me two of them. When you think about how many bats they make there, it was funny to me that this guy would remember all that."

Consider it further proof that Uncle Chuck wasn't so forgettable after all.

36

BULL

Feel like gabbing about the 1980 World Series with one of the players who won it?

Take a stroll, then, along the left-field line at Citizens Bank Park during a game. Before you get to "Harry the K's" restaurant or make a right turn into Ashburn Alley, stop and look behind Section 140, a mere 330-foot poke from home plate. That's where you will find Greg Luzinski, the Phillies' opening-day left fielder from 1972 to 1980 and now the proprietor and celebrity grillmaster at Bull's BBQ.

And he's more than happy to step away from the spicy ribs, pulled pork, and the Bull Dog—a footlong kielbasa that's considered the specialty of the house—to talk a little baseball.

"I can't ever remember being booed in Philly," Luzinski said. "I was kind of like the ethnic guy in the middle of the lineup, you know? I always had fun with the fans. They were always very good to me."

Okay, so the passage of time might have colored some of Luzinski's memories. Hugely popular among Phillies fans during his first half-dozen big-league seasons, the linebacker-sized slugger became something of a lightning rod during his final three years with the club, including the crowning 1980 season, so much so that he got sent to his native Chicago two weeks before Opening Day in '81 when the Phillies sold him to the White Sox. But we'll get back to that.

This much is undeniable: Luzinski represents one of the best reputation restorations in Phillies history. It helped, of course, that he won that World Series ring. He even had a major hand in making it all possible by delivering the winning hit in two of the three National League Championship Series victories over the Houston Astros. He hit a two-run homer off Ken Forsch in the sixth inning of Game 1, then notched an RBI double against Joe Sambito in the 10th inning of Game 4.

It was vintage "Bull," as Luzinski was known. In 11 seasons with the Phillies, he hit 223 home runs and struck out 1,098 times, ranking seventh and fifth in franchise history in those respective categories. But he also was among the Phillies' all-time best clutch hitters. In late-and-close situations—defined as the seventh inning or later with the team tied, ahead by one run, or with the tying run at least on deck—Luzinski outperformed even Mike Schmidt. From 1972 to 1980, their nine years as teammates, Luzinski hit 34 close-and-late home runs with an .844 OPS in 841 plate appearances; Schmidt hit 24 homers and had an .827 OPS in 840 plate appearances.

"Hitting home runs was part of it, but I got to the point where I took the Tony Perez idea in my head and I got to be real selfish," Luzinski said, referring to the Hall of Fame Reds first baseman. "Man on second, man on third, I used to play a game mentally and say, 'Those guys are mine.' I got a lot of big two-out key hits in my career because I thought about using the middle of the field. I became a pretty tough out with men on base and in scoring position, especially with two outs. I wanted to be in that spot. And those hits broke other teams' backs."

For instance, Luzinski cites a scoreless game in the eighth inning on July 1, 1973, at St. Louis' Busch Stadium. With the go-ahead run on second base, Cardinals manager Red Schoendienst came to the mound to discuss walking Luzinski intentionally but was overruled by Hall of Fame ace Bob Gibson. Luzinski singled to center field, driving in Bill Robinson in what turned out to be a 1–0 Phillies victory.

"I rounded first and Gibson's about 15 feet away or so and he's standing there just staring at me," Luzinski recalled. "I said to [Cardinals first baseman Joe] Torre, 'What the hell is he looking at?' Torre goes, 'You.' I said, 'What did *I* do? Sh—, he threw the pitch.' And he said, 'You weren't supposed to hit that one.' I said, 'What do you want me to do, apologize?'"

Luzinski wasn't the penitent type, not that he had anything much to be sorry for. During his four-year peak—1975 through 1978—he ranked second in the majors in runs batted in (446) and fourth in homers (129), slugging percentage (.535), and intentional walks (48). He finished as runner-up in the National League MVP voting in 1975 and 1977, falling short of Cincinnati Reds stars Joe Morgan and George Foster, respectively. Luzinski probably should've won the MVP in '77. He batted .309 with 39 homers, 130 RBI, and a .988 OPS, all career highs, and led the Phillies to an NL East crown. But Foster garnered 15 first-place votes to Luzinski's nine on the strength of 52 homers and a 1.013 OPS for the NL West runner-up Reds.

"I just wasn't supposed to win it, I guess," said Luzinski, who believes some voters may have held his league-leading strikeout total (140) against him.

Bull's homers weren't merely hit. They were crushed. He reached virtually unreachable parts of ballparks across the country, from the upper deck at Veterans Stadium and the fifth level of the Astrodome to the left-field loge seats at Dodger Stadium. Hall of Fame catcher Johnny Bench described Luzinski's power display in batting practice before the 1977 All-Star Game at Yankee Stadium by telling *The Sporting News*, "[He] made it look like he was driving golf balls. Everything he hit went out of sight."

Fittingly, the Phillies clinched their first division title in 26 years in 1976 on a Luzinski three-run homer in Montreal.

But for as much as Phillies fans adored a barrel-chested slugger who looked like he came straight out of a folktale, they soured on Luzinski after Manny Mota's double went off his glove in left field in the infamous "Black Friday" game in the 1977 NLCS. Luzinski got booed during a 7-for-61 cold spell in 1978 and every subsequent slump thereafter.

Luzinski and his wife, Jean, were also named in a *Trenton (N.J.) Times* report that alleged several Phillies players and their wives had received prescriptions of the amphetamine Desoxyn from Dr. Patrick Mazza, a physician based in Reading, Pennsylvania, home to the club's Double-A affiliate. The players denied any relationship with Mazza, who nevertheless said he knew them and claimed they wanted the pills for multiple reasons, including weight loss. Luzinski, for one, reported to spring training in 1980 after having shed 25 pounds in the offseason. The case against Mazza was dropped in 1981.

And Luzinski feuded with manager Dallas Green, who took over late in the 1979 season. By July 1980, Luzinski got so fed up with Green's tack of criticizing players in the press that he accused the skipper of "trying to be a f—ing Gestapo." The Phillies had a team meeting and nominated Luzinski to bring their complaints to Green. It didn't go well.

"I was voted upon to go in and say something to Dallas," Luzinski said. "Instead of coming to us and telling us [what was wrong], he would tell it to the press and the press was writing about it. We just said, 'Look, you said it was an open-door policy. Why don't you come out the other way and if you're mad, tell us before we've got to read about it?' It kind of didn't go over real good. There was supposedly a little rift there."

But all's well that ends well. Considering Luzinski's final act with the Phillies was riding on a float down Broad Street, things couldn't have ended any better.

He nearly returned to the Phillies early in the 1985 season. Team president Bill Giles called him to gauge his interest in re-signing to come off the bench and start at first base against left-handed pitching.

"It was a Friday night and they said, 'Let us know by Monday,'" Luzinski said. "I get a call the next day from Giles saying, 'If you come back, we can make a trade.' I said, 'It's not even 24 hours, so I don't think you better make the trade.' I decided to turn him down and never came back."

But you can hear more about that if you stop by Bull's BBQ down the left-field line. Get there early before the Bull Dogs are all gone.

37

BOONEY, DUTCH, & CHOOCH

It was April 11, 1993, and Curt Schilling had just completed a four-hit, 3–0 victory over the Chicago Cubs at Veterans Stadium. The Phillies were off to a 5–1 start in a season in which most forecasters pegged them to finish in last place. Music blared in the clubhouse. Bottles of beer were on ice. Everyone was in a good mood.

And then Mitch Williams walked in.

Often outspoken, occasionally ornery, always hyper-competitive, Williams was hot—in more ways than one. Manager Jim Fregosi called for the closer to begin loosening when the Cubs notched back-to-back one-out singles in the ninth inning. But Schilling recovered to strike out Candy Maldonado and Sammy Sosa and secure a 132-pitch shutout, leaving Williams warmed up but unused. There's little that relievers detest more.

So, Williams collected his things while the Phillies congratulated Schilling. He traversed the outfield, stepped into the dugout, and ignored his partying teammates in the clubhouse. As he approached his locker, he ripped off his uniform top and whipped his glove into the stall.

Seated at the adjacent locker, Darren Daulton wasn't amused.

"Dutch just looks at him and goes, 'What's your problem?'" reliever Larry Andersen recalled. "Mitch says something and Dutch got up and he's like, 'We just won the damn game. What's wrong with you?' He was pissed. They got kind of heated and got in each other's face. But that was Dutch. He saw to it that it was only about winning and that was all."

Ask anyone who was around that 1993 team—or the World Series–champion 1997 Florida Marlins, for that matter—and they will swear that Daulton, who died in 2017 from brain cancer, was more than merely a tough-as-nails catcher. They will insist that he was a leader unlike any they ever saw. The 1993 Phillies were a group of mulleted misfits with personalities as large as John Kruk's beer belly. They were a potential tinderbox, and without Daulton to defuse several situations along the way, they might have self-combusted long before banding together to win the franchise's only pennant in a 24-year stretch from 1984 to 2007.

But while Daulton was the consummate leader, he was far from the only catcher who doubled as the rock-solid anchor of a great Phillies team. In fact, each of the club's seven pennant-winners was backstopped by a strong-willed, no-nonsense catcher.

Go back to 1915 and Bill Killefer, who had such a good rapport with star pitcher Grover Cleveland Alexander that, legend has it, they would work an entire game without using signs. Andy Seminick was the barrel-chested, tree-trunk-legged catcher for the 1950 Whiz Kids whose influence was so profound that even All-Stars Richie Ashburn and Robin Roberts acknowledged him as the team leader. Clay Dalrymple set a tone behind the plate for the 1964 Phillies that went beyond throwing out 49 percent of runners who tried to steal against him during his career.

And it's no coincidence that the three best catchers in franchise history—Bob Boone, Daulton, and Carlos Ruiz—played on the three most beloved Phillies teams ever.

Boone caught 1,095 games over 10 seasons for the Phillies and 2,225 games overall, third-most all-time behind Hall of Famers Pudge Rodriguez (2,427) and Carlton Fisk (2,226). But he wasn't always a catcher. And he very nearly quit baseball before catching the final pitch of the 1980 World Series.

The Phillies selected Boone in the sixth round of the 1969 Draft out of Stanford. In college he played third base, just as his father, Ray, did for 13 seasons in the big leagues. Boone's sons, Bret and Aaron, went on to big-league careers as infielders.

But the Phillies had other plans. After selecting Mike Schmidt in the second round of the 1971 Draft, they figured the position would be occupied for years to come. And so, beginning that year, Boone moved behind the plate, learning the position at the triple-A level with none other than Seminick as his manager.

Boone made his major-league debut late in the 1972 season and didn't relinquish the catching job until the Phillies sold him to the California Angels in 1981. It scarcely mattered that he struggled to develop a rapport with quirky ace Steve Carlton or that the Phillies acquired catchers Johnny Oates and Tim McCarver in 1975. Boone averaged 129 games per season from 1973 to 1980 and was as much a fixture behind the plate in Philadelphia as Johnny Bench in Cincinnati, Fisk in Boston, Thurman Munson in New York, and Ted Simmons in St. Louis.

Indeed, Boone was part of a homegrown Phillies core that featured Schmidt, shortstop Larry Bowa, and left fielder Greg Luzinski. They grew up together and led an organizational resurgence that saw the Phillies go from the depths of a 59-win season in 1972 to 101 wins and the first of three consecutive division titles in 1976. And Boone was at the center of it all, even if he tends not to get as much credit as Schmidt, Carlton, or some other Phillies stars of the era.

"I know in my years with the Phillies," said Boone, now a senior advisor with the Washington Nationals, "I was as important or played as big a part as anybody."

Boone's intelligence on the field was unrivaled. It wasn't merely baseball IQ either. He was a psychology major at Stanford, which gave him an intellectual edge behind the plate and in the clubhouse. Most pitchers trusted him implicitly. He was able to outthink most hitters. He was an All-Star in 1976, '78, and '79, winning Gold Gloves in '78 and '79.

Naturally, then, Boone started all 11 postseason games for the Phillies in 1980. He got two hits in Game 5 of the epic NL Championship Series against Houston, including a single off Nolan Ryan in the legendary eighth inning. And he got a hit in all but one of the six World Series games against the Kansas City Royals, including three hits in Game 1.

"It was the biggest event of my life," said Boone, his voice cracking ever so slightly at the memory. "No, I can't say that because I've got kids and a marriage. But in my career everything was about trying to get to and win the World Series. It was very special to me."

Twenty-eight years after Boone caught the fastball from Tug McGraw that struck out Willie Wilson and clinched the 1980 World Series, Ruiz snatched the dirt-diving Brad Lidge slider that fooled Eric Hinske for the final out in 2008. But that isn't the only thing the championship catchers have in common.

Like Boone, Ruiz started as an infielder. He was 19 when the Phillies signed him for $8,000 and turned him from a squat second

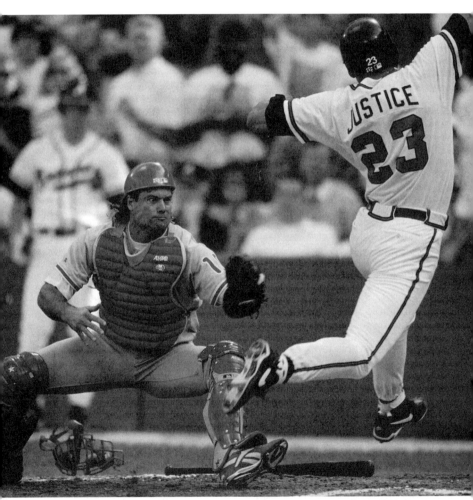

Darren Daulton lunges to tag David Justice during Game 3 of the 1993 NLCS.
(Getty Images / Ronald C. Modra)

baseman into a catcher, a position he had never played before. It was a leap of faith, not only for the Phillies but also Ruiz, who dropped out of college in his native Panama where he had been pursuing a degree in physical education. And like Boone, he emerged as a sage for Phillies pitchers and the unheralded Krazy Glue of a team that won it all.

It was a remarkable rise for a player who barely spoke English when he first arrived at the Phillies' facility in the Dominican Republic. Nicknamed "Chooch"—a shortened, cleaned-up version of the slang "chucha" moniker that was bestowed upon him as a joke by some veteran teammates—Ruiz had to learn the most basic elements of catching, from positioning himself in his crouch to getting to his feet in time to catch a foul pop behind the plate.

Ruiz progressed slowly through the minors, finally making his big-league debut at age 27 in 2006. Even then, most scouts believed he would never amount to more than a career backup. Instead, he wound up averaging 118 games per season from 2007 to 2012, during which the Phillies won five consecutive division titles.

"The thing about Chooch, he was a quarterback in a sense," Ryan Howard told reporters in 2016. "The way he handled the pitching staff, the way he prepared himself for games with the pitchers, from the defensive standpoint of knowing different situations, knowing what guy you want to beat you, what guy you don't want to beat you, just the way he played the game, he was a fireball out there."

Daulton did more than put out fires for the 1993 Phillies. He hit 24 homers, drove in 105 runs, posted an .875 on-base plus slugging percentage, and finished seventh in the NL MVP voting. It was part of a three-season peak from 1992 to '94 in which he was the best catcher in the league.

But even in his less productive years, Daulton won universal respect. A 25th-round draft pick out of tiny Cowley County (Kansas) Community College and the 629th player selected overall in 1980, he survived nine—count 'em, nine—knee surgeries, and teammates marveled at the lengths to which he went to get ready to play.

Fregosi stressed to him the importance of being a team leader, and Daulton evolved into one of the best. Stories of his hold on the clubhouse are legendary. While Andersen recalls the times that Daulton set Williams straight, longtime Phillies public-relations chief Larry Shenk remembers him once grabbing Schilling by the throat and backing him into a locker.

"I can't even think of anybody close to him as far as being a leader," former third baseman Dave Hollins said. "I didn't have the pleasure or fortune to play with anybody else like Darren. I don't know if he gets enough credit. Guys all respected him for what he went through. They didn't want to tangle with him. Without him there, obviously we don't do what we did."

Say the same for Boone and Ruiz. Like Daulton, they worked behind the plate, but were front and center in the Phillies' triumphs.

38

BILL GILES

The only job that Bill Giles ever really wanted was to be the general manager of a major-league team.

First, though, he had to rescue a franchise.

You wouldn't know it now, considering the Phillies were worth $1.85 billion at the start of the 2019 season, according to *Forbes*, but when Giles came to town from Houston in 1969, they were moribund. It wasn't so much that they had won only two pennants in 86 years, though that certainly had a lot to do with it. They played in Connie Mack Stadium, an increasingly decrepit 60-year-old ballpark located in a deteriorating neighborhood in North Philadelphia. And while baseball boomed in New York and Atlanta, Houston and Los Angeles, the Phillies lost 99 games and drew only 519,414 fans, their worst turnout in 24 years.

It didn't help either that the Phillies' best player, temperamental slugger Dick Allen, practically begged to be traded. Or that when they finally worked out a deal to send Allen to the St. Louis Cardinals, one of the players they received in return refused to come to Philadelphia. In his 1971 book *The Way It Is*, Curt Flood characterized the Phillies as "a ballclub rivaled only by the Pirates as the least cheerful organization in the league" and ripped them for "lumbering through the air in propeller jobs" rather than springing for a chartered jet.

If ever a franchise was in need of a reset, it was the Phillies. And in one of the wisest moves in his three-decade stewardship of the franchise, owner Bob Carpenter decided that Giles was the man for the job.

"Bob Carpenter was blueblood Delaware, [related by marriage to the] DuPont family, and to bring in somebody like Bill Giles to rebrand the Phillies, which was really a dead franchise for so many years, it was a brilliant idea," said Dennis Lehman, a retired Cleveland Indians executive who worked in the Phillies' public relations department in the

'70s. "He needed someone to take a fresh look at things. I don't know who he interviewed besides Bill, but it was the perfect choice."

Longtime Phillies vice president Larry Shenk put it more directly.

"To me," Shenk said, "Bill saved the franchise."

Giles comes from a baseball family. His father, Warren, was president and general manager of the Cincinnati Reds for 14 seasons before becoming president of the National League. His godfather, Branch Rickey, was the man who signed Jackie Robinson.

In 1960, after cutting his teeth working for a minor-league team in Nashville, Giles got hired by the expansion franchise in Houston. He spent 10 years with the Colt .45s/Astros and had a hand in almost everything, including the opening of the Astrodome.

Giles worked for Judge Roy Hofheinz, the Houston franchise's flamboyant owner. Known for his creativity and innovation, Hofheinz encouraged his staff to think of new ways to draw in fans. No idea was too crazy, not even a "Rocket Man" who would dress up like an astronaut and use a jetpack to fly around the dome. Giles was Hofheinz's marketing whiz, and by the late '60s, he was being directed to work on non-baseball projects, including prize fights, soccer, bull fights, and even Ringling Bros. and Barnum & Bailey Circus, Hofheinz's newest venture.

"As time went on, I felt like I was getting further and further away from baseball," Giles said. "All the non-baseball activities were fun and educational, but I wanted to be a baseball guy, not strictly a marketing guy."

By 1969, the Phillies were a year away from moving into a new stadium in South Philadelphia. Shenk, who headed up the team's public relations, marched into Carpenter's office and told the owner, "We've got to change our mode of operation. We've got to promote. We've got more seats to fill." Alas, he didn't sense that changes were imminent, not with Carpenter on the verge of retirement and planning to turn over the team to his son.

But Ruly Carpenter, who lettered in football at Yale, was more interested in player development than the business side of the organization. He needed Giles, with his marketing background in Houston, for everything else.

"Ruly gave all the business stuff to me and didn't pay a whole lot of attention," Giles said. "He didn't care if I put up dancing waters [behind the center-field wall] or a Liberty Bell [on the scoreboard] or had the 'Kiteman.' I ran all the marketing and those kinds of things, and Ruly and Paul [Owens] ran the player end of it."

Shenk feared that the new boss would clean house. Instead, Giles solicited help from a small front office that, by Shenk's recollection, numbered 11 full-time staff members.

The first order of business: Give people a reason to pay to watch a team that hadn't won anything since the "Whiz Kids" in 1950. Giles held weekly staff meetings during which he outlined what he called the "stepping stones of marketing."

"My goal was to do unusual things—cash scrambles and giveaways and all that stuff," Giles said. "If we could get them to the ballpark once, particularly when we opened the Vet, they hopefully will like it enough to where they would come back enough to become a mini-season-ticket holder for 10–15 games a year and then eventually a full season-ticket holder. It was that stepping stone of developing a fan base that started by doing a lot of nutty things."

You name it, Giles tried it. At the outset, it was very basic. The rebranding of the Phillies began with new uniforms and a redesigned logo featuring a single red 'P' with a baseball in the center. In the winter of 1969–70, Giles started a promotional caravan, in which players came in for a week to appear throughout the Delaware Valley and create a buzz about the team.

"The idea was to build a relationship between the fans and the players," Giles said. "I wanted them to get to know Bob Boone by 'Bob,' not just 'No. 8.'"

Giles' promotions got wackier and wackier. In the midst of a 10-game losing streak in 1970, he and Shenk drove to Lancaster County in search of a good-luck charm.

"He heard about hex signs that Pennsylvania Dutch people have on their barns. Those things meant some kind of good luck or something like that," Shenk said. "Well, we went shopping for a hex sign to put on the dugout roof, then we gave them away to fans at the game. And we lost."

After the Phillies moved into the 62,000-seat Vet, two 15-foot animatronic twin mannequins—Philadelphia Phil and Phillis—dressed in Revolutionary War garb were hung from the scoreboard. Giles organized cow-milking contests and other zany sideshows. On two occasions, Karl Wallenda walked a high-wire from one end of the Vet to the other.

"Bill was a P.T. Barnum," former Phillies broadcaster Chris Wheeler said. "Larry Shenk and I would try to throw cold water on some of his nonsense. We'd say, 'What do you want to do, get somebody killed out there?' He'd go, 'Ahhhh, it'll be fine.' And he got away with it. But every year on Opening Day we thought he was going to get somebody killed."

Indeed, Opening Day was always an occasion to get particularly weird. In Giles' native Cincinnati, the first game of the season was treated like a holiday. Giles wanted to make it special in Philadelphia, so he was constantly brainstorming new attractions.

In 1971, he had the first ball dropped from a helicopter to backup catcher Mike Ryan. A year later, Giles enlisted local hardware store owner Richard Johnson to ski jump off a 140-foot ramp atop the center-field seats and deliver the ball to Philadelphia mayor Frank Rizzo. But "Kiteman," as he was called, was overcome with fear when faced with the daredevil feat. With the crowd booing, he finally made it halfway down the upper deck, crashed into several rows of seats, got to his feet, and heaved the ball into the Phillies' bullpen, nowhere close to the target.

"A dead body is not a good omen for the start of the baseball season," Giles said at the time, relieved that "Kiteman" was uninjured.

Attendance rose steadily. The Phillies drew 708,247 in the final year at Connie Mack Stadium, 1.5 million in the first year at the Vet, and 1.8 million by 1974. The team started to improve, too. Led by the homegrown nucleus of Mike Schmidt, Larry Bowa, Boone, and Greg Luzinski, they won three consecutive division titles from 1976 to 1978.

But it was a Giles-orchestrated baseball move—the type he always dreamed of making—that helped put the Phillies over the top in 1980.

With Carpenter unwilling to budge on improving a three-year, $2.2 million offer for free agent Pete Rose, it seemed all but certain that the Phillies would be outbid. But Giles got WPHL-TV to agree to a $600,000 hike in rights fees by convincing the station that its ratings and advertising revenue would increase if Rose was on the team.

Giles' wish to run the baseball operations finally came true in 1981, but only after he put himself in charge.

Although Giles didn't have the money to buy a major-league team, friends suggested that his reputation within the game was strong enough that he could cobble together a group of investors who could go in with him. Sure enough, when Carpenter decided to sell the Phillies after the 1981 season, Giles put together a consortium that bought the team for $30.175 million, eight times what the Carpenter family bought it for in 1943. With a 10-percent ownership stake, Giles gave himself more of the player personnel duties. He made good moves (trading for Steve Bedrosian) and bad (including prospect Ryne Sandberg in a trade with the Cubs that was hastened by a contract squabble with Bowa).

But without Giles' marketing genius in the '70s, it isn't crazy to think the Phillies might not have even survived another decade.

"Bill had this devilishness about him and that giggle and laugh that he still has," Lehman said. "He was always the one who was sort of stirring the pot—what else can we do? How else can we get things going? It was a great era. It really was. And Bill certainly started it all."

39

DAVID MONTGOMERY

An hour or so before the start of one of the last spring-training games that he attended, David Montgomery folded his weakened body into a chair at a circular table in the Phillies' staff dining room at Spectrum Field in Clearwater, Florida.

"How do you feel, David?" Larry Bowa asked.

"Don't worry about me," Montgomery said, waving his arm. "Have you been out to see our prospects?"

Bowa smiled and shook his head. Before him sat a man who, quite clearly, had been through hell. His chin was nearly gone, a consequence of the surgeries and treatments across a five-year war with jaw-bone cancer. His voice, tinged with the twang of northwest Philadelphia, rarely rose above a whisper anymore. He was most certainly dying.

But his biggest concern was the progress of an 18-year-old shortstop from the Dominican Republic.

"What do you think about [Luis] Garcia?" Montgomery asked.

"David," Bowa said, "you're unbelievable."

"Well, I know all the guys coming up," Montgomery said. "Believe me."

Bowa laughed. "I better do my job then."

"That's right," Montgomery said. "And no more, 'How you doin', Dave?' I'm doing fine. You just keep an eye on our young kids."

It was classic Montgomery. All heart.

Is it any wonder, then, that the legacy of his 18-year Phillies presidency is the family-first culture that pervades the organization? Never mind the five division titles, two National League pennants, and one World Series crown, or the $2.5 billion television deal that was struck in 2014, or even the sparkling ballpark that opened in 2004. Under Montgomery's leadership, the Phillies became known as an inviting, uniquely collegial place to work, whether you were a million-dollar ballplayer or a part-timer on the game-day staff.

After all, that was how Montgomery got his start.

Born in 1946 in the Roxborough section of Philadelphia, he was raised on the Phillies, attending his first game at Connie Mack Stadium at age five, idolizing center fielder Richie Ashburn and sneaking a transistor radio under the pillow to listen to late-night games. In 1971, one year after graduating from the Wharton Business School at the University of Pennsylvania, he got hired by the Phillies as a sales apprentice in the ticket office, a job that paid $8,000 a year. He worked his way up to becoming director of sales and marketing and finally the head of the business department.

But never, not even after becoming the Phillies' chief executive in 1997, did he forget his roots or cease being the most down-to-earth person in the room. He would drink bottles of Bud Light at organizational gatherings in even the most posh hotels. He insisted on paying $20 for a scorebook (Montgomery kept score of nearly every game). He routinely called the team's scouts to make sure they were holding up well on the road. Not only did he know the names of almost every employee in Philadelphia and with the minor-league affiliates, but he took an interest in their families, too.

"I'd be with him and he'd stop a security guard and he'd know the security guard's wife and children," former Phillies second baseman Mickey Morandini said after Montgomery died on May 8, 2019. "Then a front office guy would come and he knew his children. Then a custodian, and he knew the wife and children. It was utterly amazing how many people's lives he touched."

But don't take Morandini's word for it. Talk to the people who worked alongside Montgomery over the years. Listen to Frank Coppenbarger, the Phillies' former traveling secretary. Or longtime public relations chief Larry Shenk. Or clubhouse manager Phil Sheridan. They all have stories about Montgomery's kindness and compassion and the way in which he made them feel like they were part of his family because, well, as far as Montgomery was concerned, they were.

At the peak of the Phillies' run of five consecutive NL East titles, the team played in a total of 10 postseason series. And by virtue of appearing in back-to-back World Series, the coaching staff was chosen to participate in the All-Star Game in 2009 and 2010. That meant an extra trip for Coppenbarger to coordinate. It was an exciting time for the organization, but also an exhausting one for its traveling secretary.

"David was always asking, 'How are you holding up?'" Coppenbarger said. "He was always trying to get me to take a trip off. He said, 'I need my closer in the postseason.' I guess I was his closer in certain areas anyway. A good word from David always meant so much."

Sheridan could relate. He was going through a divorce and struggling with living apart from his children when spring training dawned in 2006. He considered staying home rather than spending two months in Florida before eventually deciding to go. But not before Montgomery made an extraordinary offer.

"He told me, 'You've spent so many years of your life working hard for our organization. Now it is our time to take care of you,'" Sheridan told the *Philadelphia Inquirer*. "He said, 'If you need money, we'll cut you a check. If you need legal help, use our lawyers. Whenever you want to go home from Clearwater to see your kids, we will get you a flight.'"

Montgomery could be as firm as he was compassionate. He would get on Shenk's case over the most minor stat-keeping inconsistencies in the game notes. He would take copious notes on a yellow legal pad during staff meetings and circle back on topics that were discussed 10 minutes earlier. Ed Rendell, who met Montgomery in college and went on to serve as mayor of Philadelphia and governor of Pennsylvania, often talked about Montgomery's relentlessness when it came to getting Citizens Bank Park built.

"He could air you out," Shenk said. "We all got that."

Longtime Phillies broadcaster Chris Wheeler puts it this way: "He may not tell you what you want to hear, but you could take it to the bank. He was the most honest person you'll ever meet in your life."

Not even the players were exempt. Montgomery would stress the importance of giving back to the community. He would push players to establish a charity or find an organization that meant something to them and volunteer their time, and when they did, he and his wife, Lyn, would be sure to attend their events. Montgomery would also let them

PHILADELPHIA PHILLIES

know when he didn't think they represented the Phillies well. He once chastised pitcher Cole Hamels for insinuating to the media that the grounds crew didn't cover the field quickly enough to shorten a rain delay that interrupted one of his starts in 2006.

And nobody ever wanted to let Montgomery down. A month after he died, the team held a public ceremony at Citizens Bank Park to celebrate his life. A video tribute was played on Phanavision in left field, and near the end, Phillies vice president of administration Kathy Killian said she often approaches her job by asking herself, "What would David do?" It's a refrain that many other employees have applied over the years.

Montgomery's influence extended beyond the Phillies' walls. In the early '90s, he helped advise young attorney Rob Manfred, who had begun serving as outside counsel for baseball owners. Manfred often credits Montgomery with being a "mentor," and when the owners were seeking a successor for retiring commissioner Bud Selig in 2014, Montgomery was among Manfred's biggest backers.

"At the beginning of my career in the game, David helped me understand how the game operated," Manfred said after an April 2019 news conference to announce the awarding of the 2026 All-Star Game to Philadelphia. "He taught me to be a little more patient than I probably was by disposition. David was on the search committee when I was selected as commissioner, and he played an important role in my selection process."

Ask Pat Gillick why he accepted the Phillies' offer to become their general manager after the 2005 season and he will reply with two words: David Montgomery.

A free-agent executive with a Hall of Fame resume, Gillick had a lucrative offer to take over as general manager of the Los Angeles Dodgers, an attractive possibility for a Southern California native. Or he could return to scouting, his true passion. But after a four-hour meeting with Montgomery, he called his wife and said, "We're going to Philly."

"David just had a tremendous personality and a tremendous warmth to him," Gillick said. "He's one of the most wonderful human beings that I've ever come in contact with."

Bowa offered a similar characterization during a news conference to pay tribute to Montgomery after his death, calling him "the greatest person I ever met in my life." But perhaps the most poignant words spoken on that day were a variation of words that Montgomery used 10 years earlier.

"I remember when [longtime broadcaster] Harry Kalas passed away, David said, 'We lost our voice.' Well, with David's passing, we lost a very big piece of our heart," Phillies executive vice president David Buck said. "He was just a wonderful, wonderful man."

40

GILLICK & THE POPE

Nearly three decades before Pat Gillick became the second general manager to steer the Phillies to a World Series crown, he learned what it was like to do business with the first.

It was 1981, and Gillick was running the fledgling Toronto Blue Jays, an expansion franchise that hadn't won more than 67 games in any of its first five years in existence. He went into the offseason with a to-do list so lengthy that it could have stretched from Canada all the way to Hollywood, Florida, site of baseball's annual winter meetings. He wasn't going to turn the Jays into a contender in one offseason, but then, nobody actually believed that he could.

Expectations were a lot different for Gillick's counterpart in Philadelphia.

Paul Owens, known affectionately as "The Pope" because of his resemblance to Pope Paul VI, had built a homegrown nucleus that won three consecutive division titles from 1976 to '78 and finally captured the World Series crown in 1980. But the Phillies got bounced by the Montreal Expos in the Division Series in 1981, a season that was interrupted for nearly two months by a players' strike, and fans were already impatient. Heading into the winter meetings, a headline in the tabloid *Philadelphia Daily News* screamed, "PHILLIES MUST TRADE YOUTH FOR PITCHING."

It was against that backdrop that Owens dialed up Gillick to ask about Dave Stieb, a young right-hander who had a 3.19 earned-run average in 1981 and was on the verge of breaking out as one of the best pitchers in the American League.

"You had to deal with 'The Pope' very cautiously, let me put it that way," said Gillick, belching out a chortle. "He was always thinking ahead in a deal. He was honest and straightforward, but he would kind of overload a deal. He would try to give you more players than you wanted but less talent."

As Gillick recalls, Owens took that approach in the Stieb negotiations. Owens dangled backup catcher Keith Moreland and speedy outfielder Lonnie Smith. He discussed backup infielders Luis Aguayo and Len Matuszek. A young infield prospect named Ryne Sandberg would ultimately be on the table, too.

Gillick might have been more familiar with the Phillies than any other organization. By virtue of having their Florida training sites in the neighboring towns of Dunedin and Clearwater, respectively, the Blue Jays and Phillies were frequent spring-training opponents. And if their big-league teams played four or five times each March, their minor-league clubs squared off even more often.

And after listening to Owens' overtures for Stieb, Gillick took a pass.

"He knew our organization pretty well and he thought because we were down that he could get Dave Stieb," Gillick said. "It was one of those overload deals. He was trying to give me a lot of players for Stieb, who was a guy they thought would've fit in with [Steve] Carlton and [Dick] Ruthven and [Larry] Christensen. And they were right: He would've fit right in."

Indeed, Stieb went 135–90 with a 3.25 ERA over the next nine seasons for the Blue Jays en route to becoming the winningest pitcher in franchise history. Owens turned elsewhere for his pitcher, acquiring Mike Krukow from the Chicago Cubs in a three-for-one deal for Moreland and pitchers Dickie Noles and Dan Larson. Krukow went 13–11 with a 3.12 ERA in 1982 but was traded after one year to the San Francisco Giants for reliever Al Holland and aging Hall of Fame second baseman Joe Morgan.

Advantage, Gillick?

"The Pope was legendary," Gillick said. "I'll tell you, in the time I came up, he was one of the best by far."

Owens and Gillick met in 1959, when the former was managing Bakersfield in the California League and the latter was pitching for Stockton. They got better acquainted a few years later on the scouting circuit. Owens became the Phillies' farm director and got promoted to GM midway through the 1972 season. Five weeks later, he fired manager Frank Lucchesi and appointed himself interim skipper in order to get a closer look at why the team was struggling.

Before long the Phillies were the envy of other organizations because of their homegrown core. Owens oversaw the drafting and/or development of Mike Schmidt, Larry Bowa, Bob Boone, Greg Luzinski, Ruthven, and Christensen. By the mid-1970s, the Phillies had the look of an NL powerhouse.

"I think the Carpenters, [owners] Bob and Ruly, were thoroughly convinced in the early '70s that you weren't going to be able to buy yourself a team," former Phillies president and chairman Bill Giles said. "You had to start basically with the scout. If you don't have good scouts, you're never going to find the right guys. It all centered around Paul Owens and all the scouts that he had working for him. It was a great experience working with Paul Owens. I consider him really the best judge of baseball talent that I've ever been associated with."

It was a different time, to be sure. Owens reneged on a trade with the Detroit Tigers in 1974 because, as legend has it, he awoke the next morning to realize he had agreed to the deal only after having a few too many drinks. Tigers general manager Bill Campbell's reaction to Owens' change of heart: "How do you unshake a handshake?"

But there was a lot to learn from Owens, too, and as a young scout with the Houston Astros and New York Yankees, Gillick watched him closely, occasionally pressing him for advice. One lesson: Be compassionate in dealing with players, but make decisions with your head rather than your heart. Owens cried in 1975 after trading first baseman Willie Montanez to the Giants for Gold Glove outfielder Garry Maddox because he liked Montanez as a person. But he also knew it was a move he needed to make to improve the team.

"Paul was a great guy that I think the players really respected, but at the same time he had a feel of when to cut a guy loose," Gillick said. "He didn't let his personal feelings interfere with professional judgment."

Like most good general managers, Owens saw the roster as a jigsaw puzzle and understood that the moves made to strengthen the margins are often just as important as the development of the core at the center. And when Owens was out scouting or pondering a potential trade, he paid as much attention to a player's attitude and character—"makeup," in scouting parlance—as his on-field ability. If a player oozed talent but didn't have the right personality to fit with the manager or the rest of the team, Owens shied away.

"When he went out and got a Maddox or a [Richie] Hebner, he knew what he was going after," Gillick said. "It not only fit from an ability standpoint, it also fit from a makeup standpoint. That's what Pope impressed on me. He said, 'You can get players with talent, but really the key to the thing is to get the right players to fit into the puzzle.' There might be guys who have tremendous talent, but if they don't fit into what you're trying to do, it probably won't work out."

Gillick applied that philosophy throughout his career as a Hall of Fame GM. He took the Blue Jays from a laughingstock to a contender that averaged 91 victories per season from 1983 to 1993 and won five division titles and back-to-back World Series in 1992–93. He led the Baltimore Orioles to the playoffs in 1996 and 1997 and built a 116-win team with the Seattle Mariners in 2001.

When Gillick took over as the Phillies' general manager after the 2005 season, he recognized the talent in the homegrown core that was assembled by his predecessor, Ed Wade. Jimmy Rollins, Chase Utley, Ryan Howard, Cole Hamels, Carlos Ruiz, Ryan Madson, and Brett Myers looked a lot like Owens' collection of young Phillies from three decades earlier.

But it was the moves that Gillick made to round out the roster—signing non-tendered outfielder Jayson Werth, trading for ageless lefty Jamie Moyer and closer Brad Lidge, and picking up setup relievers J.C. Romero, Chad Durbin, and Scott Eyre—that enabled the Phillies to win the World Series in 2008.

"I was fortunate to inherit a group of outstanding players," Gillick said. "It was: Don't screw the thing up. They have a good nucleus. Just add the pieces to put you over the top."

Owens surely would have liked that 2008 team. He died five years earlier at age 79, though his legacy endures. Since 1986, the

Phillies have annually presented the Paul Owens Award to the best player and pitcher in their minor-league system. And when Gillick was inducted into the team's Wall of Fame in 2018, he noted the honor of joining Owens as the only general managers to receive the honor.

Gillick didn't bite on Owens' bid for Stieb, but they did make two smaller trades. In 1977, Gillick purchased first baseman Tommy Hutton from the Phillies for $15,000. Five years later, he sent outfielder Wayne Nordhagen to the Phillies for outfielder Dick Davis.

After Owens passed away, Wade recalled that he often began telling a long story by saying, "To make a long story short." But here's the long and short of it: Owens was the best general manager in Phillies history. It was only fitting that Gillick, a willing protege, walked in his shoes two decades later.

41

BOBBY ABREU

The press conference to introduce the 2019 inductee to the Phillies' Wall of Fame was called for 2:00 PM. But two o'clock turned into 2:10, which turned into 2:15. And as the cramped cafeteria at Spectrum Field in Clearwater, Florida, filled with reporters, team officials, former players, and even a group of impressionable minor leaguers, nobody had seen the honored guest. He wasn't even in the building.

"He's on 'Jimmy Time,'" former Phillies shortstop and manager Larry Bowa cracked.

"Nah," Jimmy Rollins replied. "Before there was 'Jimmy Time,' there was 'Bobby Time.'"

Indeed, Bobby Abreu operated on his own clock during his 18-year major-league career. But while teammates and coaches shared a running joke that he seemed to run perpetually late, often strolling into the clubhouse with minutes to spare before players were mandated to report, it was actually the opposite. When it came to fulfilling his goal of winning a World Series, the right fielder was always too early.

Consider this: Abreu spent nine years with the Phillies, arriving after the 1997 season in a swap with the Tampa Bay Devil Rays and leaving midway through 2006 in a trade-deadline deal with the New York Yankees. During that time, the Phillies improved from a 75-win team to an 88-win club that typically stayed in playoff contention until the final weekend of the season. But it wasn't until the year after Abreu was gone that they finally reached the postseason. In 2008, two years post-Abreu, they won the World Series.

And it wasn't only the Phillies who won it all without him. Abreu played for the Yankees for 2½ seasons, during which he batted .295 with 420 hits, 43 home runs, and an .843 on-base plus slugging percentage. But they won the World Series in 2009, the year after he signed with the Los Angeles Angels and was replaced in right field by Nick Swisher.

Neither of those championships, or the near-misses that came before them, were a reflection on Abreu. He was a two-time All-Star and received MVP votes in seven seasons. He won the home-run derby at the All-Star Game in 2005 and a Silver Slugger Award in 2004. For a period of 12 seasons, from 1998 through 2009, he had a .902 OPS, the 20th-best mark of any hitter who played a minimum of 1,200 games. He could reasonably stake his claim as the best right fielder in Phillies history. He will be considered for the Hall of Fame for the first time in 2019, and once the voters examine his candidacy, it won't be a surprise if he at least garners enough support to remain on the ballot for several years.

Like Don Mattingly, Torii Hunter, and so many others, Abreu was a very good player who simply played in the wrong places at the wrong times. His greatest nemesis: "Bobby Time."

"I have a lot of great moments over the years," Abreu said. "I did a lot of things—the 30/30 club, first homer at the new Citizens [Bank] Park. But one of the things that I really missed was winning the World Series. That's one of the things that I was looking for. I was happy for [the Phillies] because I knew how hard they built for that moment. But I missed it."

Abreu was ahead of his time in other ways, too, some of which impacted the way that he was viewed during his career.

In 1999, his second season with the Phillies, he drew 109 walks. It marked the start of an eight-year stretch in which he walked at least 100 times per season. He routinely ranked among the league leaders in pitches per plate appearance, making him one of the toughest outs in baseball. And he posted an on-base percentage of at least .400 in eight of his nine seasons with the Phillies.

But it took the publication of *Moneyball: The Art of Winning an Unfair Game*, Michael Lewis' groundbreaking 2003 book about the Oakland Athletics' approach to team-building, to shed light on the relative importance of on-base percentage over more traditional statistics such as batting average. Even then, the popularization of the Moneyball culture in baseball didn't really take root until later in Abreu's career.

If Abreu played today, he would be hailed for not chasing pitches out of the strike zone, lauded for his discipline, and valued even more highly by the influx of teams that lean heavily on analytics to influence their decision-making. Instead, he was often criticized for being too passive at the plate rather than looking to power the ball over the fence.

Abreu made nearly $125 million in his career. At a time when teams use Wins Above Replacement to judge the value of players and pay them accordingly, Abreu's 60.0 WAR—ninth among all outfielders since 1989, according to Baseball-Reference.com, and more than Ichiro Suzuki (59.4) and Vladimir Guerrero (59.4)—likely would've netted him even greater riches.

Larry Bowa looks on as Bobby Abreu speaks during his induction to the Phillies Wall of Fame. (Getty Images / Hunter Martin)

"He played in an era where we weren't quite as versed to appreciate on-base percentage and selectivity," said former Phillies center fielder Doug Glanville, Abreu's teammate from 1998 to 2002. "When you're a middle-of-the-order guy you were expected to just give me RBIs or give me power. But he would take his walks when maybe if he expanded the strike zone he could've driven in more runs. It made it so that people underestimated his value."

Abreu's skills were always evident to his teammates, though. For as much as Glanville admired Abreu's superior hand-eye coordination and his knack for driving the ball to all fields, he also marveled at the way that he picked up cues from pitchers or made intelligent reads on the bases.

"He'd be like, 'When he holds his glove like this and the laces turn, it's going to be this pitch,'" Glanville recalled. "He could figure it out by the third inning. He was like a genius when it came to that."

Abreu's instincts weren't always recognized because of what Glanville termed "nonchalance" and a "laissez-faire approach." Abreu often seemed to be gliding on the bases or in the outfield. Phillies fans, who love nothing more than a soiled uniform, would holler about Abreu's apparent aversion to colliding with the outfield wall. It could be perceived as a lack of effort when, in reality, it was an illustration of how easily the game came to him.

"He was still destroying you, but he did it so coolly," Glanville said. "He was just a pure ballplayer."

By the 2006 trade deadline, though, the Phillies reached a crossroads. They had sunk to fourth place in the National League East, leading general manager Pat Gillick to believe that changes needed to be made. He pulled off a series of smaller trades, jettisoning backup catcher Sal Fasano, third baseman David Bell, and reliever Rheal Cormier.

But Abreu was Gillick's biggest chip. He was making $13.6 million and was due for a raise to $15 million in 2007. At a time when Rollins, Chase Utley, and Ryan Howard weren't making much money, Gillick recognized an opportunity to reset the payroll. He dealt Abreu to the Yankees for four prospects, none of whom panned out, committed to the youth movement, and declared that the Phillies wouldn't seriously contend for a title until 2008.

The timeline was actually much shorter. Shane Victorino took over in right field and became a solid everyday player. The Phillies nearly made the playoffs in 2006, then overcame the collapsing New York Mets to win the NL East crown in 2007.

"I love Bobby Abreu, but I thought right at that time that with Victorino we were a little better defensive club than we were with Bobby in right field," Gillick said. "I wanted to give an opportunity for Victorino and later for [Jayson] Werth to play on a regular basis. It wasn't anything to do with Bobby or his ability."

Abreu watched the Phillies' ascendance from a safe distance up the New Jersey Turnpike. But he had not yet sold his South Jersey home when they reached the World Series in 2008. He was staying there during the postseason and watching on television when he noticed something.

Rollins was 0-for-10 with three strikeouts through the first two games against the Rays. After Game 2, with the series headed back to Philadelphia, Abreu decided it was time for a phone call—and a pep talk.

"I told him, 'My brother, you're too excited. Calm down. There's things that you can do better. You want to do too much,'" Abreu said. "I told him, 'Talk to the guys. Just go out there and play the game. You guys deserve to be there. You guys already know how to play the game. Don't try to do too much.' I told him, 'I'm with you guys. My heart is going to be there.'"

Abreu watched the final out of the 2008 World Series with his mother. He was a few months from signing a one-year, $5 million contract with the Angels. But when the celebration began at Citizens Bank Park, Abreu wept.

"I cried because I believe it's something that every player wants to do," he said. "You're here just to win the ring. I was crying for happiness for them."

It was a moment that resonated, even on Bobby Time.

42

THE STAR OF ALL-STARS

When the Phillies returned from the All-Star break on July 9, 1964, Johnny Callison walked into the home clubhouse at Connie Mack Stadium, got dressed in his uniform, and went out for batting practice, just as he did before almost all of the nearly 1,900 games in his 16-year major-league career.

It was impossible to tell that he had just hit the biggest home run of his life.

Two days earlier, at Shea Stadium in New York, Callison came to the plate in the ninth inning of the 35th All-Star Game in baseball history. The score was tied, 4–4, after Willie Mays worked a leadoff walk, stole second base, and scored on Orlando Cepeda's bloop single that landed in shallow right field, where second baseman Bobby Richardson might have caught it if he hadn't been so preoccupied by the threat of Mays swiping third. The winning run was now on second base. There were two outs. Hard-throwing Boston Red Sox reliever Dick Radatz was on the mound. And a crowd of 50,850 was waiting to see what would happen next.

Bang.

"He reared and threw me a high hard one," Callison wrote in *The Johnny Callison Story*, his 1991 autobiography co-authored with John Austin Sletten. "As soon as I swung, I thought it was a homer. You can just feel it—hear it! I was on cloud nine as I rounded the bases. By the time I rounded second, I saw Radatz throw his glove into the dugout. Curt Flood, Johnny Edwards, and the rest of the National League All-Stars mobbed me at home plate."

Since the inception of the All-Star Game in 1933, there have been only three walk-off home runs. Ted Williams hit one for the American League in 1941 at Briggs Stadium in Detroit. Stan Musial did it for the National Leaguers to end a 12-inning game in 1955 at County Stadium in Milwaukee.

And then there was Callison.

At 5-foot-10 and 175 pounds, the Phillies right fielder from Bakersfield, California, was the smallest player on the NL's 1964 roster and had an even slighter ego. With 226 career home runs, including four consecutive seasons with 20 or more from 1962 through 1965, he belonged in a group of NL outfielders that included Mays, Hank Aaron, Roberto Clemente, Willie Stargell, Flood, and Billy Williams, even if he would die from embarrassment before he ever admitted it.

"Johnny was very quiet, very laid back," former Phillies shortstop Bobby Wine said. "Probably the best all-around player we had on the team as far as everything goes—good contact, home-run power, the most accurate arm in the outfield. But he was a real quiet, laid-back person. That's probably why he didn't get a lot of the recognition that other guys got."

Indeed, you wouldn't catch Callison bragging about his achievements, be they his league-leading 16 triples in 1965, or his majors-leading 40 doubles in 1966, or even his runner-up finish to St. Louis' Ken Boyer for the NL MVP Award in 1964. He drove in 104 runs that year and bashed 31 homers, including three against the Milwaukee Braves in a September 27 game when the Phillies were collapsing down the stretch and he was sick with the flu. Callison was so ill, in fact, that he was shivering in the dugout.

But despite his exceeding talent and matinee-idol looks, Callison never sought the spotlight. If anything, he was proud of his defense, specifically his 90 outfield assists from 1962 through 1965. Even the cannon-armed Clemente had only 59 assists during that span.

"Johnny loved the game of baseball," said former Phillies catcher Clay Dalrymple, Callison's road roommate. "He enjoyed hitting, but he was a really good outfielder, too. He had a good arm, and he concentrated on throwing the ball right and catching the ball and getting rid of it back to the infield. He was a good ballplayer."

And he certainly wasn't about to strut over turning on a belt-high fastball from Radatz, a mountain of a man at 6-foot-6 and 230 pounds, and tagging it into the upper deck in right field to fuel the NL's 7–4 victory. Never mind that the AL team was led by Chicago White Sox manager Al Lopez, who had a hand in trading Callison to the Phillies for infielder Gene Freese after the 1959 season. Callison still wasn't about to gloat.

"Heck, no," he told the late Stan Hochman of the *Philadelphia Daily News*. "Al's a nice guy. If you hit .170, people don't keep you."

It's little wonder that Hochman wrote of Callison, "He can run, throw, hit, and hit with power, and his only flaw is his shyness."

Three Phillies players were selected to the All-Star team in 1964. Ace pitcher Jim Bunning tossed two scoreless innings in relief of starter Don Drysdale, then lefty Chris Short gave up two runs in the sixth on back-to-back singles by Mickey Mantle and Harmon Killebrew and a two-out triple by Brooks Robinson.

Think of those names. Even now, they are baseball mythology. Mantle. Mays. Aaron. Clemente. Drysdale. Killebrew. And although Callison had been an All-Star two years earlier and was in the midst of his near-MVP season, he never figured Los Angeles Dodgers manager Walter Alston would pick him for the All-Star team. Once he did get selected, he had modest expectations for his role in the game.

"I figured I'd pinch hit," he told Hochman, "and that would be it."

Callison did pinch-hit for Bunning in the fifth inning. Facing Camilo Pascual, he popped out to shortstop. And that might have been the end of his 1964 All-Star experience had Aaron not been sick and unable to play the outfield. So, Alston kept Callison in the game, sending him out to replace Clemente in right field as part of a double switch in the top of the sixth.

Due to hit again in the seventh inning, Callison asked to borrow Cubs outfielder Billy Williams' bat. Williams swung a 34-inch, 32-ounce Louisville Slugger that was lighter than Callison's lumber. Callison figured a lighter bat would make it easier to get around on Radatz's heat. It worked, too. He hit a deep fly ball to center field, but Mantle hauled it in.

Callison used Williams' bat again in the ninth inning, and well, you know what happened.

"I was there as a fan," said longtime Phillies public relations chief Larry Shenk, who was in his first year with the team in 1964. "I was in the last row behind home plate watching it. He's the only All-Star MVP that the Phillies ever had. How could it get any better than that?"

There would've been one way. Entering play on September 21, 1964, the Phillies were leading the NL by 6½ games with 12 games remaining. But they lost 10 games in a row, slipped to third place, and wound up losing the pennant by one game when the Cardinals rallied to beat the Giants on the final day of the season.

It was Callison's best chance to reach the playoffs. Even the two years that he spent with the Yankees at the tail end of his career came during the lull between the end of the Mantle dynasty and the Bronx Zoo teams of the late '70s.

Callison retired after the Yankees released him in August 1973. He worked as a sales rep for a Philadelphia bakery, sold used cars for Avis, even tended bar near his home in Doylestown, Pennsylvania. He died from a long illness in 2006 at age 67.

If Dalrymple and Callison ever talked about the All-Star Game homer, Dalrymple can't recall the conversation. He's sure that he congratulated his old pal, but that was probably the extent of it.

"I watched the game and I watched the home run, and I was thrilled to death that he hit that home run to win the game," Dalrymple said. "It meant a lot to me because it was important to my roommate, and I was really thrilled. But as far as making a big thing out of it, Johnny wasn't really that good about talking about things like that anyway. He didn't blow himself up."

Dalrymple never had any trouble doing it for him, though.

"If Johnny had been 30 or 40 pounds heavier, with his ability, he'd have been in the Hall of Fame. I have no doubt about that," Dalrymple said. "He just wasn't big enough to quite do all the things that he had to do to get in the Hall of Fame."

Callison could certainly hang with Hall of Famers, though. And for one day, at an All-Star Game in New York, he was the star of stars.

43

THE ANALYTICS REVOLUTION

ohn Middleton stood outside the visitors' clubhouse at Yankee Stadium, unsure of whether he should enter. The 2009 World Series had ended a few minutes earlier. After 372 days at the pinnacle of baseball, the Phillies had been dethroned, and the pain was acute.

But Middleton saw an opportunity. A co-owner of the Phillies since 1994, he wanted to thank each player for a pennant-winning season. So, he went locker to locker, without drawing attention from the media throng until, at last, he knelt beside Ryan Howard, who bashed 45 home runs in the regular season and was the Most Valuable Player of the National League Championship Series before going 4-for-23 with 13 strikeouts in the World Series. They spoke quietly, Middleton doing his best to console the hulking slugger before issuing a directive.

"Ryan," he said, "I want my f—king trophy back."

Six years later, Middleton took a bold step to try getting it.

The Phillies regressed in each of the six seasons after their World Series disappointment. They lost to the San Francisco Giants in the NLCS in 2010. After winning a franchise-record 102 games in 2011, they fell to the St. Louis Cardinals in the NL Division Series. They went 81–81 and missed the playoffs in 2012 and had back-to-back 73–89 finishes in 2013 and 2014. By the midpoint of the 2015 season, they were 27–54 en route to 99 losses.

Even worse, they were woefully behind the times. While other teams tapped into the waterfall of data that was newly available through Statcast and other technological advances, the Phillies under general manager Ruben Amaro Jr. and team president Pat Gillick remained stubbornly old-school, relying almost entirely on boots-on-the-ground scouting to procure information and influence their decision-making in terms of both roster-building and in-game strategy.

So after years of existing out of public view with his fellow Phillies owners, Middleton finally spoke up, loudly and clearly. At the June

30, 2015, news conference to introduce new team president Andy MacPhail, the cigar magnate from Haverford, Pennsylvania, who sold his father's tobacco company for $2.9 billion in 2007 and now owned 48 percent of the Phillies, made two things clear: He had a vision for the future of the franchise and was ready to take the lead role in seeing it through.

"The way I've run my businesses, I look at my competitors," Middleton told reporters. "If my competitors are doing something better than I am, I want to understand what they're doing and why they're doing it, and then I want to figure out how I can do it at least as well, if not better. So I think there are organizations that have done a better job of transitioning between eras, and we need to look at that and we need to find out what they're doing that we're not doing."

Middleton began to reshape the Phillies' front office. He kicked Amaro to the curb near the end of the 2015 season and directed MacPhail to hire a general manager who was literate in analytics. Behold the Dartmouth-educated Matt Klentak, who became the youngest GM in club history when he took over at age 35 after the 2015 season. Ned Rice, who MacPhail credited with explaining analytics to him when they worked together with the Baltimore Orioles, was brought on as assistant GM.

The objective, Middleton told the *Philadelphia Inquirer* in the spring of 2017, was to achieve a "sustainable competitive advantage." And "the best way to achieve that goal," he added, "is to combine people who are thoroughly grounded in baseball and baseball analytics—Matt and Ned—with extraordinarily bright people who can think critically and creatively and have a proven track record in analytic jobs outside baseball."

In that vein, the Phillies hired Andy Galdi away from Google to head up their beefed-up research-and-development department. They pried principal software engineer Zo Obradovic from a Silicon Valley start-up and senior quantitative analyst Alex Nakahara from Northrup Grumman, the aerospace and defense company.

The next step was to find a manager who would fit with the Phillies' new direction. It surely wasn't Pete Mackanin, the longtime scout and coach who worked on Charlie Manuel's staff from 2009 to

2012 and took over as manager when Ryne Sandberg stepped down midway through the 2015 season. Klentak inherited Mackanin and didn't see much point in replacing him right away. The 66-year-old was suited to steward the team through a teardown and the early stages of the rebuild.

But after a 37–38 finish to the 2017 season, the Phillies believed they were getting closer to contention again. Klentak wanted a fresh perspective in the dugout, someone who could better connect with a young team.

Enter Gabe Kapler.

Despite having neither coached nor managed at the big-league level, Kapler was the progressive manager that the Phillies wanted. He also didn't look, sound, or act like any skipper the city had ever seen. With the tanned physique of a bodybuilder from Malibu, the unfailingly positive oratory style of Tony Robbins, and a devotion to the data-driven tenets of the analytics era, fans didn't know what to make of Kapler.

A former outfielder who spent 12 years in the big leagues and won the World Series as a member of the Curse-busting 2004 Boston Red Sox, Kapler insisted he never set out to be an iconoclast. He's also hardly the only modern manager who pores over the information provided to every team by new-age systems such as PITCHf/x and TrackMan or is guided by the alphabet soup of predictive new metrics, including FIP and wOBA.

"I have no interest—zero interest—in being different for the sake of being different," Kapler said after the 2018 season. "I have no interest in pushing the envelope for the sake of pushing the envelope. I just want us to have better practices."

In the next breath, though, he separated himself from the establishment.

"I understand that I don't look or sound or behave like Dallas Green," he said, "and I'm not going to."

Kapler immersed himself in the city. He opted to live in Philly in the off-season rather than returning to the warmth of his native Southern California and wasn't shy about being spotted around town. He became a regular at Cafe La Maude in Northern Liberties on weekday mornings and Suraya in Fishtown in the evenings.

But Kapler was always going to be a tough sell in hardscrabble Philadelphia. Almost immediately, he had a polarizing effect on a fanbase that he was only going to win over if the Phillies won. Therein lied his—and overall, the organization's—problem. By the end of the 2019 season, it was fair to question whether the new Phillies Way was going to succeed.

The Phillies surprised everyone by spending 39 days in first place in 2018. They were atop the division at the All-Star break and made a prospect-laden bid to trade for star shortstop Manny Machado. (The Orioles dealt him instead to the Los Angeles Dodgers.) On August 7, the Phillies were 64–49.

But they lost 33 of their next 47 games and were eliminated from playoff contention on September 22. Three days later, they slid below .500 en route to an 80–82 finish.

Middleton spent nearly half a billion dollars on roster improvements before the 2019 season, including the signing of Bryce Harper to a free-agent-record 13-year, $330 million contract. The Phillies traded top pitching prospect Sixto Sanchez to the Miami Marlins for All-Star catcher J.T. Realmuto, who came with only two years of club control. It was clear they were through rebuilding; they were determined to win immediately.

But a raft of injuries and the regression of several young starting pitchers caused the Phillies to stumble to an 11–16 mark in June 2019. They didn't win more than four games in a row all season, fell far behind the first-place Atlanta Braves, and were on the outskirts of the wild-card race entering the season's final month. They finished 12–16 in September, including a five-game sweep by the Washington Nationals, and went 81–81 overall, missing the playoffs for an eighth consecutive year.

Klentak received a three-year contract extension in March 2019; MacPhail got a three-year extension late in 2017 and although they both advocated for Kapler to keep his job, Middleton decided 11 days after the conclusion of the season to fire him, ending a managerial tenure that always felt more like an experiment.

PHILADELPHIA PHILLIES

The Phillies hired veteran manager Joe Girardi on October 24, 2019. An industrial engineering major from Northwestern University and the decade-long skipper of a New York Yankees team that was at the forefront of the analytics revolution in baseball, Girardi understands how to use data to gain an advantage. But he also wasn't afraid to push back in New York when he felt the reliance on metrics became too overbearing. He seemingly hasn't forgotten that the game is still played by human beings with feelings and emotions rather than programmable robots.

Middleton insists the Phillies aren't running from analytics. At the very least, though, Girardi appears to be a vote for balance.

"We had no analytics department before I came on the scene," Middleton said in October 2019. "I'm the guy who is driving that bus. Not Matt, not Andy, not Gabe, not even Andy Galdi, who runs that department. I'm the person. It's my vision. And I and the Bucks [co-owners David and Jim] are the ones who are funding that. We're committed to that. Look at the postseason teams. They're all analytically driven. We just need to be better at what we do. A lot of times it's not so much the data, but it's the delivery of that data [to the players] that has to be thought through. We need to sit down and talk about that."

Klentak put it another way during Girardi's introductory news conference.

"We've reached a place where it is time to win, no questions asked," he said. "It is time to win right now."

Middleton, after all, still doesn't have his f—king trophy back.

44

NOLA & THE NEXT GENERATION

When the Phillies took Aaron Nola with the seventh overall pick in the 2014 Draft, they reasoned that a polished pitcher from a major college program wouldn't need much time to be ready for the big leagues.

On that point, at least, they were correct.

But the Phillies' talent evaluators, like their counterparts from other organizations, suspected that Nola had limitations. He doesn't throw as hard as, say, University of Oklahoma right-hander Jon Gray, the third overall pick in the 2013 Draft. He isn't as physically imposing as 6-foot-6 right-hander Lucas Giolito, a first-round pick in 2012. Most of the scouts who came to Louisiana State University to watch Nola pegged him as a middle-of-the-rotation starter rather than a top-of-the-line ace.

"We viewed his ceiling as probably a [No.] 3 or 4 [starter], really, in retrospect," former Phillies general manager Ruben Amaro Jr. said.

Nola wound up being worth considerably more. Actually, he's the rarest of baseball creatures: a homegrown, cost-controlled ace. To a baseball executive, he's akin to the Hope Diamond, a 1963 Ferrari GTO, a winning Powerball ticket. There's almost no limit to his value.

When the Phillies traded for catcher J.T. Realmuto on February 7, 2019, and signed star right fielder Bryce Harper to a 13-year, $330 million contract a few weeks later, they signaled to the baseball universe that they were ready to transition from a rebuilding team to a serious playoff contender. The core of what they believe will be their next great team was taking shape, and it featured Realmuto, Harper, homegrown slugger Rhys Hoskins, and 2015 second-rounder Scott Kingery, a sparkplug with the versatility to play six positions and the upside of an All-Star.

At the center of it all, though, was Nola, without whom the Phillies would still be searching for the anchor of their starting rotation.

Aaron Nola in his windup in a September 2018 game against the Braves.
(Getty Images / Rich Schultz)

"From an organizational perspective, there really is no greater feeling than when you're able to see a pitcher who was drafted and developed and came through the system make the kind of impact that [Nola] has made," general manager Matt Klentak said at a February 2019 news conference to announce Nola's four-year, $45 million contract extension, the easiest decision a club executive could possibly make. "For what he's done on the field, for the work ethic that he brings to our team, for the humility that he brings, Aaron really is the perfect fit for our team and our city."

It's possible, of course, to rebuild a team without drafting and developing a No. 1 starter. The Boston Red Sox, for example, procured two of them by spending $217 million on free agent David Price and emptying their farm system in a trade for Chris Sale. But it's more economical to grow your own. The Los Angeles Dodgers' decade-long success has come on the back of Clayton Kershaw. The San Francisco Giants won three World Series with Madison Bumgarner. The Detroit Tigers captured four consecutive division titles with Justin Verlander.

Once that ace is in place, it emboldens an organization to package a top pitching prospect (Sixto Sanchez) in a trade for a catcher with two years of contractual control (Realmuto) and an owner to drop nearly half a billion dollars in a free-agent binge for a veteran reliever (David Robertson) and two former MVPs (left fielder Andrew McCutchen and Harper).

But the Phillies had more modest ideas in the fall of 2013, when they dispatched area scout Mike Stauffer to Baton Rouge, Louisiana, to watch Nola.

"Starting pitching was something that we were short on in our organization at the time after having lost most of the big boys," said Amaro, referring to the "Four Aces" rotation of Roy Halladay, Cliff Lee, Cole Hamels, and Roy Oswalt in 2011. "It was important for us to replenish that. We drafted [Nola] because we knew that he'd be a major-league pitcher in a very short period of time."

Indeed, Stauffer's notes on Nola indicated that the junior "manipulated the baseball." He also wrote in his reports that Nola exhibited uncommon poise in front of 10,000 fans at LSU home games and hostile crowds on the road at Ole Miss, Arkansas, and elsewhere in the Southeastern Conference.

"He has a lot of moxie up there when he takes the mound. He's a cool cat, a quiet competitor," Stauffer told the *Philadelphia Inquirer*. "But what he did was just be himself there. He stayed focused. He attacked hitters, threw strikes, changed speeds, and he really finished. That's what you're looking for."

The Phillies sent cross-checkers and other talent evaluators to LSU to confirm what Stauffer was seeing. When it came time to make the first-round pick, Amaro and then–scouting director Marti Wolever were on board. Nola was their man.

Nola rocketed through the minors and made his debut midway through the 2015 season, 11 months after being drafted. Two years later, Hoskins burst onto the scene with a historic home-run spree—18 in only 170 at-bats. It was easy to see them becoming the fresh, young faces of the Phillies' new generation.

In 2018, though, Nola emerged as one of the top pitchers in all of baseball. He finished third in the National League Cy Young Award voting with one of the best seasons ever by a Phillies pitcher.

Hyperbole? Hardly. Consider this: In the franchise's 136-year history, only seven pitchers worked at least 200 innings, struck out at least 200 batters, and posted an earned-run average of less than 2.50 in a season. Nola joined Lee (2011), Halladay (2010–11), Steve Carlton (1972 and 1980), Jim Bunning (1966–67), Grover Cleveland Alexander (1914–15 and 1917), and Charlie Ferguson (1886) in the 200/200/2.50 club.

Then-manager Gabe Kapler called it "maybe the best season I've ever seen a pitcher have up close—and I was with Pedro Martinez, arguably in his prime. I think Nola's season was right up there with Roy Halladay's best, Cliff Lee's best, Steve Carlton's best. A jaw-dropping season."

Nola does it with a fastball that scrapes 94–95 mph on occasion but averages closer to 92–93, a solid change-up, and one of the best curveballs in the game. He also has precision control and a competitive streak that enables him to reach back for something extra in the later innings of starts when he's feeling fatigued.

"He's become an incredible pitcher," Atlanta Braves slugger Freddie Freeman said at the 2018 All-Star Game. "His two-seamer, he starts it almost behind you and it comes back over. His curveball, you think you can hit it, and it drops to the ground every time. The change-up is obviously very effective. He throws everything for strikes. It's not fun facing him."

It's all slightly hard for A.J. and Stacie Nola to believe. Their youngest son is unfailingly humble. He barely speaks above a whisper and prefers to keep his head down. His reaction to finalizing the contract extension: a low-key call to his parents, who "pretty much screamed" upon getting the news.

When the Nolas visit Philadelphia and see Aaron's likeness on a SEPTA bus or a city billboard, or when they saw him chatting with fellow 2018 Cy Young finalists Jacob deGrom and Max Scherzer in the outfield before the All-Star Game, it's what A.J. Nola describes as a "wow moment."

"It's weird," Stacie Nola said. "To see his name on someone's jersey or hear people talking about him, or people want his autograph, it's like, 'It's just Aaron.' When we're in Philadelphia and we see his banner when you're walking down the street, you're like, 'Let's get a picture with it!'"

There's plenty of time for that. Nola, like Harper and probably Hoskins and Kingery, isn't going anywhere.

If the Phillies didn't know quite what they had when they drafted Nola, his college coach did. In 2015, before Nola's major-league debut against the Tampa Bay Rays, LSU coach Paul Mainieri texted his old friend, Phillies president Andy MacPhail.

"I just wrote, 'I just want you to know that you may not realize how special this kid is, but you will find out in a very short time,'" Mainieri said. "He's seen a gazillion ballplayers, and I'm sure he's heard that a lot. But I honestly felt that way. I think everybody in Philadelphia is starting to understand why I felt this kid was so special."

45

BEST OUTFIELD EVER?

Every spirited baseball debate is a matter of perspective. Deciding on the best outfield of all time isn't any different.

Baby Boomers from New York may be partial to Mickey Mantle, Roger Maris, and Yogi Berra, a left fielder for the Yankees by 1961. Their generational counterparts on the West Coast would likely argue for Willie Mays, Willie McCovey, and Felipe Alou of the 1963 San Francisco Giants. If you grew up in New England in the 1970s, you're probably inclined to point to the Red Sox's trio of Jim Rice, Fred Lynn, and Dwight Evans. Barry Bonds, Andy Van Slyke, and Bobby Bonilla were terrific for the Pittsburgh Pirates in the early 1990s, just as Manny Ramirez, Kenny Lofton, and Albert Belle were for the Cleveland Indians in the middle of that decade.

In 1982, a *Sports Illustrated* senior editor submitted his admittedly outside-the-box opinion. The late Richard W. Creamer, authoring the "Perspective" column in the magazine's October 17 issue, took up the case for the Phillies' outfield from 1891–95, prefacing his argument by writing, "Before you dismiss that best-outfield claim as the raving of a hidebound antiquarian, consider the exploits of Del, Big Sam, and Sliding Billy."

Okay then, let's fire up Marty McFly's DeLorean and dive into the careers of Ed Delahanty, Sam Thompson, and Billy Hamilton.

Delahanty, Thompson, and Hamilton played together for five seasons and are believed to be the only three–Hall of Famer outfield ever. Each was posthumously inducted into Cooperstown, their legacies rooted in grainy photos taken in the 19th century and eye-popping statistics that somehow don't seem to translate across place or time.

But when it comes to their individual accomplishments, well, good luck finding an outfield trio that can top their 1894 season, in which they each batted .400 and combined for 19.5 Wins Above Replacement, according to Baseball-Reference.com. By comparison— and 19th century baseball was so much different that it's virtually impossible to compare—the '61 Yankees outfield also had a 19.5 bWAR, while the '63 Giants trio had a 22.3 bWAR. In their best season together, Rice, Lynn, and Evans combined for a 19.0 bWAR in 1979.

Delahanty, the left fielder, had the most all-around talent. A right-handed hitter with big power relative to the deadball era, his .346 career average ranks fifth all-time behind Ty Cobb (.366), Rogers Hornsby (.359), Shoeless Joe Jackson (.356), and Lefty O'Doul (.349). He hit four home runs in a game on July 13, 1896, at West Side Park in Chicago—and the Phillies still lost, 9–8. Sam Crawford, a Hall of Fame contemporary, once called Delahanty "the best right-handed hitter I ever saw."

Hamilton, the center fielder, had blazing speed on the bases and in the outfield. A left-handed hitter with a .455 career on-base percentage that ranks fourth all-time behind Ted Williams (.482), Babe Ruth (.474), and John McGraw (.466), he led the league in runs four times and stolen bases seven times, although it's worth noting that players of that era were credited for steals when they advanced on a fly out or an error or took more than one base on a hit. Hamilton was nevertheless a force, widely credited for pioneering the headfirst slide. On May 17, 1893, he led off a game with a homer and ended it with a walkoff blast, a feat accomplished by only five other players. In their 1953 book, *The Philadelphia Phillies*, co-authors Frederick G. Lieb and Stan Baumgartner wrote that Hamilton was "fast as a deer, and he could wriggle around a baseman—waiting with ball in hand—like a slippery eel."

Thompson, the right fielder, was the most prolific run-producer of the time. At 6-foot-2 and 207 pounds and with a powerful left-handed swing, he led the league in slugging three times and home runs twice. In 1889, he became the first player ever with 20 homers and 20 steals in the same season. His 166 RBI in 1887 stood as the single-season record until Ruth drove in 168 runs for the Yankees in 1921. Defensively, he mastered the one-hop throw to the infield and home plate.

Delahanty signed with the Phillies in 1888 at age 20, jumped to the upstart Players' League in 1890, then returned a year later after that league folded. Thompson was already established when the Phillies signed him away from Detroit for $5,000 before the 1889 season.

Hamilton joined the team in 1890 after playing two seasons in Kansas City.

The Phillies brought the three outfielders together for the 1891 season. Initially, Delahanty was the primary center fielder and Hamilton played left. They switched midway through the season in 1892, and by the following year, they comprised the top third of the batting order, with Hamilton leading off, Thompson batting second, and Delahanty third. According to the research for Creamer's column, each player had an 11-game hitting streak at one point in the 1893 season. Between them, they had 12 hits in one game, 10 in another, and at least seven hits in a game 14 times. While Hamilton won the batting title with a .380 average, Thompson finished second at .370, and Delahanty third at .368.

The only thing that could stop the three outfielders from leading the Phillies to their first pennant was typhoid fever, a bacterial infection for which a vaccine was not yet developed in the United States. When Hamilton fell ill in August of 1893, the Phillies were in first place. But he missed the rest of the season and the Phillies faded from contention en route to a fourth-place finish.

A fire destroyed much of Baker Bowl, the Phillies' home ballpark, in 1894, forcing the team to play several home games at the University of Pennsylvania's field. The disruption didn't seem to bother the outfielders. Thompson batted .415, Delahanty .405 and Hamilton .403, accomplishments that look even more impressive now considering a player hasn't hit .400 since 1941. There have been only twenty-eight .400 seasons, 15 of which occurred before the turn of the century. Still, the Phillies finished in fourth place again.

In 1895, Delahanty batted .404 while Thompson notched 211 hits and Hamilton picked up 201. But the Phillies came in a distant third place, and Hamilton got traded to Boston for third baseman Billy Nash.

From that point, it wasn't merely their careers that diverged.

Hamilton played six seasons in Boston, then nine in the minor leagues. He managed in the minors and scouted for the Boston Braves before leaving the game to work at a leather manufacturing plant in Worcester, Massachusetts, where he lived with his wife, four daughters, and two grandchildren until he died of heart disease in 1940 at age

74. Twenty-one years later, he was elected to the Hall of Fame by the Veterans' Committee.

Thompson played for the Phillies through 1898, though his last full season was 1896. He made a brief return in 1906 when the Detroit Tigers were short players, but mostly spent his post-playing days out of baseball. He invested in real estate in Detroit and was appointed a U.S. Deputy Marshall during World War I before dying of a heart attack in 1922 at age 62. It wasn't until 1974 that he was elected to the Hall of Fame.

Delahanty's life was both tortured and tragic. He remained with the Phillies through 1901 before jumping to the newly formed American League when the Washington Senators offered him $4,000 per year. But he drank heavily, separated from his wife, and was embroiled in contract squabbles. He took leave of the Senators in the midst of a Detroit-to-Washington road trip in 1903 to visit his wife in New York but got kicked off a train near the Canadian border for being "loud and belligerent," according to Creamer's recounting. The ensuing details remain fuzzy, but Delahanty went missing and was later found dead in the Niagara River at age 35. He was elected to the Hall of Fame in 1945.

For five years, though, Delahanty was part of perhaps the best outfield ever assembled, even if there's no longer anybody alive who can attest to its greatness.

"They were an odd, disparate trio, as different off the field as on it," Creamer wrote in *Sports Illustrated*, "but they were all Hall of Famers and in the five seasons they played together they did more than any other outfield before or since. You want to argue?"

Go ahead and try.

46

THE ONES THAT GOT AWAY

Pat Gillick signed the player who ripped out the Phillies' beating heart in Game 6 of the 1993 World Series. But it was his acquisition of an outfielder other than Joe Carter that annoyed the heck out of his front-office and scouting counterparts from Philadelphia.

"We got George Bell off them," Gillick said, his voice tinged with pride even now.

It happened in 1980 at the winter meetings in Dallas. Phillies general manager Paul Owens was the envy of the annual event after the team won the World Series two months earlier. The Toronto Blue Jays were at the other end of baseball's social class. They lost 107, 102, 109, and 95 games in their first four years of existence, and as their GM, Gillick was looking under every rock for talent.

That search took him to the back fields of the Phillies' spring-training complex in 1980, where he saw Bell take a few right-handed swings. Known for his photographic memory, Gillick took a mental note.

Bell played only 22 games that season at Double-A Reading before being sidelined by a back injury. He didn't hit any home runs. And when the time came to protect players who were eligible for the Rule 5 Draft, the Phillies figured they weren't at risk of losing the 21-year-old if they left him exposed.

"We got that little bit of a look and decided to take him, and I don't think they were expecting it," Gillick said. "[Phillies scout] Hugh Alexander always used to say, 'I don't know how you guys knew about that guy.' I think they were a little bit stunned, actually."

The Blue Jays stashed Bell on their big-league roster for the entire 1981 season, a requirement for retaining a Rule 5 pick. He went to Triple-A in 1982, returned to the majors in 1983, and stayed for the next decade. He batted .288, slugged .493, and led all American League hitters with 195 homers from 1984 to 1990, a period in which the

Phillies had seven Opening Day left fielders—Glenn Wilson, Jeff Stone, Gary Redus, Mike Easler, Phil Bradley, Chris James, John Kruk—and 36 players at the position overall who combined for 91 homers.

Clearly, then, Bell is one that got away. But there have been others.

Hank Aaron tried out for the Phillies but never received an offer, in part because of owner Bob Carpenter's refusal to sign black players until 1957, 10 years after Jackie Robinson's debut. The Phillies were interested in Al Kaline as an 18-year-old in 1952 but instead gave a $100,000 bonus to a high-school pitcher named Tom Qualters, who posted a 5.64 ERA in 34 games and never recorded a win. They hosted Carl Yastrzemski for a tryout in 1957, then made a low-ball offer before he signed with the Boston Red Sox for $108,000.

The Phillies tried to acquire Gold Glove center fielder Curt Flood in the 1969 trade that sent Dick Allen to St. Louis, but Flood didn't report, choosing instead to challenge baseball's reserve clause in a case that went to the Supreme Court. Twenty-eight years later, outfielder J.D. Drew didn't sign with the Phillies after being selected with the second overall pick. He reentered the draft in 1998 and was taken fifth overall by the Cardinals.

After the 1982 season, team president Bill Giles thought he was pulling off the heist of the century when he acquired lefty-hitting outfielder/first baseman Von Hayes from the Cleveland Indians. It was a five-for-one trade, but the Phillies were giving away, as Giles wrote in his memoir, "a solid but past-his-prime second baseman, a reserve outfielder, a minor league pitcher that we weren't real high on, a minor league catcher that we weren't real high on, and a 24-year-old shortstop we suspected was older than that and who had a very awkward stance that we didn't think would allow him to hit major league pitching."

The Phillies scarcely missed the first four players: Manny Trillo, George Vukovich, Jay Baller, and Jerry Willard. But the fifth? That 24-year-old (at least) shortstop with the weird stance? Julio Franco wound up batting .298 over a 23-year big-league career that lasted until he was 48 (at least).

"[Indians president] Gabe Paul kept telling me how his wife, Mary—who helped raise me—loved Hayes and that he might have to get a divorce over this trade," Giles said. "I think he told me this so he would get more in return."

But the Phillies' biggest mistakes were a pair of trades that sent two Hall of Famers to the Chicago Cubs 16 years apart.

Ferguson Jenkins signed with the Phillies in 1962 and spent four years in the minors before coming up late in the 1965 season. He made eight relief appearances and posted a 2.45 ERA. With the help of pitching coach Cal McLish, who taught him to throw a slider, he flashed the potential to be successful in the big leagues. But manager Gene Mauch didn't have much tolerance for young pitchers, according to Jenkins.

"Mauch had that reputation as the 'Little General.' He did what he wanted," Jenkins said. "He was a veteran-type manager that wanted guys that had more experience than myself and the other young pitchers. We had Grant Jackson, Rick Wise, Dave Bennett, myself. There were a few guys that were chomping at the bit waiting for our chance. A lot of us got traded away."

Jenkins got dealt early in the 1966 season over McLish's objection. With Mauch looking for veteran pitching, the Phillies sent Jenkins, lefty pinch-hitter John Herrnstein, and young outfielder Adolfo Phillips to the Cubs for 34-year-old right-hander Larry Jackson and 37-year-old reliever Bob Buhl. Jackson had a few good years but retired after the 1968 season.

In 1968, Jenkins notched the second of his six consecutive 20-win seasons.

Oops.

Jenkins developed into a prototypical workhorse. He topped 300 innings in a season five times, tossed at least 20 complete games eight times, and won 20 or more games seven times. He won the Cy Young Award in 1971 and was elected to the Hall of Fame in 1991.

As great as Jenkins was, he was nearly unbeatable against the Phillies, going 26–8 with a 2.39 ERA in 43 career appearances, including 38 starts. He had more wins, shutouts (7), and strikeouts (266) against the Phillies than any other opponent.

Coincidence?

"I always tried to beat 'em," Jenkins said. "I always tried to show them that they made a mistake. It's instinctive. In my eyes, when I became a starter I always thought that I was capable of winning. But I guess in their eyes, maybe not."

Jenkins was in his second-to-last season in 1982—and back with the Cubs after stints with the Texas Rangers and Boston Red Sox—when the Phillies made another regrettable deal with Chicago.

Giles had put together a group of investors to buy the Phillies from the Carpenter family for $30.5 million and taken over a player-personnel role. He knew the team would have to move on from some core members of the 1980 World Series club, many of whom were beginning to decline. Among those players: popular shortstop Larry Bowa.

But Bowa insisted that outgoing owner Ruly Carpenter pledged to give him a four-year extension even though he was about to turn 36. Giles told Bowa that he had no intention of upholding that promise, prompting Bowa to go public with a demand to be traded.

A logical landing spot was the Cubs, who hired 1980 Phillies manager Dallas Green as president/general manager. The Cubs were also looking for a shortstop after Ivan DeJesus batted .194 with a .509 on-base plus slugging percentage in 1981.

"We agreed that a straight-up swap of Ivan DeJesus for Bowa wasn't fair because DeJesus was seven years younger," Giles wrote in his memoir. "Green wanted us to throw in a prospect, and he said he would take any one of five young players, including a kid named Ryne Sandberg."

It was a deal. DeJesus for Bowa and Sandberg.

"The scouting report on Sandberg from our baseball people was that he couldn't hit well enough to play third and couldn't field well enough to play second," Giles said. "Even the Cubs had some of the same concerns that we did, toying with the idea of converting him to a center fielder. History shows that we were all wrong on Ryne Sandberg."

Phillies fans adored Bowa and loathed the trade. By the end of the 1984 season, it was a total steal for the Cubs.

DeJesus batted .249 with seven home runs and a .637 OPS in three seasons with the Phillies. He was the shortstop on a pennant-winning team in 1983 but went 2-for-16 and made an error in the World Series.

Sandberg, meanwhile, was crowned NL Most Valuable Player in 1984, the first of 10 consecutive seasons in which he was named an All-Star. He won nine Gold Gloves, hit 282 home runs—fourth-most ever by a second baseman—and was elected to the Hall of Fame in 2005. Not bad for a former 20th-round pick.

One that got away?

Maybe the biggest one ever.

47

FROM THE VET TO THE BANK

From the groundbreaking in 1967 to the grand opening in 1971, through design changes, labor strife, and enough political drama to fill an episode of *The West Wing*, it took 3½ years to build Veterans Stadium.

And 62 seconds to destroy it.

By the end, the Vet outlived its welcome. Years of neglect had stolen whatever luster once existed beneath its concrete austerity. Many players panned it every chance they got, adding fuel to the narrative that it was, at best, a cookie-cutter, artificial-turf relic and, at worst, a rat-infested dump.

Still, Bill Giles wept on the morning of March 21, 2004, when the button was pushed and the old place imploded.

"The Vet was a big deal in the beginning," said Giles, the former Phillies president. "It was a gem. That was the style of stadiums back then, and everybody thought they were fantastic. I got goosebumps every day that I went to the Vet. There were so many fond memories spent there."

Indeed, on the eve of the first game ever played at the corner of Broad Street and Pattison Avenue, longtime Phillies public-relations chief Larry Shenk remembers Giles staying until midnight and cleaning the glass door at the front entrance with Windex. Giles recalls *Sports Illustrated* hailing the new stadium as "beautiful."

Really, though, the Vet was splendid in its utilitarianism. Like so many stadiums of the time, it featured an artificial playing surface that was cheaper and easier to maintain than natural grass and allowed for greater usage. The Phillies played there in the spring and summer, the NFL's Philadelphia Eagles in the fall and winter.

In time, the Vet became the site of the first golden era in franchise history. The Phillies made the playoffs six times from 1976 to 1983. They hosted the All-Star Game in 1976 and 1996. And they celebrated their first World Series title on that hideous carpeted surface in 1980.

The Vet might have been a dump, but it was the Phillies' dump. And believe it or not, the club's longest-tenured employees were nostalgic about seeing it go.

"We wound up spending a lot of money to keep it up because the city didn't," Shenk said. "The Eagles were the opposite. They hated the place. It was our home for 33 years."

But Giles, elevated to the role of team chairman by 1997, and team president David Montgomery were also realists. They understood that the Phillies needed a new ballpark if they were going to be competitive. Giles is also a baseball romantic. He grew up going to games at Crosley Field in Cincinnati and had an affinity for old classic parks. And once the Orioles opened Camden Yards in Baltimore's Inner Harbor in 1992, it became fashionable for teams to go retro with ballpark designs.

Giles wanted to build a new park in Center City. He proposed several sites, including 16th Street and Spring Garden, but ran into opposition. Ultimately, the Phillies settled on a site adjacent to the Vet. Citizens Bank Park, as it would be called after a $95 million naming rights deal, was designed by Philadelphia architect Ewing Cole and HOK Sports of Kansas City and scheduled to open in 2004.

First, though, there was the matter of giving the Vet a grand sendoff.

Shenk was reassigned from day-to-day duties with the team to planning season-long tributes and a closing ceremony on September 28, 2003. He didn't take that responsibility lightly. He led a contingent of team employees to Cincinnati to observe the closing of Riverfront Stadium at the end of the 2002 season. They also watched video from the final games at Atlanta-Fulton County Stadium, San Francisco's Candlestick Park, Memorial Stadium in Baltimore, and others.

"We wanted to pay the proper tribute," Shenk said.

The Phillies spared little expense. Former players were invited back throughout the 2003 season for various events. Fans were asked to vote for the All-Vet Team, and the selected players were outfitted in red-pinstriped blazers from Mitchell & Ness and introduced before the second-to-last game. Shenk lined up former players, managers, coaches, executives, and even media members to remove a number from the "Vet Countdown" chart on the outfield fence before each game. The biggest names were saved for last.

"[Steve] Carlton, [Mike] Schmidt, and Harry [Kalas]," Shenk said. "Harry pulled off the No. 1 at the last game. There were a lot of tears."

The pregame ceremony before the finale resembled the opening ceremonies at the Olympics. Long-tenured front-office staffers marched onto the field with flags representing each year of the Vet's existence. Kalas and longtime public-address announcer Dan Baker introduced former players beginning with Jim Bunning, the winning pitcher in the first game at the Vet in 1971.

Carlton took the mound for one last pitch and Schmidt swung a bat and circled the bases a final time, while Kalas repeated his calls of Carlton's 3,000th strikeout and Schmidt's 500th home run. Finally, Tug McGraw mimed the clinching pitch of the 1980 World Series, a moment made even more poignant because he was dying of brain cancer.

At one point during the ceremony, Schmidt raised Jim Thome's arm to symbolize the transition from the old ballpark to the new one. Thome had signed a six-year, $85 million contract before the 2003 season and was viewed as the bridge between the Vet and Citizens Bank Park.

"I'll never forget that," Thome said. "I have a picture of that, actually, in my office that I always cherish because that was such a cool memory in my career. Here I was, the rookie, still the new guy in town, and it was very humbling to have Mike Schmidt walk out and raise your hand. It was just amazing."

The Phillies lost the last game, 5–2, to the Atlanta Braves. For posterity, Chase Utley made the last out, a 5-4-3 double play; Pat Burrell had the final hit; Jason Marquis threw the last pitch; Thome hit the last home run in the second-to-last game.

Bulldozers were still removing the crumpled remains of the Vet when Citizens Bank Park opened on April 3, 2004. And if the Vet was ever considered beautiful, this $458 million gem was the starlet of ballparks. From the red-brick facade to a 360-degree open concourse, a 50-foot high Liberty Bell that looms over right-center field, and even a children's play area, it had all the amenities of a contemporary ballpark with the desired retro charm.

Citizens Bank Park stands behind the rubble of Veterans Stadium on March 21, 2004, the morning the Vet was demolished. (AP Photo / Michael Bryant)

The Phillies paid homage to their history, too. A food and entertainment section beyond the outfield fence was named Ashburn Alley after late Hall of Fame center fielder and broadcaster Richie Ashburn, and the bi-level restaurant in left field was dubbed "Harry The K's" in honor of Kalas. Statues were unveiled outside the ballpark to pay tribute to the Phillies' Hall of Famers: Schmidt, Carlton, Ashburn, and Robin Roberts. A statue of Kalas was added later.

Pregame ceremonies for the inaugural game at Citizens Bank Park included the players entering the field from a set of stairs in the outfield. For the record, the Phillies lost the opener, 4–1, to the Reds. Randy Wolf threw the first pitch. Cincinnati's D'Angelo Jimenez notched the first hit. Bobby Abreu clocked the first home run.

"I couldn't believe that this beautiful new place was really in Philadelphia," Shenk said.

It seemed everybody loved Citizens Bank Park. Well, almost. Pitchers weren't big fans.

Home runs flew out in every direction, especially to left field, where seemingly harmless fly balls dropped into flower beds just beyond the railing over the fence. The park allowed 218 homers in 2004 and 201 in 2005. More than half went to left field, prompting the Phillies to push back the left-field wall by five feet after the '05 season. John Smoltz called the new place "a joke."

"I loved it," Thome said. "To be honest, I had to calm myself down. The thing I noticed most is you didn't really have to do too much. If you just made contact, you get into those hot days, the ball will jump out of there like no other. There was a little bit of the fight of, how do I control myself in the box knowing you could hit a homer but you didn't want to try too hard."

A few other adjustments needed to be made, too. Initially, the Phillies were supposed to occupy the upper level of a two-tier bullpen. But when several relievers complained about being within reach of fans—or at least objects that could be easily thrown by fans—they were moved to the lower level and the visiting team was put in the line of fire. After the inaugural game, Cincinnati's Todd Jones told reporters that the Reds relievers "felt like monkeys in an exhibition."

The Phillies drew 3.25 million fans in the first year at Citizens Bank Park, a franchise record that was topped in 2008 and again in each of the next four seasons. At one point, from 2009 to 2012, they sold out 257 consecutive games.

Giles might not have wanted to see the Vet go, but upon the opening of the Bank, he said he was "proud as a peacock."

"This was one time," he said, "where reality was better than my dream."

48

THE CARPENTER FAMILY

In 2009, the Phillies closed out the Colorado Rockies in Game 4 of the best-of-five Division Series on a Monday night in Denver and opened the National League Championship Series three nights later in Los Angeles. But because of the unpredictability of the playoffs and the impracticality of reserving rooms for nights that might go unused, the team flew home for one day between series rather than going directly to Southern California.

Ruly Carpenter thought the itinerary was bonkers.

"What the hell are they doing?" Carpenter said in a telephone call to longtime Phillies public relations honcho Larry Shenk. "It doesn't make any sense."

Shenk interrupted his old boss. "Ruly," he said, "it's not your money anymore. Don't worry about it."

Sorry, Carpenter said, but he couldn't help himself. It was another illustration of how much baseball has changed since 1981, when he sold the Phillies for eight times the purchase price 38 years earlier.

Carpenter was a third-generation owner. His family stewarded the franchise from the depths of second-class baseball citizenry in Philadelphia to nearly four decades of solvency and eventually even prosperity.

It all began with his grandfather, Robert Ruliph Morgan Carpenter Sr., who married into the ultra-wealthy and powerful du Pont family of Delaware and decided in 1943 to buy the bankrupt Phillies for $400,000. With little interest in running the team, he appointed his 28-year-old son as the youngest club president in baseball, putting him in charge of day-to-day operations.

Bob Carpenter Jr. became principal owner when his father died in 1949. A year later, led by star pitcher Robin Roberts and center fielder Richie Ashburn, the Phillies reached the World Series for the first time since 1915. Although the "Whiz Kids," as they became known, got swept by the dynastic New York Yankees, they lost by one run in three of the four games in a series that stuck with Ruly Carpenter, who was 10 years old.

"Joe DiMaggio, in one of those games that were played in old Connie Mack Stadium, hit a home run to left-center field that hit up and might have gone over the roof in left field," Carpenter said, referring to the decisive 10th-inning blow against Roberts in a 2–1 loss in Game 2. "It was a double-deck stadium in the outfield, and it either hit on the roof or went over the roof."

Another memory: the daily ribbing from some players.

"They used to give me hell because I was the owner's bratty little son," he said. "I had a lot of fun with them teasing me."

The Phillies weren't particularly good during Ruly Carpenter's adolescence. They had only two winning seasons from 1951 to 1961, but nevertheless outlasted the Athletics, Philadelphia's American League club that moved to Kansas City after the 1954 season. The Phillies became the sole occupant of Connie Mack Stadium and drew upwards of 900,000 fans per season. They even cracked the one-million mark in 1957 despite posting only a 77–77 record.

Carpenter went to Yale, where he lettered in football and baseball. And when he decided to work for his father in 1963, he was interested less in the business side of the organization than the player-development system.

"The Carpenter family were not businessmen. They were sportsmen," Shenk said. "They wanted to be around tall, strong pitchers who could throw the heck out of the ball. That's all they wanted to talk about."

Ruly, in fact, grew close with Paul Owens, a former minor league infielder who became a scout for the Phillies in 1960 and field coordinator in 1963. While Owens worked with the team's prospects, Ruly handled administrative duties at minor-league camps in Florida.

"I was able to see firsthand how bad our farm system was," Carpenter said. "I took care of the paperwork in the office, but I really got to know Paul and some of the other managers and had a firsthand experience as to what our problems were."

Carpenter recommended to his father that Owens be promoted to oversee the minor-league operation. He also took a closer look at the Phillies' scouting staff. Some scouts, such as Tony Lucadello, were retained. Others were fired and replaced by the likes of Eddie Bockman and Hugh Alexander.

Slowly, the Phillies began drafting the core of their next great team. Lucadello found Mike Schmidt in Ohio; Bockman turned up Larry Bowa in California. The Phillies drafted Bob Boone out of Stanford in 1969 and turned him from an infielder into a catcher. They signed Manny Trillo as a catcher out of Venezuela in 1968 and converted him into a second baseman before losing him to Oakland in the Rule 5 Draft a year later and reacquiring him in a 1979 trade.

"[Trillo] had tremendous arm strength but threw from a high-three-quarters position and the ball kind of tailed on him," Carpenter said. "He didn't really get on top of it like a catcher who throws more like a quarterback. We converted Trillo to a second baseman because we realized, as a catcher, you weren't going to be able to change the way he'd been throwing for his entire life as a kid.

"In those days, you didn't have all the computers and technology that you have today. Most of these major-league teams have a dozen or so techie-type guys that just sit there and crunch numbers all day. They come up with statistics that I never heard of before. We basically would grade arm strength and running speed and things like that, but when it comes down to it, the hitting, the pitching, it was all very subjective."

Sounds more like a scout than an owner, doesn't he?

Even as free agency entered the game and players were allowed to change teams more freely, the Carpenters were more interested in developing players than buying them.

Bob Carpenter retired in 1972, turning over the team presidency to Ruly. Over the next 10 years, the Phillies won four division titles, including three in a row from 1976 to 1978, and captured their first World Series crown in 1980.

"It was our good fortune to acquire Steve Carlton from the Cardinals [in a 1971 trade]. That was key," Ruly said. "But Schmidt,

Bowa, [Greg] Luzinski, Boone, those were guys that we drafted and signed and brought through our farm system, and they became the core of our team. None of that would've happened without Paul and Dallas [Green, the farm director]. Those two guys were really critical to the development of the Phillies teams that you saw in the '70s and early '80s."

But the game was changing. With the advent of free agency in 1976, salaries skyrocketed, and Phillies players reaped the benefits. In 1977, Schmidt became baseball's first half-a-million dollar player, taking home $560,000 annually. A year later, despite Carpenter's holding firm to an offer that wasn't as strong as some other suitors, free-agent star Pete Rose signed with the Phillies for four years and $3.24 million.

The contract that really boggled Carpenter's mind was the Atlanta Braves' five-year, $3.5 million deal in 1981 with Claudell Washington, an outfielder who had been an All-Star once in seven previous seasons.

Labor strife was growing, too. The Phillies' World Series title defense was derailed, at least in part, by a players' strike that interrupted the 1981 season for two months. They were 34–21 and leading the National League East by 3½ games when the strike began. After it ended, they went 25–27 and lost in five games to the Montreal Expos in the Division Series.

By then, Carpenter made up his mind that he was going to sell the team. He told *The New York Times* that the Phillies' player payroll totaled $7 million and that the team needed to draw at least 2.7 million fans per season just to break even. They drew 2.6 million in the regular season in 1980.

In the fall of 1981, team president Bill Giles put together a group that bought the Phillies for $30.175 million. Carpenter insists he doesn't regret selling, even though the franchise is worth more than $1 billion, according to *Forbes*.

"Bryce Harper is making almost as much money in one year as what we sold the franchise for in the '80s," Carpenter said. "I just didn't see a future for single-family ownership because of the amount of money it takes to keep your best players. It's just a different world."

The Phillies' post-Carpenter era has now lasted as long as the family's ownership. Ruly Carpenter, who turned 79 in 2019, lives in Wilmington, Delaware, and still follows the team closely. He's acquainted, though not particularly well, with the current owners, including billionaire John Middleton.

"I watch most every game," he said. "Once you get addicted to baseball, it's kind of hard to turn your back on it."

Especially if you aren't paying the salaries.

49

AL REACH

If ever John Middleton felt a twinge of doubt about the wisdom of signing Bryce Harper to the longest and richest contract in franchise history, he might have considered strolling through the heart of Center City Philadelphia.

There, at Al Reach's old office, Middleton would've found all the inspiration he needed.

Reach would have loved Harper. Before becoming the Phillies first owner in 1883, he manufactured and sold sporting goods. That's how he made his millions. His company was among the first to make baseball bats, balls, and gloves. It says so right there on the 36-word historical marker outside the door to 1820 Chestnut Street, once the site of Reach's prominent downtown store.

Just imagine, then, what Reach would've done with Harper, whose on-field style exceeds even the substance of his playing ability. Harper signed the largest endorsement deal ever for a baseball player in 2016 when he agreed to a 10-year extension with Under Armour, undeniably a 21st century descendant of early sporting goods titans such as A.G. Spalding Co. and, yes, A.J. Reach & Co. He's among the most fashionable of today's players, with a color-coordinated cleat (and matching compression arm sleeve) for every occasion, from Mother's Day to Memorial Day to the Fourth of July. He even wore neon green Phanatic-themed cleats on Opening Day in 2019 to mark his Phillies debut.

Indeed, it's easy to imagine Harper as Reach's dream superstar.

Reach was a star player in his own right. Born in London but raised in New York before the Civil War, he played second base for the Philadelphia Athletics, a touring independent team, for $25 a week in the 1860s. Despite his slight stature (5-foot-6, 155 pounds, according to records that were kept), he was a proficient left-handed hitter. When the Athletics joined the new National Association, they offered him $1,000 per year to lead their offense with a .353 average in 1871.

As Reach got older and his performance slipped, he turned his attention to sporting goods. Noting that Philadelphia lacked places to buy bats, balls, and other equipment, he opened his first store on South Eighth Street in 1874. Seven years later, he partnered with Ben Shibe, a leather manufacturer, and built a factory in Fishtown, a working-class neighborhood located to the northeast of Center City. By 1883, they were producing 1.3 million baseballs and 100,000 bats per year.

Reach maintained his contacts in the game, too. He was approached by National League president A.G. Mills about moving the failing Worcester, Massachusetts-based team to Philadelphia, a larger market. Reach's interest existed on several levels, including a chance to expand his friendly rivalry with Spalding, president of the Chicago White Stockings franchise that would eventually become the Cubs.

"It didn't take much of a sales talk to sell Reach on the idea of a Philadelphia National League club," Frederick G. Lieb and Stan Baumgartner wrote in *The Philadelphia Phillies*, published in 1953. "Though Al was English born, the son of a London cricketer, he was baseball all the way and loved the game with real fervor. 'I'm in,' he told Mills, and he was in to stay for two decades as Phillie president and the club's leading stockholder."

Reach joined local attorney John Rogers to take ownership of the team for the 1883 season. He bought an old field on a block between 24th and 25th streets and Ridge and Columbia Avenues in North Philadelphia, built a small wooden grandstand and bleachers to boost the seating capacity to 6,500, and named the place Recreation Park.

And with that, the Phillies—or the Quakers, as they were often called in those early years—were born.

One problem: Worcester's best players were already dispersed among other teams, leaving the Phillies to cobble together a roster. They dropped their first game, 4–3, to the Providence Grays on May 1, 1883, the first of many losses for a talent-deficient club that finished with a 17–81 record. Meanwhile, across town, the Athletics won the pennant in the American Association.

Undeterred, Reach vowed to make the Phillies successful.

"We spent a year finding ourselves," Reach said, according to Lieb and Baumgartner. "Of course, it was expensive; we made mistakes, but we learned from our experiences. Philadelphia has the population and interest to support a second club, and some day the Philadelphia National League club will be famous—more famous than the Athletics."

It took time, but Reach's promise came true. In his 17 years as team president, the Phillies had 11 winning seasons. They boasted several star players, including the outfield trio of Billy Hamilton, Sam Thompson, and Ed Delahanty, the latter of whom was signed for $1,900, a sum that was nearly as staggering then as Harper's $330 million contract today.

Things began to turn after Reach hired manager Harry Wright in 1884. Three years later, with the Phillies drawing more fans than Recreation Park could hold, Reach achieved his greatest ownership triumph. He built Philadelphia Baseball Grounds, which later became known as Baker Bowl. It was the most advanced ballpark of the late 19th century and served as the Phillies' home for 51½ years until Shibe Park opened in 1938.

Reach's son, George, recalled his father taking him to see the site of the new 12,500-seat ballpark before it was erected at the corner of Broad Street and Lehigh Avenue in North Philadelphia, with estimates of the cost ranging from $80,000 to $101,000.

"Dad stopped the buggy and said, 'George, what do you think of that for a ball ground?'" George Reach told Lieb and Baumgartner. "I thought he was joshing me, as the field was covered with tin cans and other debris, while a dirty steam ran through it. I began to laugh, and I said: 'I know, father, you are joking and having some fun with me.' He replied, 'Not at all. What's more I intend to erect a ballpark here of which we all can be proud.'"

Reach's ownership was also marked by disappointment and even tragedy. Star pitcher Charlie Ferguson died of typhoid fever in 1888 at the age of 25 after only four standout seasons with the Phillies. In 1894, fire destroyed the grandstand and bleachers of Reach's new ballpark, which was rebuilt with the first cantilevered upper deck in a sports stadium.

Also, Reach grew disenchanted with increasingly bitter labor fights to keep star players—"jumpers," as they were dubbed by owners—from defecting to the Players' League in the 1890s and eventually the fledgling American League at the turn of the century. He was often stung by the players' lack of loyalty, never more than when middling first baseman Sid Farrar, a member of the inaugural 1883 Phillies, jumped to the Players' League in 1890.

"He was always a good first baseman, but he never hit much; yet year after year, we kept him on," Reach said, according to Lieb and Baumgartner. "Of all my players, I thought Sid would be the one to remain loyal."

As Reach gave more attention to his sporting-goods company, his impetuous partner Rogers took on a more involved role with the Phillies. Reach turned over the team presidency to Rogers in 1899, and three years later, they sold the Phillies to a syndicate led by stockbroker James Potter for $170,000.

Reach poured everything into sporting goods. The factory on Tulip Street in Fishtown expanded into what *The Sporting News* called "the largest and most complete in the world." Reach also developed a prototype batting helmet that was ahead of its time. The company later expanded into boxing equipment. A 1916 industrial census indicated that more than 1,000 people were employed by A.J. Reach & Co., while many others worked from their nearby homes to stitch laces onto baseballs.

A.J. Reach & Co. also manufactured the official baseball of the American League, and *Reach's Official Baseball Guide* was published annually until 1939 and recognized as the AL's official publication.

Reach retired to Atlantic City, New Jersey, until his death at age 87 in 1928. In his later years, he often noted the irony of someone who played without a glove selling mitts to the next generation of players. More than a century later, major-league clubhouses overflow with gloves and bats. Most players have endorsement deals with the company of their choice, with Harper leading the way.

Let there be no doubt, then, that the Phillies' first owner would approve of the team's 21st century star.

50

THE
PHANATIC

There wasn't a news conference, or even a press release, to announce the arrival of the most beloved character in Phillies history.

The Phanatic just showed up one day and never left.

He is impossible to miss, what with his googly eyes, purple eyelashes, blue eyebrows, trumpet-shaped snout, curled-up tongue, gawking neck, 90-inch waistline, bulging pot belly, oversized shoes, and electric green fur. And there's seemingly nothing that the 6-foot-6 creature from the Galapagos Islands won't do, from dancing atop the dugout to mocking an opposing player and launching hot dogs out of a cannon into the stands while driving a motorized ATV.

The Phanatic appeared on April 25, 1978, and has outlasted thousands of players. He has hung around for nine division titles, four World Series, and two championship parades down Broad Street. Through it all, his enduring popularity has been unrivaled.

"No disrespect to Schmitty," former shortstop Larry Bowa said, referring to Hall of Fame third baseman Mike Schmidt, "but the Phanatic rules over everybody that's ever played here."

The Phanatic's reach is larger than that, actually. He has become a mascot for the city of Philadelphia and the Delaware Valley at large, making hundreds of appearances each year. He has entertained at birthday parties and visited countless schools. He has made sick children laugh in their hospital beds and brightened the days of who knows how many people.

"Fortunately I was given the liberty of doing whatever I wanted," said David Raymond, the Phanatic's original alter-ego from 1978 to 1993, "as long as it was—as [team president] Bill Giles would say—'G-rated.'"

The Phanatic—or at least the notion of a Phillies-themed mascot—was the brainchild of Dennis Lehman. A member of the public relations department in the late 70s, Lehman operated the scoreboard at Veterans Stadium and made occasional road trips with the team. He was always on the lookout for new in-game entertainment ideas, alternatives to the clapping hands and other standbys that were so common.

During a trip to San Diego, Lehman got a glimpse of "The Famous Chicken," a radio station mascot that entertained fans during Padres games. When Lehman returned home, he attended Giles' weekly Tuesday staff meeting and proposed the idea of a Phillies mascot.

"I just said to Bill, 'This guy's unbelievable,'" said Lehman. "It was a sideshow. It didn't really distract from the game. It actually enhanced the experience of coming to the ballpark."

Giles had his doubts. But he was also willing to try just about anything at least once if it might attract a few more fans to the Vet. He told director of promotions Frank Sullivan to contact *Sesame Street* and speak with the designers of Big Bird. Giles even tracked down Muppets creator Jim Henson—"Bill was always able to get whoever he needed on the phone," Raymond said—who referred the Phillies to Bonnie Erickson and Wayde Harrison, the wife-and-husband team that created Miss Piggy, Statler and Waldorf, and other characters on *The Muppet Show*.

The Phillies commissioned Erickson and Harrison to come up with a mascot. Giles insisted on only a few specifications: "Fat, green, indefinable... and lovable," he said.

But once the Phanatic was created, the Phillies needed someone to climb into the costume. Raymond, an intern from the University of Delaware and the son of legendary Blue Hens football coach Tubby Raymond, turned out to be the perfect choice. Not only was he willing to do absolutely anything for a full-time job, but as a former college punter, he had the athleticism and flexibility to move around in the 35-pound suit.

"They seemed to be a little bit careful to dodge around exactly what they wanted me to do, but I didn't care. I wanted a job," Raymond said. "I didn't care if they asked me to jump, to skydive, whatever. I could've been shot out of a cannon. I could've ridden an ostrich. I would say yes to anything."

The Phanatic basks in the glory of a Phillies win. (Getty Images / Christopher Szagola / Icon Sport Media)

Giles still was leery. The Phillies didn't make a grand announcement. Giles also decided not to buy the copyright from Erickson and Harrison. The costume cost the Phillies $2,900; the rights would've been an extra $2,100, an expenditure that Giles knew he couldn't talk owner Ruly Carpenter into for something that might be a bust.

"What a mistake," Giles said.

Five years later, after putting together the group that bought the Phillies from the Carpenter family, Giles spent $200,000 for the copyright to the Phanatic, already one of the most iconic mascots in sports. (At the time of this writing, the Phillies were suing Erickson and Harrison for threatening to withdraw from a 1984 agreement to allow the Phillies use the Big Fella "forever.")

Raymond's biggest concern, at least at the outset: "I thought people were going to kill me or set me on fire." But it didn't take long, just a few days actually, to realize that the Phanatic was going to work.

It was the middle of the fifth inning of one of the Phanatic's first games when he grabbed a rake and ran onto the field with the grounds crew in an attempt at between-innings hilarity. By accident, one of the groundskeepers tripped over the Phanatic's big ol' shoe.

"And everybody roared," Raymond said. "I mean, you would've thought Jackie Gleason just did one of his '*and awaaay we go!*' I was like, 'Wow, they're really watching us.' We were just a bunch of morons running around like idiots and we were getting standing ovations. That's when I knew, okay, this is really working."

Like an actor playing a role, Raymond developed a personality for the Phanatic. He also was unafraid to drag players, managers, and even umpires into the joke. Eric Gregg, an umpire and native Philadelphian, memorably danced with the Phanatic between innings. Pittsburgh Pirates catcher Manny Sanguillen was one of the first players to interact with the Phanatic on the third-base line during pregame warm-ups.

Raymond took miming classes, but more than anything, it probably helped his non-verbal communication skills that he grew up with a mother who was hearing impaired.

"She told me a funny story about how, when I was a teenager, when she'd get into an argument with me, she'd turn off the hearing aid," Raymond said. "She'd joke with me and say, 'That's when I saw what was to become the Phanatic's personality evolve.' I would jump around in front of her, waving my arms, and say, 'You can't take away the car!'"

Favorite shticks? Raymond has a few. He was always partial to the Phanatic's smashing of a Dodgers helmet to the tune of "I Love L.A." by Randy Newman or a Yankees helmet to Frank Sinatra's "New York, New York."

And who could forget the 1988 run-in with Dodgers manager Tommy Lasorda? The Phanatic likes to mock opposing players and managers, many of whom play along. But after years of the Phanatic dressing up a life-sized dummy with Lasorda's jersey, which was often secretly provided to him by Dodgers second baseman Steve Sax, Lasorda charged out of the dugout, knocked over the Phanatic, and hit him with the dummy, nearly decapitating him in the process.

"I remember running into Tommy years later and thinking that I told this story so much that maybe it didn't really happen," Raymond said. "I saw him at the winter meetings and he had a bunch of friends around, and he told the whole story the way I always told it. I said, 'Yes, this actually really did happen.'"

Raymond stepped aside after the 1993 World Series, passing the torch to Tom Burgoyne, his backup for many years. Raymond founded a character-branding company that develops and trains mascots for sports teams and businesses, including Gritty, the Philadelphia Flyers' wild-eyed mascot that achieved national attention upon its creation in 2018.

But for 41 years, the Phillies' big, green, hot-dog-firing machine has been the standard for all sports mascots to follow.

Just as Lehman envisioned when he came back from San Diego, right?

"I guess it would really sound smart if I said, 'Yeah, sure,'" Lehman said. "But no, I was just thinking, *It's better than clapping hands and charges*. [Raymond] set the standard. It didn't take very long for him to steal the show. He didn't kill something that wasn't that funny. He would let it go and try something else. That, to me, was his special sauce, his ability to modify things and not fall in love with how funny he was.

"And it was a great brand for the Phillies."

A brand like no other.

Acknowledgments

In 1982, my dad took me to my first baseball game. We drove an hour up the New Jersey Turnpike to watch the Yankees get walloped, 14–1, by the Kansas City Royals. The extent of the Yanks' offense came on Butch Wynegar's home run in the eighth inning—as we were walking out of the stadium.

A year later, we tried again. This time, we drove an hour down the Turnpike to see the Phillies. I have no recollection of what happened, most likely because I was six. But my dad doesn't either, probably as a consequence of spending half the game in the parking lot with a wire hanger after locking the keys inside his blue Oldsmobile Delta 88.

It's a wonder that I ever wanted to go to another game.

As it turned out, I couldn't get enough. Thirty-seven years later, I work in that South Philly parking lot, which is now more or less Citizens Bank Park. I have attended several hundred games, either as a fan or a writer, in ballparks across the country. It's an understatement to say that I feel lucky to work in the field that I always considered to be a dream.

My interest in baseball, as well as my passion for it and curiosity about it, only multiplied over the years. Here's hoping I ask better questions now than I did when I was six, though I will let all the players, managers, coaches, executives, scouts, broadcasters, and fellow writers with whom I have been fortunate to come into contact be the judge.

This book would not have been possible without the time and memories of so many of those people. I conducted original interviews with, in alphabetical order: Larry Andersen, Mike Arbuckle, Bob Boone, Larry Bowa, Mark Carfagno, Ruly Carpenter, Frank Coppenbarger, Chris Coste, Clay Dalyrmple, Rich Dubee, Bill Giles, Pat Gillick, Doug Glanville, Dave Hollins, Ferguson Jenkins, Geoff Jenkins, Todd Kalas, Bob Klein,

Jerry Lafferty, Dennis Lehman, Brad Lidge, Greg Luzinski, Charlie Manuel, Gary Matthews, Tim McCarver, Mickey Morandini, Dickie Noles, Dave Raymond, Pete Rose, Aaron Rowand, Rick Schu, Larry Shenk, Jim Thome, Shane Victorino, Chris Welsh, Chris Wheeler, and Bobby Wine. I also relied on press conferences or one-on-one conversations for the *Philadelphia Inquirer* with Bobby Abreu, Ruben Amaro Jr., Cole Hamels, Ryan Howard, Gabe Kapler, Matt Klentak, John Middleton, Aaron Nola, Jimmy Rollins, Mike Schmidt, Chase Utley, and others. A huge thank you to all.

Special thanks, too, to Larry Andersen, one of the all-time great baseball storytellers, for his wonderful foreword.

Without question, my favorite thing about baseball is its history. The Phillies have existed since 1883 and lost more games than any team in North American professional sports. But they also celebrated twin World Series triumphs in 1980 and 2008. All of it makes the franchise unique. And I am grateful to Triumph Books, especially Josh Williams and my editor, Jesse Jordan, for enabling me to dive into that history and giving me the creative freedom to do so.

I owe enormous gratitude to my bosses at the *Philadelphia Inquirer*—Stan Wischnowski, Pat McLoone, and Gary Potosky—for bringing me back before the 2018 season. Your leadership and unyielding support reinforce how fortunate I am to work for the *Inquirer*, a remarkable institution with devoted people. Two of the best are Matt Breen and Bob Brookover, my amazing baseball-writing teammates.

Along those lines, I am eternally thankful to my sportswriting mentors, from the late Jack Falla at Boston University to Jay Greenberg, and the editors who took chances on me along the way: Sandy Smith at the *Concord Monitor*, Charlie Jaworski at the *Binghamton Press & Sun-Bulletin*, Ron Fritz at the *Wilmington News Journal*, Hank Hryniewicz and Mark Murphy at the *Boston Herald*, and Dave Kull and Matt Marrone at ESPN.com.

The quality of baseball writing across the country is at an all-time high. For 15 years, I have been so awed by the work of my co-workers and competitors on the Phillies and Red Sox beats that I mostly hoped to keep up. More importantly, I am proud to call so many of them friends. Hat tips to Rob Bradford, Tim Britton, Ian Browne, Steve Buckley, Kevin Cooney, Jerry Crasnick, Evan Drellich, Martin Frank, Matt Gelb, Paul Hagen, Chad Jennings, Brian MacPherson, Jason Mastrodonato, Sean McAdam, Jen McCaffrey, Meghan Montemurro, Jim Salisbury, Michael Silverman, Alex Speier, Jayson Stark, John Tomase, and Todd Zolecki. Thanks, too, to the Phillies media relations folks, led by Bonnie Clark and Greg Casterioto.

No offense to everyone listed above, but I haven't met a more passionate baseball fan than my father-in-law, Howie Frisch (no relation to Frankie, despite what he says). He's a pretty good copy editor, too. I draw inspiration from my late mother-in-law, Phyllis Gotlib, who had such a big heart and ever more zeal for life. David and Debby Frisch are the best bro- and sister-in-law around. It took me too long to say it, but my sister, Robyn Lauber, is pretty darn cool. Thanks always, Beenie.

My mom, Barbara Lauber, passed away during the writing of this book. Somehow I was able to finish it without her. She would have bought every copy in every bookstore in New Jersey, and I know she would expect our family to pick up the slack. No pressure, everyone.

None of this happens without my dad, Richard Lauber, who grew up in New York when it was the mecca of baseball. He remembers Bobby Thomson's "Shot Heard 'Round the World" in 1951 and was at Yankee Stadium for Reggie Jackson's three-homer game in the 1977 World Series. He also bought me my first glove... and bat... and catcher's mask... and on and on. Thanks for saving all of my baseball cards, Dad. Let's open a pack together soon.

My son, Jake, lights up my life and brings me more joy than I ever imagined. I'll miss hearing him ask, "How many more chapters do you have left, Daddy?" Suffice it to say, I owe the J-Man a lot of trips to the playground.

And to my wife, Becca: You're the most amazing, wonderful, supportive, caring person and partner. There isn't anyone with whom I would rather share everything. What else can I say, Babes? I love you the most.

Sources

Books

Fitzpatrick, Frank. *You Can't Lose 'Em All: The Year the Phillies Finally Won the World Series.* Taylor Trade Publishing (2001).

Giles, Bill; Myers, Doug. *Pouring Six Beers at One Time: Stories From A Lifetime in Baseball.* Triumph Books (2007).

Kashatus, Bill. *Macho Row: The '93 Phillies and Baseball's Unwritten Code.* University of Nebraska Press (2017).

Lieb, Frederick G.; Baumgartner, Stan. *The Philadelphia Phillies.* A.S. Barnes and Co. (1953).

Maadi, Rob. *Mike Schmidt: The Phillies' Legendary Slugger.* Triumph Books (2010).

Roberts, Robin; Rogers, C. Paul III. *The Whiz Kids and the 1950 Pennant.* Temple University Press (1996).

Salisbury, Jim; Zolecki, Todd. *The Rotation.* Running Press (2012).

Shenk, Larry. *If These Walls Could Talk: Stories From the Philadelphia Phillies' Dugout, Locker Room, and Press Box.* Triumph Books (2014).

Shenk, Larry. *The Fightin' Phillies: 100 Years of Philadelphia Baseball from the Whiz Kids to the Misfits.* Triumph Books (2016).

Wheeler, Chris. *View from the Booth: Four Decades with the Phillies.* Camino Books, Inc. (2009).

Zolecki, Todd. *The Good, The Bad & The Ugly: Philadelphia Phillies.* Triumph Books (2010).

Newspapers & Periodicals

Breen, Matt. "Jamie Moyer wants to know: Where were you when the Phillies won the World Series?" *Philadelphia Inquirer*. October 25, 2018.

Creamer, Robert W. "The Best Outfield Ever? Why, Del, Big Sam and Sliding Billy, For Sure." *Sports Illustrated.* October 18, 1982.

Doyel, Gregg. "The Rise, Fall and Redemption of Indy Baseball Great Chuck Klein." *Indianapolis Star*. August 4, 2017.

Durso, Joseph. "Carpenter's Motive: Prod Other Owners." *The New York Times*. March 8, 1981.

Fitzpatrick, Frank. "Dallas Green, first Phillies manager to win the World Series, dies at 82." *Philadelphia Inquirer*. March 22, 2017.

Fitzpatrick, Frank. "A look back at '93 Phillies offers sobering lesson in ruthlessness of time." *Philadelphia Inquirer*. July 19, 2018.

Hochman, Stan. "Johnny Callison was the Phillies' shy All-Star MVP." *Philadelphia Daily News*. July 8, 1964.

Huber, Robert. "Ryan Howard Is Not a Creep, a Cheat, a Liar or a Fraud." *Philadelphia Magazine.* March 22, 2007.

Lauber, Scott; Brookover, Bob. "2008 World Series Game 5, and all the rain that delayed the Phillies' reign." *Philadelphia Inquirer.* Aug. 3, 2018.

Marcus, Steven. "Bob Boone, Aaron Boone have faced personal-catcher situations." *Newsday*. May 5, 2018.

Wulf, Steve. "A Hard-Knock Life." ESPN.com. July 11, 2013.

Websites

asapsports.com
baseballhall.org
baseball-reference.com
delawareonline.com
ESPN.com
inquirer.com
MLB.com

NBCSportsPhilly.com
newspapers.com
sabr.org/bioproject
si.com/vault
theathletic.com
youtube.com

About the Author

Scott Lauber is a baseball writer for the *Philadelphia Inquirer* and *Philadelphia Daily News*. He has a Bachelor of Science in journalism from Boston University, graduating in 1998. After stops at the *Concord* (N.H.) *Monitor* and *Binghamton* (N.Y.) *Press & Sun-Bulletin*, he began covering the Phillies for the *Wilmington* (Del.) *News Journal* in 2005. He wrote about the Red Sox for the *Boston Herald* and ESPN.com from 2010 to '18 before returning to his baseball roots in Philadelphia early in the 2018 season. He's a member of the Baseball Writers Association of America and a Hall of Fame voter.

The Big 50 is Lauber's second book. He co-authored *Phillies Confidential: The Untold Inside Story of the 2008 Championship Season* with former Phillies outfielder Gary Matthews. Lauber lives in Moorestown, New Jersey, with his wife, Rebecca, and their son, Jacob.